Decolonizing Maasai History

Decolonizing Maasai History

A Path to Indigenous African Futures

Meitamei Olol Dapash and Mary Poole

ZED

LONDON • NEW YORK • OXFORD • NEW DELHI • SYDNEY

ZED
Bloomsbury Publishing Plc
50 Bedford Square, London, WC1B 3DP, UK
1385 Broadway, New York, NY 10018, USA
29 Earlsfort Terrace, Dublin 2, Ireland

BLOOMSBURY, Zed and the Zed logo are trademarks of Bloomsbury Publishing Plc

First published in Great Britain 2025

Cover design by Holly Capper
Cover image © lifehouseimage/Getty Images

Bloomsbury Publishing Plc does not have any control over, or responsibility for, any
third-party websites referred to or in this book. All internet addresses given in this
book were correct at the time of going to press. The author and publisher regret
any inconvenience caused if addresses have changed or sites have ceased
to exist, but can accept no responsibility for any such changes.

A catalogue record for this book is available from the British Library.

A catalog record for this book is available from the Library of Congress.

ISBN.	HB.	978-1-3504-2744-0
	PB:	978-1-3504-2743-3
	ePDF:	978-1-3504-2742-6
	eBook:	978-1-3504-2741-9

Typeset by Integra Software Services Pvt. Ltd.

To find out more about our authors and books visit www.bloomsbury.com
and sign up for our newsletters.

BLOOMSBURY
OPEN ACCESS

An ebook edition of this book is available open access on bloomsburycollections.com. Open access was funded by the Bloomsbury Open Collections Library Collective. Bloomsbury Open Collections is a collective-action approach to funding open access books that allows select authors to publish their books open access at no cost to them. Through this model, we make open access publication available to a wider range of authors by spreading the cost across multiple organizations, while providing additional benefits to participating libraries. The aim is to engage a more diverse set of authors and bring their work to a wider global audience. More details, including how to participate and a list of contributing libraries, are available from http://www.bloomsbury.com/bloomsbury-open-collections.

Contents

Illustrations

Acknowledgments

This book was born through over twenty years of conversation about history in Maasailand, and it has benefited from the knowledge, wisdom, and insistence on correctness of the Maa Nation of East Africa. We held two history conferences to receive guidance and feedback from elders and youth about our approach to this book, over a dozen community presentations to groups of as many as several hundred people, and countless smaller gatherings, where we received critical feedback.

We recognize especially members of our leadership who contributed to this book, those who live between worlds and negotiate the power of the state and Maa Nation. We thank first the late Honorable Justice Ole Tipis, whose life under colonization was given to Maasai land rights and sovereignty. We recognize the late Honorable William Ole Ntimama who became later in life a fearless warrior and foremost Maasai land rights hero, the late former member of Parliament Honorable John Keen, Honorable Moses Ole Marima, the late Honorable Justice Ole Keiwa, former Chairman Olkaijiado County Council Alex Ole Likimani, Honorable former Narok Senator mpapa Philip Ole Lemein, the late mpapa and former Council member Jame Ole Naeku, Chairman of Maasai Counsel of Elders Kelena Ole Nchoe, Honorable Council member Salankat Ole Nchoe, Council member Murera Ole Saoli, Council member Maranga Ole Oltuni, Council member Joseph Ole Sayialel of Olkejuado County Council, former Chairman Olkejuado County Council, Hon. Tarayia Kores, and all the leaders in both Narok and Kajiado Counties who extended their goodwill and/or moral support during the initial stages of this work.

The wisdom of the Maasai community is contained most in our Elders, today of the *Ilnyangusi, Ilseuri and Ilkitoip* age groups. We recognize especially the contribution to this book of the late mpapa Oljikooi Ole Nkuyiayu who until his going to sleep spoke passionately for truth and for the recentering and decolonization of Maasai history.

Many colleagues contributed to presentations, research, analysis, and to accessing interviews and information, most of whom are activists involved in campaigns in Maasai Mara, Mau Narok or Rose Farm (as it is popularly known), and Amboseli National Park. We recognize a core group of these incredible community leaders and activists: Our lifelong colleagues Daniel Ole Leturesh, Donkol Ole Keiwa, (Charles) Parkisiaa Ole Takai, Nenkoroi Ole Taki, Justus Ole Kiok, Meya Ole Patu, Morome Ole Naikumi, and our son and brother the late (George) Risa Ole Kosen, who must be smiling from above on seeing this work come to fruition. His contribution to the struggle will forever be remembered. We thank Joseph Ole Mpoe, and his brother the late Moses Ole Mpoe, who continues to whisper, "keep the good fight going!" We thank Logela Olol Melita, Sammy Ole Kiminta, Joseph Ole Kipila, Simintei Ole Lemurt, and Enoch Ole Kiminta. Our deep gratitude to Kaitlin Nolkiponi Noss, Kate Levy, and Zoe Naini Caras for your important contributions. Thank you, Kai Daniel and the Prescott College class of 2015, for the maps presented in the book.

This book germinated in the powerful commitment of land rights activism of the entire Maa Nation. We recognize all of those who have remained steadfast in the struggle for the first liberation of Maasai lands in Loliondo and *Korongoro* (Ngorongoro) in Tanzania, *Ilaikipa*, *IlKeekonyokie* (Kajiado), Transmara, and *Ilpurko* in Narok. The journey to complete liberation is long but we remember that our forefathers overcame the time of death, the emutai, on the arrival of the first Europeans, and so shall the future generations of the Maa Nation overcome adversity in whatever manifestation.

Our hope for that survival rests in the ability of our leadership to remain true to our integrity and resist corruption. Many of our leaders have fallen down in recent years. But others have remained tall, and we honor especially H.E. Hon. Jamal Ole Lenku, the current governor of Olkejuado County, an outspoken advocate for Maasai land rights and sovereignty. We trust that such visionary leaders will continue to be born into the future, as they have through history, and we hope that Hon. Lenku's example will inspire the current emerging generation of Maasai leadership.

During the Mau Narok/Rose Farm land struggle, Maasai youth led by Dr. Nchorira Naikuni and Gideon (Booster) Ole Kisio and others built a movement of university students across Kenya, and they brought a powerful new historic dimension to the struggle. As a generation of Western-educated youth of this community, they led fearless and well-organized protests in Narok town and Mau Narok, and the seriousness of this campaign reverberated in the seat of government in Nairobi. Thank you to Linus Ole Kaikai for his courage in giving much needed coverage to the Mau Narok land struggle.

The power of Maasai women has been the unshakable beacon of our struggle and, in the Rose Farm of Mau Narok especially, many women paid a costly price to defend the land from the state's politically engineered and criminal resettlement agenda, where they endured brutality and torture, including of pregnant women, and saw their livestock destroyed. We honor each one of them and acknowledge their individual and collective sacrifice, dedication, and intellectual contribution to the liberation of Maasailand. Eunice ene Marima, Naneu ene Ntimama (*Entito Orkingiy*), Margaret ene Kioleken, Mary ene Simat, Karsis ene Mpoe, Naisuaku Ene Leto, and many others not mentioned here are Maasailand's face of resistance.

We wish to honor the fifty-one community members who were arrested with Meitamei, detained and tried for more than two years, for protesting the illegal reoccupation of Rose Farm. All of these refused to be intimidated into pleading guilty in exchange for freedom, knowing the destructive impact of such deals made behind closed doors.

The struggle to safeguard Maasai Mara for the present and future generations of Maasailand and of the world could not have been won without the fearless commitment of all the residents of the Mara. We thank campaign organizers, including Meja Ole Ketikai, Parsaloi Olol Dapash, Ntalameya Olol Dapash, Mark Ole Kasoe, Kirrinkai Ole Ikayo, Geofrey Ole Narok, Lenkaina Ole Tira, Somoine Ole Tira, Peter Ole Narok, as well as many other Maasai Mara residents across the country.

Prescott College in Arizona has been a unique and essential partner in this work. The College has supported the development of a semester in Indigenous solidarity studies for twenty years, one that has fed Maasai land rights and other community priorities. We thank the many Prescott College students and faculty whose work contributed to this book through archival research and interviews of community members, under our direction, and who presented research findings through community presentations.

This book was written at the Dopoi Center in Maasai Mara, a hub of community organizing, education, and decolonizing research that is also home to Prescott College in Maasailand. The early vision of Dopoi was understood by a few special people: Dan Garvey, Richard Bakal, Kate Mayian Cabot, Mike Stone, Dan Boyce, and Suzanne Pfister, the later two being the former and current chairs of Dopoi's other partner organization, the Maasai Education, Research and Conservation Institute (MERC). We thank the US and Kenyan MERC board for its steadfast support.

Writing and then publishing this book have been both the gift and the challenge of a lifetime. The challenges included navigating distance between East Africa and the United States, as we lived on different continents much of the time. Internet and electricity are intermittently available in rural Kenya which slowed the work at points. Even more, the project required us to translate between our different cultural ways of seeing history, and so it changed us both as we taught each other and found our way to a shared line of sight.

Publishing the book was even more difficult. We received such negative feedback at several points that we began to doubt whether this book would ever come to light. Small groups of colleagues and friends waded into the project with us at important moments and they told us to keep going: we are deeply grateful especially to Beryl Satter, Alice-Kessler Harris, Carol Poole, and Roxanne Dunbar Ortiz. We also found community through the words of many historians whom we have never met, especially Toyin Falola and B.A. Ogot. We maintained an imaginary council of elders of Indigenous scholars whose brave work inspires and informs us. We are forever indebted to Nick Wolterman, our editor, and to Zed Books and Bloomsbury. Nick read every word of our manuscript and made it better by nuancing language in some critical passages. But we are grateful most for his belief and commitment to this project.

It is important to admit that at one point the negative feedback we received caused us to doubt not just that the book would be published, but even our own judgment. We share that to encourage all Indigenous and other minoritized scholars to stand firm in what you know to be real and true. In the end, it was the doubts themselves that inspired us to a deeper push to clarify and communicate. We both feel humbled by our chance to write this book, this privilege of a lifetime to sink so deeply into the history of the Maa Nation, like spending years in ceremony sitting at the feet of elders. We are grateful to have been part of a community conversation with a purpose.

I am grateful to my close and extended family who have supported me in this work in Maasailand for decades, and especially for the example set by my parents Mark Poole and Jean Poole, of life lived for justice. I am also grateful to my students whose questions have pushed me to teach beyond what is broken and to identify "where the hope lies." It is my hope that this book contributes to the work of other historians imagining postcolonial futures. Kara entito olosho le Maa, and I am eternally grateful that the Maa Nation has chosen to survive and that I have been welcomed to that journey.

—Mary Nashipae Poole, PhD

My father Dopoi Olol Dapash, who lived between 1886 and 2001, was a radical anticolonial leader of the Maa Nation; my mother, Loshe ene Olol Dapash, is the reason I became educated and thus able to continue to lead resistance to the neocolonization of Maasailand today. I want to thank my children for their

unconditional love over the years as I stayed away to pursue the rights of the
Maasai people in Kenya, Tanzania and other parts of the world.

For many years, our history, as it has been told by others, has been used to
appropriate Maasailand. Generations of our people have been eroded in the process.
It is my prayer that by reclaiming our history we will mark a new beginning in our
own true liberation and a restoration of our culture, land rights, and future as a
community. It is my challenge to the new generations of the community to begin to
write about yourselves, speak for yourselves, to challenge the appropriation of our
history. This liberation should, and must, create a new ground for collaboration
with all of those interested in learning about us and sharing the struggle.

—Meitamei Olol Dapash, PhD

Introduction

This book was written to speak back to the history produced in the West of the Indigenous Maasai people of East Africa, a history that has been used to deny our claims to cultural survival and to land rights. Maasai are a pastoralist people, one cultural community of *Olosho le Maa*, the Maa nation, whose lands were bisected under colonization in the late nineteenth century and further divided by the states of Kenya and Tanzania in the early 1960s. This book suggests a new narrative outline for Maasai in Kenya, one that reflects Maasai historical knowledge and common sense.

Why might this intervention matter beyond Maasailand? One reason is that we describe the role that Western history has played in the expansion of neocolonial power in Maasailand, a story that we believe has relevance to other colonized contexts. Another is that a restored Maasai history disrupts the bigger story of African history and its pivot on the myth of African decolonization. This book demonstrates that it was the Kenyan state, not the British Empire, that finally achieved the colonial agenda for the permanent occupation of Maasailand. Most importantly, we wrote this book to share our discovery of the power of decolonized history to ignite determination for justice, which can engender an actual decolonization of land. We learned that lesson at a place called Mau Narok, a corner of the world where the skills of Western history production were taken into the hands of a community in resistance, and a broader movement for Maasai land recovery was born.

This book is born of collaboration. Meitamei Olol Dapash is an activist leader, scholar, and cultural traditionalist of the Maasai community in Narok, Kenya. Mary Poole is a US historian of race, gender, and social policy, who was named in Maasailand many years ago. Beyond us literally hundreds of people have contributed to the book, which was undertaken to respond to questions raised in the Maasai community about gaps in oral history, especially the mechanics of land occupation.[1] It was such a question that led us to research the history of Mau Narok, and that is where our story beings.

Mau Narok and the Power of Righting History

Mau Narok is the Maasai name for a belt of verdant forest and grasses where the Maasai community converged with their cattle in times of drought. As pastoralists, the life of a Maasai person, even today under changing times, revolves around finding sufficient grasses for the community's cattle, goats, and sheep, which has historically involved moving around a dry landscape following rain and the grasses it brings. Through history, Maasai have reserved the richest land—the forests, swamps, and highlands—as drought reserves, which may remain untouched for months or years during wet seasons when grasses can be found at greater distances. Drought reserves tend to be sources of medicines, and thus shared with other communities, especially the Indigenous Ogiek forest hunters and beekeepers. Hundreds of wildlife communities also considered Mau Narok home during the centuries of Maasai stewardship of the land; as hunting for food is forbidden in Maasai culture, large and small mammals, prey and predators, lived mostly unmolested in Maasai territory, creating their own worlds through conflict and coexistence. As a place of survival and restoration, as a drought reserve, Mau Narok was essential to the larger social ecology of Maasailand and the ability of the people to live most of their lives on the drier landscape.

When the British began their conquest of Maasailand near the end of the nineteenth century, they set their sights quickly on Mau Narok. But what they saw was not the abundant evidence that the landscape had been formed through the disciplined environmental management of Maasai society. They saw a "natural" world of an impossible vitality that they could transform through a capitalist logic into profit. Some Maasai were removed through forced evictions that in 1911 culminated three decades of violent conflict and the decimation of people and cattle by European diseases. Others remained behind.

The British set out to transform Mau Narok to commercial agriculture, though this agenda was never accomplished during the era of formal colonization. A single Welsh settler laid claim to most of the eventual 30,000 acres of Mau Narok.[2] Nevertheless, Maasai continued to graze the land, and it was not until the British left and the Kenyan state established in the early 1960s that Mau

Narok was fully colonized. The landscape was transformed at that time into huge private absentee ranches. It was occupied by Kenya's first president and distributed among his friends and allies to produce their personal wealth which translated into hegemonic political power. Mau Narok's forests were leveled, and fences constructed, rivers depleted for irrigation, and land poisoned with pesticides to create wheat and barley farms, while landless Maasai were pushed to borders policed by state security. These changes decimated the wildlife—the elephants, lions, and hundreds of other wildlife communities that had also called Mau Narok home.

The quiet theft of Maasai futures was underway at the same moment that the world celebrated the end of colonization through much of Africa, the "Independence Era" of the early 1960s. Independence was meant to mark the end of the previous 500 years of international slave trade and then formal colonization that had caused African communities to be forcibly dispossessed from homelands. This severing of people from land had enabled Europe to pillage the continent's untapped wealth for its own profit—its gems and minerals, rich soils, ivory, and its people and their uncompensated labor. Europeans presented themselves as a superior civilization and they decimated African governances, economies, and cultures in their wake. The African people who organized movements for decolonization gave their lives not only to end European occupation but to restore African sovereignties, cultures, social, and political systems.

Many argue that the promised Independence never reached the African continent; we can say ourselves that it never reached Maasailand. Instead "Independence" brought a new African class of colonizers to facilitate the same movement of resources from people who were impoverished to expand the wealth of the already wealthy. Under Kenyan statehood, Maasailand was more deeply penetrated through corruption and privatization, sale, and state-sponsored theft of land. Resources were more violently plundered, typically under the management of the very same administrators and foreign corporations that had enriched themselves in the British colonial era. Thus, the multibillion-dollar corporate rape of land and water for soda ash at Magadi in eastern Maasailand continued apace through the transfer of power from the British Empire to the Kenyan state. The global tourism industry established in the transition to the Kenyan state, which reaps the wealth of Maasai culture and coexistence with wildlife, barely compensates the Maasai protectors of the wildlife with a fraction of what the industry generates. Mau Narok and other ancestral land continue to be occupied, and the food grown there feeds Nairobi and beyond, while hunger grows in Maasailand especially in times of drought. Water from Mt. Kilimanjaro in Maasailand is piped beneath the feet of thirsty villages, to grow tulips for export in Nairobi.[3]

The Kenyan state used the same tactics of displacement against Maasai that had once been used by the British against all Africans. Maasai were not provided education and the means to vote, though these were extended to many urban Kenyans. They were subjected to unaccountable state violence when they resisted further removal. This new form of colonization rejected the racist colorline of the old but continued to function through the same basic ideology, as Westernized Africans joined the mission to civilize the "backward," and Indigenous Africans were cast as an embarrassment to modernizing states, as roadblocks to development. Slain Maasai land rights lawyer Elijah Sempeta famously—within the Maasai community—defined Independence to be nothing more than a "myth."[4]

By the early 1960s, Maasai society saw that Independence would bring an intensified and more permanent loss of land. They formed the Maasai United Front (MUF) under the leadership of Justus Ole Tipis to advocate their rights and claims to cultural sovereignty. After a series of meetings held to gather information about local land issues and determine a collective position, they made their way, uninvited, to London where the Kenyan constitution was being drafted. They demanded that the British honor its commitment that all occupied Maasai lands be returned to the Maa-speaking peoples, just as land was being returned to the ethnic communities that would assume the power of the state. They demanded that *Olosho le Maa*, the Maa nation, be recognized in a semi-autonomous coexistence with the Kenyan state.[5]

Maasai lost that fight for political determination. Even more, they lost the ability to be seen and understood in their new condition, as colonized subjects in an ostensibly "postcolonial" world. Through the first five decades of statehood, through the cascading plunder of Maasailand, Maasai were isolated by their invisibility. The African political left, those who had theorized decolonization, did not acknowledge the condition of Maasai and other Indigenous peoples, those whose full humanity was not recognized by the states that forcibly encompassed them, and who also resisted expectations that they would relinquish their lands and cultures. They did not recognize that Indigenous lands were the frontiers of neocolonialism, settled anew after the retreat of Europeans by African communities that inherited the power of states. The few fragile networks of solidarity Maasai had built with Western allies lost their organizing principle with the end of formal colonization. Through the myth of Independence, there was no path to common ground with other oppressed classes, the growing numbers of landless urban poor in Kenya or exploited farm workers.

The myth of Independence also dissembled and confused the Maasai community internally. Those few with Western education recognized that Maasainess was a newly scorned identity in the emerging assemblages of the Kenyan state, and they began to seek distance from their own "primitive" selves. The MUF leadership was eventually destroyed in the chaotic scramble for land, as former activists were coerced, some of them participating in the plunder. Some joined a small elite class of Maasai whose interests eventually diverged from that of the larger impoverished and politically powerless community. It was not just in Maasailand that people were confused by the myth. Landlessness increased, urban slums swelled, and the revolutionaries that had forced an end to British rule were re-incarcerated by an emerging political class. These elites grabbed the personal wealth necessary to maintain political power, as Kenya was shaped to feed the newly structured demands of global capitalism.

African history had never been written in the West until Independence. At that point, it was reasoned that new African nation-states needed histories to unify the diverse peoples contained by their borders. European historians went to work crafting a past for Africa that pivoted on Independence and positioned Western-styled nation-states as Africa's inevitable salvation from its own primitivism. Specific histories of Maasai and other pastoral people were written to rationalize the deeper theft of their lands. These histories challenged Maasai identity in the past while producing them into invisibility in the present.

Decolonizing history is thus a necessary part of the actual decolonization of land. Decolonized history inevitably challenges the wealth and power gaps perpetuated through these structures of state power. History is weapon, one which can be wielded either by states or by occupied communities. As a tool of liberation, a written history that resonates with the lived experience and historical memory of a community can serve actual, not metaphoric, decolonization of land.[6] Mau Narok was the place that we learned this lesson.

Because it turns out that the land at Mau Narok itself had not been defeated through its half-century of occupation by corporate agriculture, through the tilling of its soil, burning of its forests, and mining of its water. In the early 2000s, the land had begun to call again to the people. Moses Ole Mpoe, a Maasai manager on one of the large Mau Narok ranches, set out to investigate whether these 5,000 acres were bound by an actual legal title. At that time, people were raising other questions: for example, who had authorized the police who were beating and detaining Maasai women for collecting firewood or water at the edges of barley and wheat fields? People remembered a former settler, Ethyl Powys Cobb, who tried to give land back to the Maasai community—what happened with that attempt?

We responded by heading to Kenya's capital city for information with a class of undergraduate students from Prescott College. In Nairobi we found many surprises, including that no title deeds could be located to verify the ownership of the entire 30,000 acres—a map of the sizes and borders of the actual ranches would have to be built through knowledge on the ground. That took us also to the Kenya National Archive to reconstruct the history of this place where we learned that Maasai did not relinquish their rights to this land. We realized that there was an argument, bound for court, that the land was occupied today illegally under Kenyan law.

It was the Prescott students who presented our findings to several hundred members of the Maasai community in a packed conference room of the Seasons Hotel in Narok Town in August of 2008. Afterward, we discussed what to do with the information into the night. Three days later 700 people moved with their cattle, goats, and sheep back onto Mau Narok, and they began building villages. The reoccupation of Rose, Muthera, and Cecil and other farms that form the larger part of Mau Narok land continues to this day. In March of 2010, fifty-two claimants filed suit in Kenyan High Court under the African Charter and UNDRIP for the return of Mau Narok to the Maasai families that had been displaced.[7]

Government retaliation heated up at that time. Growing numbers of Maasai people were subject to violence by state police and private security forces, to mass arrest, specifically targeted torture of women, threats and assassination of movement leadership. After Ole Mpoe and a companion were assassinated outside of Nakuru following one of many canceled court dates in December of 2010, an estimated 15,000 Maasai people gathered at Mau Narok from across Maasailand to mourn his passing. For three days they fasted, chanting "Melo Enkop," "the land of our forefathers will not go." Draconian state actions that followed included an attempt to give free Mau Narok land to Kenyans from the dominant Kikuyu ethnic community in an apparent attempt to incite "ethnic" violence on the ground. Maasai resistance resulted in roiling civil unrest and daily coverage in Kenyan media.[8] Through many subsequent and equally unsuccessful government attempts, the movement for Maasai land justice continued to grow.

A portion of the land has been returned to the community through a lower court ruling while the National Land Commission has resumed its investigation. It appears that Mau Narok is coming home. But as that happens, it will not be to feed a world designed by the colonizers.

Instead, land rights in Maasailand is a commitment to a restoration of ecological justice through Maasai stewardship. The movement of Maasai people for land justice, known broadly and inclusively by the Swahili word for land, "Shamba," aims to end the assignment of land to death as a commodity. That is the call of the global Indigenous people's movement as it is understood here. Beginning in the 1980s, Maasai embraced Indigenous identity as a new framing that orders the chaos of their condition as neocolonized subjects in an ostensibly post-colonial world. Indigenous identity offers solidarity with other communities colonized by nation-states, whose cultures together may contain the planet's most necessary knowledge on which to build a different future.

Olosho le Maa and Indigenous Futures

A great deal of confusion exists about what it means to be Indigenous in an African context. Indigenous peoples are not recognized by most African nation-states, including Kenya.[9] These describe "indigenous" apolitically, to mean "originating in a place," and indeed all African people are "indigenous" in that way to the continent. But with a capital *I*, the word expresses an identity of solidarity of peoples, communities, and nations throughout the world. These communities share both a condition of a particular oppression within nation-states and are united in a resistance to relinquishing culture and land. The United Nations has acknowledged that the identity does in fact include "marginalized" groups in Africa who identify as Indigenous:

> Domination and colonisation has not exclusively been practiced by white settlers and colonialists. In Africa, dominant groups have also after independence suppressed marginalized groups, and it is this sort of present-day internal suppression within African states that the contemporary African indigenous movement seeks to address.[10]

As it has been used in Maasailand, "Indigenous" describes a collectivizing identity embraced by thousands of unique communities across the globe. These communities are distinct on the landscape of capitalist exploitation because they are cultures structured around accountability to specific and commonly held land. They therefore exist as a roadblock to privatization and unsustainable extractive industry. For Indigenous peoples, total assimilation into nation-states is neither an option nor a solution, because cultural death is equivalent to personal death. Maasai have been treated under Kenya through policies modeled on US Indian policy. Treaties were fabricated and ignored, land subjected to allotment, and boarding schools erected for forced assimilation. Like other Indigenous peoples, Maasai have been repurposed under statehood to represent the "primitive" contrast to the modern state, an identity that was once attributed to all colonized peoples in what is now Kenya. Maasai poverty is rationalized by the supposed backwardness of their culture.

Indigenous communities through their refusal to die are inherently fronts of resistance to the entwined phenomena of 500 years of colonization and expansion of global capitalism. Indigenous peoples defy through their lives the notion that there are no alternatives to the modern organization of life to which much of the world has become accustomed. From Maasailand, much of the common sense of Western culture appears irrational, and other possibilities appear obvious. Possible futures are evidenced by practical solutions currently explored. These include,

1) Communal Use of Land. The pressures to privatize Maasailand are enormous. Following the model of US allotment policy, with funding from the British and US governments, Kenya took steps at Independence to eventually transform Maasailand into privately titled plots. The process was overseen by corrupt agents and land boards backed up by the juridical and police power of the state.[11] Yet in the deepest of rural areas Maasai continue to resist by using titled land communally. Shared use of land is necessary for the survival of pastoralism, which is a form of coexistence with cattle rather than of commodification.[12] Maasailand's economy and its primary management strategy depend upon deferred grazing, which involves strategically migrating around landscapes, and are not possible under relations of private property. Today this traditional science of land management is being applied to changing conditions throughout the community, as tourism and other economic opportunities are compensating for reduced grazing lands. Maasai know through centuries of cycles of drought and rain that it is possible to sustain and even reignite the vibrance of the land's own intelligence and to strengthen and reknit its ecology.

2) Dense and Resilient Community. Shared use of un-partitioned land and other resources requires a strong and flexible social system to manage grazing rights and thus all other aspects of decision-making. The culture itself is a product of shared land use. Its layers of governance and dense social scaffolding web individuals to thousands of other specific individuals, creating a structural basis for consensus decision-making. The density of this scaffolding produces social visibility in Maasailand; there is no "private" space imagined to be only the business of an individual family. The communal nature of Maasai society prevents any form of incarceration of any social group, and there is even no *Maa* word for "freedom," as there is no grasp in the language of an opposite condition.[13] Today Maasai cultural courts, not the courts of the Kenyan state, are the first avenue of redress for crimes committed in the community. Entire clans rather than mere individuals are held accountable for the behavior of their members and fines assessed with livestock for all crimes, even those as serious as murder.[14]

The social scaffolding is maintained through ritual. Colonization waged war on Maasai ceremonial life for decades, yet it has survived and recently a cultural resurgence has flooded the land, and many thousands of people gather for ceremonies. Young Maasai men and women have been leaving jobs in Nairobi for months to join age-mates who maintain the herding economy, together smearing ochre on their bodies and sleeping on the skins in ceremonial villages.[15] In its social scaffolding, which balances the needs of individuals, the community, and the land, Maasai culture has practical insight to share about how to rebuild a society after the collapse of externally induced incentives to civility. Maasai society is not defined by any measure of blood quantum but by accountability to the community and the land, and Maasailand has welcomed outsiders who accept those terms through its history.

3) Conservation of Ecosystems through Coexistence. Communal use of land is also the chief conservation strategy in Maasai culture and the reason that Africa's greatest wildlife are found in Maasailand and virtually nowhere else in East Africa outside of parks and reserves. To share grasses, forests, and water with wildlife communities requires respect and recognition of equal rights to exist and to negotiate resource use. Communal use of land also forms the basis of Maasailand's approach to development. While the Kenyan government receives close to 14 percent

of its revenue from tourism, mining, agriculture, and other industries in Maasailand, it does not build infrastructure there as it does in even the poorest parts of Central Kenya. What that has meant is that Maasailand is dependent on outside donors for basic infrastructure—schools, clinics, and water sources. In some cases, this has created the opportunity for locally led development that embeds a Maasai approach to sharing resources. For example, water projects have in some cases been located through community consensus processes that ensures that water will not be privatized or sold for profit, and that elephant migratory routes will not be disturbed—community priorities like schools, clinics, and cooperatives will be watered, but not undesirable activities like commercial agriculture.[16] One of the greatest challenges and opportunities facing Maasailand today is of extreme variations in weather patterns that seemingly overnight have brought floods and continuous rain to some historically dry land, swelling dry rivers and rapidly growing forested areas, while others face unrelenting drought. Climate variance is not new in Maasailand and strategies of adaptation draw on centuries of experience.

Maasai culture can be described as a structural relationship to land, a humility, and a specifically grounded expertise in ways of shaping human economies to the long-term sustenance of life. Maasailand demonstrates that alternatives to the global culture of capitalism not only exist but are being practiced today. But the profound resource of Maasai culture can be missed by outsiders, those who have been trained to cognitively dismiss Indigenous cultures as relics of past worlds, impossible as features of the present. The colonization of history may be the most potent source of this false and destructive construct, and that awareness led to this book.

Decolonizing Maasai History

Though many younger Maasai people are now being "educated" out of their historical sense, Maasai elders still know their history. History in Maasailand is a body of knowledge produced through processes of interpretation by consensus and transmitted orally. It is a story that extends back in time through many generations and is periodized not by years but by the names chosen by age groups in ceremony. It is structured around wars, droughts, migrations, and times of conflict within the community. Recent history pivots on the near destruction of Maasai society 150 years ago with the arrival of British military in Maasailand, "the time of death," or *emutai* in the Maa language. It is a story of the strategies, betrayal, conflicts, defeats, and ultimate survival of people living under foreign, and then—after Kenyan Independence—domestic occupation. History exists to pass on to each new generation stories of how survival has been achieved and threatened through time, and what the past implies about future efforts.

But that is not typically the history found in books about the Maasai published in the West, even in those otherwise expressing support for Maasai people. In many of these, before their colonization, Maasai are depicted not as a society with a dense and complex social polity but as bands of nomadic peoples who shared a language. Maasai are said to have only developed a consciousness of themselves as a community and culture through their removal onto reservations by the British, so through the agency of their colonizers. Generally, published works describe the near-destruction of Maasai society in the early years of British colonization as the "triple disasters," primarily the result of acts of god— disease and drought, not of intentional violence.[17] Even when the violence is acknowledged, notably in Lotte Hughes' influential *Moving the Maasai*, it is nevertheless presented as "a colonial misadventure." That is, Hughes focuses on missteps, bungling, and individual pernicious actors within the colonial apparatus, rather than on violence as a structural element of colonization itself.[18] However, Hughes rightly points out how often Western Maasai history overlooks Maasai resistance to colonization and thus "downplays African agency."[19] The idea that Maasai society did not substantially resist colonization is the most destructive in written Maasai history, and it has led to a popular interpretation of Maasai as British collaborators.[20] This particular silencing, in the words of Michel-Rolph Trouillot, these "forces" of historical production "are no less powerful" than "gunfire, class property, or political crusades."[21] This silencing creates an illusion that acts of rebellion are disconnected from historical context, are nothing more than emotional reactions to fleeting dissatisfactions, masking evidence of a commitment to liberation expressed through generations.

Although contemporary Western historians would no doubt be harshly critical of such viewpoints, it is nevertheless also worth noting that the primary sources on which Maasai history was first framed demonstrated through their hostility that Maasai were indeed enemies. They included statements like this one from an official "Masai Reserve Annual Report" in 1921:

The Maasai are a decadent race and have survived through being brought under the protection of British rule. But for this they would certainly have been exterminated by the more virile and numerous African tribes. They remain primitive savages who have never evolved and who under present condition, in all probability, never can evolve. Their environment is fatal. They live under conditions of indescribable filth in an atmosphere of moral, physical and mental degeneration. A large proportion of them are diseased or deformed. The infant mortality is appalling, and the birth rate an extraordinary one.[22]

British functionaries in the Kenyan colony demonstrated a willingness to lie to their superiors in London to maintain a story that the Maasai were willing to go quietly, and that they were handling Maasai evictions peacefully. Thus, British sources must be read with care and nothing they claim about Maasai society, or about military engagements and massacres, can be taken at face value; they must be supported with other evidence and aligned with oral history.

Written history of the Maasai ends at Kenyan Independence where an even more totalizing erasure occurs. At this point, the Maasai are absorbed with all other Kenyan communities who did not inherit power into an amorphous collective. The word "Maasai" barely exists in histories of the Kenyan state. This erasure erodes the ground on which Maasai can assert a right to self-representation and to land.

Looking at history outward from Maasailand requires that we revise the broad strokes of Kenyan, and then African, history. This is mainly because for the Maasai people colonization did not end with Independence. In some critical ways, colonization was not accomplished *until* the advent of Kenyan statehood. What Maasai people have experienced, and the archival evidence supports, is that Mau Narok and other Maasai lands were not fully and permanently occupied until the Kenyan state assumed power from the British colony in 1963. The transition from colonial to neocolonial power in Kenya is a story of continuity and expansion rather than rupture and reinvention. Thus, the book adopts the language of African intellectuals who have interrogated *neocolonialism* in Africa since Independence. The book also engages with critiques of nation-statehood beyond Kenya. It pursues obvious parallels with other neocolonial and especially settler colonial contexts, and with the work of Indigenous scholars in other parts of the world.[23]

In presenting Maasai history through the years of Kenyan statehood, this book breaks with some current academic conventions in African history that treat the assertion of identity by an "ethnic community" such as the Maasai as threatening to the cohesion of nation-states and even dangerous in its utterance. In Kenya in particular, ethnic difference is often blamed as the source of post-election violence.[24] We argue instead that the roots of such conflict are found in the consolidation of power of the Kenyan state and its function on behalf of structures of global capitalism that funnel the wealth, the land, and labor of Kenya, for capture elsewhere. Post-election violence has actually been engineered by, and undertaken among, competing political parties in a contest over state power, not the Indigenous communities asserting their rights to identity.[25] Yet it is the Indigenous communities that are targeted for their claim to identity, and even expression of "being Maasai" risks potential censure from the Kenyan state. More broadly, Indigenous scholar Rudolph Ryser found that the conflicts following Independence throughout Africa, while known in history as "civil wars" produced through "ethnic violence," are better characterized as wars of states against Indigenous peoples asserting the right to exist.[26]

An important step in the decolonization of Maasai history has been to undertake a study of the history itself—the academic production of Maasai people as a historical object. The field of Maasai history was established, along with all African history, as nation-states were formed at Independence. Maasai historical studies centered on the question of whether Maasai (and other Indigenous) identity is real and provable. The assumption would have been in the negative as no African people were granted historical subjectivity at that time in the Western academy. As late as 1963, Oxford's senior historian argued that there was no African history. He claimed that any search would uncover only a timeless, "unrewarding gyrations of barbarous tribes."[27] The field of Maasai history has been animated ever since through a tension between identity and rights to land and sovereignty. In this book, we trace its origins.

To understand the origins of the field of Maasai history, we need to understand the recent part that Western history has played in the longer 500-year project of Western colonization of the world. History as an academic discipline produces a universal perspective about colonization, that of the colonizing societies. It also creates a complex discursive landscape, body of knowledge, and mechanisms for establishing truth, which Stuart Hall has called the "western cultural archive."[28] Linda Tuhiwai Smith describes how one aspect of this arm of imperial power works in her Māori community.[29] The raw materials of a community's own knowledge, information, data such as the use of a plant for medicine, or the story of a people's origin in the world—a version of their history—are useful in the fashioning of Western hegemonic power through a process similar to other forms of mining. The information extracted from colonized places is brought to centers of imperial power, the universities, museums, institutions, publishing apparatuses in Europe and the United States. There it is made "meaningful," and used to contribute to the stories produced in Western cultures that together create the deep structures of thought through which colonization is normalized and made sensical. History was brought into new service in the formation of nation-states after the Second World War as a mechanism for building national identities for peoples encompassed by state borders. These were often the same borders produced under formal colonization. History produces "knowledge" essential to the illusion that nation-states are founded on the will of the people they claim. It produces knowledge that the occupation of Indigenous peoples occurred in the past and is settled in the present. It reifies the idea that the nation-state itself is the truest form of governance invented by human societies. History is essential to rationalizing the incoherence of modern nation-states. It does so by producing a story in which democracy and freedom can coexist with slavery and genocide for example, a story that masks the obvious and actually impossible contradictions.

The power of history in particular is wielded most effectively through those characteristics of academic history that are taken for granted. For example, we often take for granted in the West that the purpose of history is to produce one universal coherent narrative. We thus treat history as a mapping project that must incorporate all parts of the world into a single picture in order to be complete. It is not accidental but inherent in this approach that Western history will extinguish, rather than coexist with, non-Western histories. Equally, the questions taken into the archives are often assumed to be the entitlement of individual historians who are encouraged to follow their own curiosity and are not subject to any structural accountability to the people they represent. They need only conform their writing with current conventions in the Western academy. A third example is the division of human history into "prehistory" and "history" as different fields organized around different methods. This separation can lead to an unconscious location of non-literate, non-capitalist societies backward in time to a pre-civilized past, eclipsing their existence in the present.

These conventions produce Indigenous and other minoritized peoples into what Trouillot calls "silences," the aggressive production of colonized peoples into nonexistence through narrative. This silencing is actively performed.

> [O]ne "silences" a fact or an individual as a silencer silences a gun. One engages in the practices of silencing. Mentions and silences are thus active, dialectical counterparts of which history is the synthesis.[30]

Silencing occurs through the process of the production of archives, the institutions that collect and assemble sources, vetting what is true and "debatable," and determining "the difference between a historian, amateur or professional, and a charlatan."[31] Silencing occurs in the lack of recognition that non-Western societies *have* history themselves, have their own rules to distinguish between history and fiction, and assert "epistemic validity" in non-Western ways.[32]

Maasailand, its resources and its knowledge, continues to be mined today through similar means and infrastructure as other apparatuses of extraction built under British colonization. Researchers abound, some of whom have lived in their tented camps for years. They track cheetah populations, the promise of certain herbs for pharmaceutical production, or Maasai folklore or gender systems. These researchers sometimes develop genuine friendships with individual Maasai people. But they also, and more typically, may have no relationship with the surrounding Maasai community even after years of living, in essence, in the community's living room. "History" has arrived in the form of a researcher with a tape recorder and list of interview questions vetted by a university IRB process. A local interpreter/guide will be hired and will secure interviews with their relatives, so information will be randomly gathered rather than through the recognized structures of knowledge production in the community under study. The researcher will often promise to return and share what they have learned, though it is rare for them to follow through.

Thus, academic research has been experienced not as a means to knowledge, but as another means of extraction, similar to what is experienced through tourism, where a piece of something precious in Maasai culture is exchanged for very little money. People know that their words have more value than what they are getting in return. It is common to hear an elder express some version of "how many dissertations and articles have I helped to write? How many people who already have jobs have a I helped get better jobs, while I cannot afford to send my own children to school?" Historians are likely unaware of the power they wield by following a research agenda through their own curiosity, the questions that align with their common sense. If pursued unconsciously, questions about Maasai society by a non-Maasai historian will inevitably frame Maasai history through imperial epistemologies. It will center a Western line of sight, draw too uncritically on colonial sources, and essentially feed an assumption that Maasai are objects of their own history.

Sometimes work by Western historians recognized as experts on Maasai history and society has helped to support political positions opposed to the community's own. For example, David Western has argued for decades that Maasai society hunts and eats wildlife in times of drought, considering them to be "second cattle." He based this claim on an anomalous, uncited, and individual example.[33] The practice is in fact generally unknown throughout Maasailand and offensive to Maasai common sense, but Maasai people have not been present at the academic conferences where this claim has been made, nor have they been aware of its dissemination through English language journals. Western's work has been used to dismiss the universal Maasai resistance to a proposed reintroduction of commercial hunting in Maasailand, while Western himself, a British Kenyan raised to hunt African wildlife, actively promotes such a reintroduction of hunting to fund "conservation."[34]

The written history has also challenged the ability of the Maasai community to remember and interpret the meaning of its own past, and its ability to differentiate between fact and fantasy. One example is found in the telling of the meaning of *Entorror*, the northern homeland from which Maasai were violently evicted and sought to reclaim through the early twentieth century. To Maasai, *Entorror* has deep significance to Maasai identity; it evokes the oral knowledge of the long history of resistance to British occupation, and thus articulates a commitment to land justice in the present. But in written history, the significance of *Entorror* has been reduced instead to an "attachment" to lost territory that "represents a larger nostalgia for the past."

> "The Purko's last foothold in Entorror, Laikipia has taken on the status of a lost Eden in social memory. It is said to have been sweet, disease-free, blessed by good pastures and plentiful rain, in contrast to the bitterness" of the south. Intertwined with this idea is nostalgia for the concept of a Maasai nation and nationalist identity ... Entorror was both a place and a defining moment, which many Maasai set against the disharmony and disunity of the present time. The current political struggles over land, resources and power can only be understood in this context.[35]

In this quotation from Hughes's *Moving the Maasai*, the longing for a "lost Eden" is a mythology produced by the culture of the historians but not of those they have been empowered to interpret, and the metaphor is not benign.[36] Elsewhere, Hughes has said that the struggle and strategies of Maasai communities making claims to their traditional lands are a problematic example of "what happens when 'memory' [and its uses in political agitation] becomes confused with 'history.'"[37] Just two years before *Moving the Maasai* was published, Maasai people had launched the first land rights campaign of a generation in a larger century-long fight for the return of *Entorror*, Laikipia.[38]

Decolonizing Maasai history requires that we carefully consider the impact of theories produced in the West as they have been used to frame African and Indigenous histories. Social constructivism emerged in the 1960s as a brilliant interrogation of the deep structures of Western thought through which imperialism could have appeared rational.[39] It provides a means to explore *Western cultures*, the fracturing in the Western mind of the world's peoples into "civilized" and "savage," the distribution of power by socially constructed categories of identity.[40] A core element of this theory is a critique of Western universalisms. But the search for the social construction of identity has often been applied in pedestrian ways to Indigenous African cultures that instead silence their self-representation. As will be discussed further in Chapter 1, historians of written Maasai history have suggested that since "all identity is socially constructed," any cultural change over time can be treated as evidence that Maasai identity is "fluid" beyond the grasp of Maasai people themselves, and therefore Maasai's own self-identification can be deemed unsophisticated and inauthentic through interrogation by Western scholarship.[41]

Gender theory is another area of Western scholarship that has been applied reductively to African contexts.[42] "Gender" as it is known in the West was introduced to Africa by colonization, where in the words of Yoruban scholar, Oyèrónkẹ́ Oyěwùmí, the "creation of 'women' was one of the very first accomplishments of the colonial state."[43] Europeans did not *discover* African women to be an oppressed social class, but rather *invented* them as such, through the colonial apparatus that stripped women of their traditional leadership and denied them all powers controlled by the colonial state: education and literacy, land ownership and rights under customary law.[44] In many African places, including Maasailand, that discrimination continues deep into statehood, and today Maasai women are disadvantaged in all arenas of power introduced or monopolized by the West.[45] But this historical context has been missed in much Western scholarship which has assumed entitlement to probe all manner of African women's personal lives in the name of "sisterhood." Such scholarship has claimed that African women are oppressed instead by the men of their own cultures, especially through 'cultural practices.'[46] Since Independence, some Western feminist activists have pushed for criminalization of the practices of rural African societies, especially marriage and circumcision, and their campaigns have actually undermined women's health and autonomy. The history reconstructed by Dorothy Hodgson demonstrates that such efforts promote colonizing agendas:

Even the "awareness" campaigns had little resonance with Maasai communities. Most of the campaigns echoed the rhetoric and assumptions of colonial and postcolonial development initiatives, with their emphasis on "educating" Maasai about their "backward" and "primitive" practices in an effort to develop and modernize them.[47]

As all but a fraction of Maasai women have had no access to Western education, they cannot speak directly to conversations about them and are typically objects of scholarship where they show up. Maasai women are thus among those "third world women" identified by Gayiatri Spivak, who are denied their own enunciation, and used to rationalize neocolonial intervention undertaken "on their behalf."[48]

It is in fact Maasai culture that provides spaces of resistance to women's disempowerment, through traditional means of asserting voice and by strengthening non-capitalist economies. Maasai women continue to build and "own" houses and their share of livestock, direct many aspects of the community's internal economy, control the distribution of food, maintain exclusive control of courts assembled for crimes against women, and determine many parts of ceremonial life and education. In her recent work, Dorothy Hodgson offers a radical and necessary new direction for the study of "gender" in Maasailand, reconstructing the use of Western gender systems in the colonial project.[49] Entering the topic through new doors, she discovered that Maasai women's collective action in Tanzania has focused on land rights, not "cultural practices," which aligns with our own experience. While we applaud this redirection, we ourselves do not wade into analyzing gender in Maasailand. We await the input of a broader representation of Maasai people empowered through Western education to enter the conversation on their own behalf.

Olosho le Maa and Writing History

To "decolonize" Maasai history requires that we start over from the beginning and orient the field differently through different questions. The field of Maasai history was established by people who are not themselves Maasai and who do not speak Maa. Their orienting question was "who are these people and when did they begin?" We turn to the same published and archival sources that they used but with different questions, ones that respond to gaps in Maasai society's historical knowledge. We ask, "what do British or Kenyan records say about how we lost this particular land?" and "what happened behind doors in the secret meetings at which our treaty rights were denied?" The community's own historical process directed us to the right places to look for the silenced story, a history of resistance undertaken through every conceivable means from the first moment of occupation to the present.

This requires empowering Maasai society's own processes of history production. The frames of Maasai research methodologies are recognizable to those trained in Western methods. An entire language exists in Maa to describe aspects of research, *Enjurore*, literally translated as investigation, or *Enkikilikuanare*, inquiry. They involve data collection methods similar to qualitative methods in English, and similar safeguards to ensure rigor.[50] To that end, research is conducted with transparency. No accounts are incorporated if the speaker is not willing to have their words repeated and attributed. A recognition of the researcher's positionality is essential to the process as is impartiality. A single lie told by a Maasai person will have the effect of discrediting that person forever, so great care is taken to repeat only what is known to be accurate.

Research in Maasailand is conducted through the structure of age groups. The oldest generations have the two most important responsibilities: first to ensure that the history their generation received is accurately passed down, and second to conduct the process through which more recent events and phenomena are interpreted and added to the historical narrative. Today these are the elders of the *Ilinguesi* and *Ilseuri* age groups. They function as a university press might in a Western context: soliciting information, vetting the accuracy of accounts, debating interpretations, and adjusting larger narratives. History will be retained in this fashion for roughly twenty generations after which time most of the detailed knowledge will be allowed to fade. These elders are responsible for disseminating history, which is undertaken through families. Children are taught history at home and more formally through ceremonies. History is one of the main subjects taught at *Eunoto*, *Olng'esherr*, and other graduation ceremonies between age groups, and the skills taught include repetition of oral narratives to develop the capacity for memorization, enabling a Maasai person to recite long testimony verbatim at courts and other forums. This training begins for Maasai children in childhood. The preparation for each graduation ceremony typically takes years as historical interpretations are forged, and whatever is taught at ceremonies will stand from that point as the reigning historical canon.

The production of history in Maasailand, both the past, *Erishata Tulusotie*, and the process of historical production, *Enjurrore e Enkatitin*, differs from

Western history in some important ways. While some Maasai people take a particular interest in history and thus become recognized as "historians," these do not form a special class of experts. All Maasai people participate with equal weight in the production of narrative. Second, Maasai speak in poetics and with continuous metaphoric reference to historical memory. That has been presented in an undignified way by those who capture these words but not their meaning, as "primitive" speech. The vetting process for Maasai history is necessarily different as it does not rely on citation, as these paragraphs demonstrate. However, this book and all the knowledge it contains, including these uncited claims about the historical processes in Maasailand, will be "published" orally, disseminated through the community, and subject to intense scrutiny. Any inaccurate claims will be challenged and corrected. Finally, Maasai history has not historically benefitted from the archival sources in Nairobi and London. These hold the promise to not only support but also expand and challenge Maasai narratives in productive ways.

The process of interpreting Maasai history has afforded great attention to violent incidents. These include the event known as the *Laikipiak* wars of the mid-nineteenth century, where the decision of all *iloshon*, sections of Maasai society, to undertake a totalizing war against one that had become dominant, has been repeatedly interrogated. It includes what is known as the Kedong massacre of 1895, the events of the early 1920s known collectively by the name *Ololulunga* massacre, and many other moments. It includes more recent violent encounters in Likia forest over agricultural settlement, as well as the violent clashes at Entasapukia between Maasai and Kikuyu settlers in the late 1990s. This knowledge, similar to what is contained in a Western archive, has great potential value beyond Maasailand and could be shared.

History is recognized as an expression of power in Maasailand. When we notice that the field of Maasai history is written, debated, interpreted, and even typically researched in Europe and the United States, many thousands of miles from Maasailand, other more basic inequalities are cast in deeper relief. The resources necessary for a Maasai person to pursue even a secondary degree are often prohibitive. Maasai people with PhDs can be counted on one's fingers. Decolonizing history requires that we recognize that these inequalities are not facts of nature but have been historically produced.

Yet Western researchers can be essential partners in decolonizing projects. This book could not have been written without the information gathered and published by Kenyan and other Africanist historians. As our project required us to begin with the common sense of Maasai oral history rather than the framing of published history, the interpretations of this book and those published histories are often misaligned. It is our hope that different interpretations of African, Kenyan, and Maasai history can coexist and inform each other through dialogue rather than in competition over a "one true narrative" that favors a Western line of sight and discourages books such as this one from being published.

Narrative coexistence in Maasai history is necessary because the alternative has led to silencing, and the erasure of a people's history is a form of violence that enables and masks other more tangible violence. A colonized history engenders a splitting of the self of the colonized, an intimate rupture between what one knows and "the truth," and a diminishment of the value of everything one loves. For Maasai people to be recognized as modern subjects, they must accept that their assignment as objects is natural, and that others are inherently better equipped to represent them than they themselves. In other words, to colonize a people's history is to induce madness. While this book is intended to be an intervention into academic conversations, its deeper purpose is thus far from academic. Hopefully it will be the first of many written by the people of Maasailand, especially the young people as they continue their educations in Western as well as Maasai historical knowledge. In these pages we critique specific works and in some cases historians themselves. Our intention is never to offend or harm, but rather to expose specific ways that history has been wielded as a weapon of neocolonial structures of power beyond the intention of historians. We consider the Maasai community to have a right to this knowledge. The book is written for the whole of *Olosho le Maa* and all Indigenous communities in East Africa, in commitment to our common purpose. It is written for the other minoritized peoples of Kenya and Africa to support fronts of anticolonial solidarity among us. Finally, this book is written to give back to the Indigenous peoples engaged in similar work throughout the world from whom we have gained tremendous knowledge and understanding ourselves.

To decolonize Maasai history is to shift the role of Western researchers from gatekeepers to collaborators, and this inevitably involves sharing resources. That may look like devoting time to securing tuition remission for Maasai scholars, sharing access to journals, to paid work, opportunities to teach, to publishing networks and conferences, to libraries and computers, and to all levels of formal education. Time is a valuable resource that can be shared among colleagues, as is fluency in English and in academic culture and discourses. From that place, we have found that the tools of Western scholarship can in fact be used in the service of redistribution of power and to the decolonization of history, and Western academics can be critical partners in that work. With our deepest respect to the insight of Audrey Lorde, in Maasailand we find that the master's tools can in fact be used to dismantle the master's house. But only if all of those holding the tools can step outside of the house and be willing to let it fall.[51]

Chapters

In Chapter 1, "Maasai History and the Strategies of Neocolonialism," we pursue a gap in the historical knowledge of Maasai society about why and how a field of study came to be produced about Maasai history that excluded the involvement of Maasai people. This search led to a realization that the broader field of African history was strategically produced at the time of African Independence as a mechanism to create imaginary pasts for African states and to produce into silence the diversity of African people, especially those who would come to identify as Indigenous. The chapter thus contextualizes the academic field of Maasai history within an alternative periodization and narrative framing of Independence, one that reflects the "good sense" of Maasailand that Kenyan statehood did not end colonization. It revives earlier critiques of Kwame Nkrumah and other decolonial activists that used a language of neocolonialism.

Chapter 2, "*Kenyamal Enkop*: The History of Maasailand Occupation," retraces the continuity of land occupation through the twentieth century under British colonization and the Kenyan state. Maasailand was imagined at this time to be an empty territory, whitened through a relatively short period of British occupation, and specifically used after Independence to build the personal wealth and political power of Kenya's neocolonial ruling class. This chapter responds to the primary interest of Maasai scholars, oral historians, and activists in archival historical reconstruction, articulated through versions of the question: "How specifically did we lose our land?"

Chapter 3, "*Melo Enkop*: The Story of Mau Narok," presents the research that contributed to sparking the land rights movement and court case at Mau Narok. It describes the deliberate economic segregation and disempowerment of Maasai people through tribalist politics of the Kenyan government and the production of Maasai society as impoverished and politically powerless, to facilitate land occupation. This chapter also details the activism of the Maasai United Front and their alternative vision in the era of Kenyan Independence for a coexistence of a Maa nation and Kenyan state.

Chapter 4, "*Amboseli*: The Past and Future of Conservation in Maasailand," presents research conducted on a Kenyan government seizure of another area of Maasai land through the creation of the Amboseli National Park. It presents an example of how poverty and underdevelopment are strategically produced in the reconstruction of Maasailand to facilitate wildlife tourism. It shows how the collusion of the conservation and tourism industries has prevented Maasai assumption of their historical role as stewards of wildlife ecosystems and communities.

Chapter 5, "*Olosho le Maa* and the Long Century of Anticolonial Resistance," offers a new narrative frame of Maasai history. It brings archival and secondary source history into focus through the common sense and historical knowledge of *Olosho le Maa*.

The concluding chapter "Conclusion: *Entaisere* (the Future)" presents the hope for decolonizing Maasai history and the future of Maasailand.

This book is drawn from our engagement with the history of Kenyan Maasai, those living north of the Tanzanian border, and what is written in English. The histories of Kenyan and Tanzanian Maasai must be reknitted, with the whole of *Olosho le Maa*. That is a future project for Maasai historians, but one not undertaken in this book.

Maasai History and the Strategies of Neocolonialism

How does it feel to be an object in your own history?

"Everyone 'knows' the Maasai," begins the current authoritative book on Maasai history. "Men wearing red capes while balancing on one leg and a long spear, gazing out over the semi-arid plains stretching endlessly to the horizon."[1] A Western reader will recognize the setup: this book begins with a romanticized imaginary of the "noble primitive" in order to debunk it, exposing instead a grittier more authentic reality. But look again these words through the eyes of a Maasai person: the "everyone" invited into this exploration of Maasai identity does not include Maasai people themselves. Thumbing through the pages of this book, a Maasai reader will see that Maasai people are not among its authors or even sources.[2] If they have sufficient literacy in English and sit down to read the book, they will discover that the chapters together culminate in a challenge to the idea that Maasai have an historical identity. They will see no evidence that their own oral history has been consulted in this claim. If a Maasai person encounters this book through their work as a tour guide in a lodge gift shop, they might shrug off such a strange and disorienting discovery.

But that option will not exist for a Maasai person encountering the book through formal education. For them, becoming educated will mean accepting that Maasai identity is a thing knowable, and perhaps only knowable, through the expertise of Western scholarship. They will have to begin to see the identity of their community as a property of the West. It is the nonchalance of this assumption that demonstrates how Western history serves the coloniality of power in Maasailand. Maasailand is imagined to be empty of its own historians and historical narratives, a virgin territory on which the Western academy can explore and settle itself.

The first step to decolonizing Maasai History has thus been to understand how power works through it, and this chapter reflects that effort. We reconstruct the historical moment into which Maasai History was born as an academic field of study in the West. That moment is known as the era of "African Independence," during which scholars wrote for the first time a historical narrative that encompassed the African continent. African history was primarily established to create stories of unified pasts for new African nation-states, and that narrative pivoted on Independence as the moment of Africa's awakening into modernity. Histories were also written at this time for the communities like the Maasai who defied the call to abandon their cultures, who practiced ecological economies across borders, and who stood in the way of the colonizing severance of people from land. Those histories, of Africa's Indigenous peoples, engaged with the authenticity of their claimed identities as a central theme.

To read this history through a Maasai line of sight is to see continuity in the long century of colonization, and to see African Independence as something other than an anticolonial event. From Maasailand, African decolonization not only remains unachieved, it has yet to be undertaken.

The Myth of Independence

Beginning in the late 1950s and following anticolonial movements across the continent, some fifty African states were founded within the borders of former European colonies into Cold War geopolitics. The era is known as African Independence. Kenya was created in this era, in 1963 as a capitalist nation-state in the sphere of the West. Kenya emerged into statehood with a new ruling class, dominated by one of Kenya's over forty-two ethnic communities, from the Kiambu region of Kikuyu homeland in Central Kenya. For Kikuyu people, Independence meant a return of all colonized homeland. For its entitled classes, it also meant inheritance of the financial, governmental, and policing infrastructure through which power over African peoples had been built and wielded by the British.

But what this era brought to Maasailand was instead a new deeper, "hyper" form of colonization. Not an acre of occupied Maasailand was returned to the Maasai people.[3] Some Europeans were enabled by the new state to hold on to the hundreds of thousands of the most fertile acres of Maasailand settled by themselves or their parents. Other huge tracts of Maasailand were occupied without title by Kenya's president and his family and political associates. Central Kenyan people were given still other tracts through settlement schemes that dispersed the Kikuyu base of political power throughout the country. As a new government and civil society were being formed in Nairobi of primarily Kikuyu people, the British colonial administration in Maasailand was retained virtually intact. Correspondence among local administrators in the Maasailand headquarters of Narok and Ngong barely recognizes the political revolution supposed to have been underway in 1963.[4] Even high-ranking British colonial administrators were retained in Nairobi to oversee resource extraction in Maasailand. These included Bruce McKenzie, Minister of Agriculture, who engineered the dismantling of grazing land and introduction of fully commercial agriculture in the Mau Narok region, which will be discussed at length in Chapter 3. Magadi, one of the richest soda ash mines in the world, had been carved out of Maasailand in the early twentieth century. Under statehood, it continued to produce behind the same fortressed walls built by the British for the same international corporation, Tata Industries.[5]

What changed under the Kenyan state was the speed of the seizure of Maasai land and removal of Maasai from it. This was accomplished through settlement schemes and elite land grabbing as mentioned, and also new national parks and through individual sale as communal land was privatized. Towns in Maasailand grew to facilitate the movement of wealth from rural areas. They were constructed to house grainaries, cattle markets, and breweries, and they swelled with Central Kenyan business people. These towns quickly became unlivable. Narok, the biggest town in Kenyan Maasailand, has 40,000 residents but not a single park, no sewage system, and a faulty electrical grid restricted to the business class. The town regularly floods, killing people and livestock, as it has no functional city planning. Narok epitomizes the neocolonial African state model of unequal development as a typical "funnel" town between big cities like Nairobi, "dense, high-technology islands" and the lifeless "surrounding peasant economy."[6] The new Chinese-funded dry port railroad system under development cuts through Kedong and Suswa, similarly to the British railroad of the colonial era, without the informed consent of the community.[7] To this day, the Kenyan government has barely built any schools or clinics or boreholes in Maasailand. It has barely built or then maintained roads or built electrical grids. In Central Kenya however, children in government-funded schools have computers and labs. Middle-class government workers travel eight-lane highways in their SUVs between their comfortable homes in Central Kenya and their jobs in Nairobi. Fifty-plus years since the supposed end of colonization in Kenya, Maasai women spend their lives walking the landscape to find enough drinkable water for their families for a day. They sometimes die in childbirth within view of five-star lodges that line the river banks as part a billion-shilling wildlife tourism industry existing on Maasai land. The industry brings almost no benefit to the Maasai people.

Maasais were not alone in this new condition. Maasailand is but one local point of extraction within a new formation of global imperialism that continued the colonizing project in a different form, a new "coloniality of power" in the words of Anibal Quijano.[8] After the Second World War, the center of Western power shifted from Europe to the United States and has been distributed among new international actors over time. But "the west," defined here with Stuart Hall as a "*historical*, not a geographical construct," remained dominant. It continued to be the beneficiary of wealth that continued to be mined from the African continent and other once formerly colonized spaces.[9] Not just Maasai land but the lands of people across the world have been reoccupied under ostensibly "post-colonial" conditions. Two-thirds of outside purchases of agricultural land in the Global South in the first decade of the twenty-first century, typically for biofuel, food, and mineral production, have occurred in countries with "serious hunger problems." Land is purchased through typically ninety-year leases for mineral extraction, fuel crops like palm, and as a hedge against anticipated global food and water wars. An estimated 20 to 50 million hectares of African land has already been taken in what is being compared to a present-day Berlin-style[10] agreement between developed countries for control of African resources, this time around including China, South Korea, India, and Gulf Arab states. This reoccupation of land requires the removal of communities and creates classes of landless urban people.[11] In regard to Africa, these dynamics have been described as a "new colonization."

> Tragically, a silent recolonisation on a mass scale is happening through further dispossession in areas where the original colonisation had not been complete. The new colonisation is dressed in the language of economic development and fighting poverty but its interest is the satisfaction of the needs of multinational companies for markets and land to grow food for export.[12]

Wealth has flowed from Africa to the West through structures built into the economies and governances of African states. New African governments were loaned funds that had strings attached, and their economies were typically manipulated after through stipulations on debt repayment, interest rates, and currency valuation. Western investors have used price controls and other market restrictions to push investments friendly to international capital, forcing African governments to limit their investment in education and health care and similar priorities. There are many mechanisms of the flow of wealth outward from

Africa, including the interest on loans never repaid, and "debt cancellation ... workers remittances, and unrecorded capital flight" through tax havens. When we consider these, says a recent study, we see that the much-touted Western humanitarian aid to Africa is a drop compared to the flow of "aid" from Africa to the West, a net of more than $16 trillion between 1980 and 2016, an amount roughly the size of the US GDP.[13] David Harvey and Ellen Meiksins Wood call this "the new imperialism" of a world now defined by universal capitalism and dissemination of economic power to new actors in Southeast Asia and China.[14]

The West has tried for decades to mystify these dynamics and naturalize Global South poverty as a problem, not of this wealth transfer, but of a lack of "development." The story told is that the West has unlocked the key to abundant wealth which will also eventually rain on the former colonies if they accept Western control: in essence, the poison of Western intervention will become the cure in time.[15] The story is a version of the "dual mandate" through which European colonization was rationalized as a "civilizing project" undertaken for the benefit of the "natives." Its roots run even deeper, in the evolution of Western thought through 500 years of colonization and its radical reinvention of the meaning of history and of time. Quijano describes the process through which Europe reimagined those societies they conquered as not merely inferior, but actually existing in the past along a storyline of progress "whose culmination was Europe."[16] Europeans came to imagine, he says, "non-Europeans" to be in fact "pre-Europeans," on a path from "the traditional to the modern, from the magic-mythic to the scientific."[17] Quijano says that this core idea was retained as Europe's colonies transitioned to states, as an attempt to produce among the colonized an unattainable desire to become Western, the new face of the "civilized" and the end goal of development.[18] "Development theory" enabled the United States to justify its assumption of the helm of the new coloniality after the Second World War while maintaining its self-image as the global moral standard bearer. Through the lens of development, "the world" became a monolith in the Western imagination. In the words of Gustavo Esteva, development discourse prevents the peoples of the Global South from "being what they were, in all their diversity" as they had become "transmogrified into an inverted mirror of others reality: a mirror that belittles them and sends them off to the end of the queue."[19]

Decades later, development theory has undergone constant reinvention and critique in the West and the Global South as failure after failure are acknowledged.[20] But still the basic premise continues to structure discourse in the West, where the problem of Africa is of lack of development, which is calculated on the bloated "needs" of an idealized Western lifestyle. The idea was embedded in the new global financial institutions, the "Bretton Woods" of the World Bank and IMF.

At this same time however, African people had begun to use a different language to describe their own encounters with the new power matrix: neocolonialism. In 1965, the same year that the United Nations Development Programme was established, Kwame Nkrumah wrote,

> The essence of neo-colonialism is that the State which is subject to it is, in theory, independent and has all the outward trappings of international sovereignty. In reality its economic system and thus its political policy is directed from outside.[21]

African states in the former French colonies, Nkrumah says, were kept small and dependent on Western powers for their security while Western Europe and the United States consolidated their own economic power.[22] Shortly after Independence the new European Economic Community (EEC) placed a 27 percent tariff on chocolate, a finished import, which prevented the establishment of a chocolate industry in Ghana. Prices for the raw material were also kept so low that Ghanian people had to "slave" to grow cocoa for export.[23] Julius Nyerere, Tanzania's first president, said that his country was prevented from developing a manufacturing sector for their main export crop, sisal, by the EEC's 12 percent duty on finished imported "twines and cordage." The energy and ambition unleashed by the end of formal colonization were quickly grounded. Nyerere said,

> When we were preparing our first five year development plan, the price of our sisal was 148 British old pounds [per ton] .... We felt that this price was not likely to continue [after Independence.] So we planned on the basis that we might average 95 pounds per ton. It dropped down to less than 70.
> We can't win ... What can we do? What really can we do? ... What do we do with our sisal? Eat it? ... in a world of vultures, really, what can we do?"[24]

African leadership that articulated plans for actual decolonization were ousted or assassinated through the collusion of Western powers and replaced by those willing to facilitate the continued transfer of wealth, and to share in the spoils. Patrice Lumumba, the first prime minister of Congo,[25] expressed the awareness of that possibility when he said,

> Dead, living, free, or in prison on the orders of the colonialists, it is not I who counts. It is the Congo, it is our people for whom independence has been transformed into a cage where we are regarded from the outside ... History will one day have its say, but it will not be the history that Brussels, Paris,

Washington, or the United Nations will teach, but that which they will teach in the countries emancipated from colonialism and its puppets … a history of glory and dignity.[26]

After Lumumba was assassinated in 1961, he was replaced by Joseph Mobutu Sese Seko, a "U.S. strategic ally for 30 years," who enabled the West's pillage of the Congo's resources. Kenya emerged as a state in debt to Britain and the United States, as it was required to borrow millions of pounds to pay repatriating European settlers for "their" Kenyan land.[27] That debt grew for Kenya and many African countries in the era of Structural Adjustment moving into the 1980s, which formalized the external manipulation of African economies to support continued development of resources for global capitalism.[28]

Africa became even further isolated from the West in the new era of statehood—ostensibly liberated yet sunk in corruption, a continent defined in the Western imagination by an unsolvable poverty resulting from the deficits of Africa itself. Nkrumah said that "neocolonialism" was in fact "worse" than the conditions of European colonization, as the underlying theft of African modes of production had been openly pursued but now were hidden.

> For those who practise it, it means power without responsibility and for those who suffer from it, it means exploitation without redress. In the days of old-fashioned colonialism, the imperial power had at least to explain and justify at home the actions it was taking abroad.[29]

Before Independence, British workers knew that the tea they drank was grown in the highlands of the Kenyan colony by people whose lands were occupied for the benefit of the same capitalist classes positioned to squeeze as much profit as possible from their own labor. This knowledge led Britain's Labour Party to support decolonization in Africa from 1951. But the sisal and cocoa exported to Europe as cheap raw materials after Independence created more jobs for Europeans who made them into rope and chocolate. As those workers fought their governments, successfully, for expanded rights including expensive welfare states, they did not have to recognize the wealth and employment transfers from the African continent that factored into their government's ability to cede ground. The exploitation was mystified in the tangle of the rules of the "free" market and illusion that African nations were in fact independent.[30]

Ramon Grosfoguel says,

> One of the most powerful myths of the twentieth century was the notion that the elimination of colonial administration amounted to the decolonization of the world. The heterogeneous and multiple global structures put in place over

a period of 450 years did not evaporate with the juridical-political decolonization
of the periphery over the past 50 years.[31]

Neocolonialism is masked by a realignment of power in the West. Old colonial
empires have given way to new Western blocks which monopolize specific arenas
of global power: technology, military and atomic weaponry, finance, natural
resources, and media and communications.[32] Neocolonialism is also cultural,
disseminating across the world, in the words of Sabelo Ndlovu-Gatsheni,
"negative processes of Western modernity." In regard to Africa, he says that
neocolonialism is most destructive in the confusion it produces, mystifying the
actual predicament of African people. It is,

> a domain of myths of decolonization and illusions of freedom and a terrain
> of unfinished nation-building, fragmented identities and failing economic
> development. At its centre is the reign of epistemological colonization. The
> "postcolonial neocolonized world" lacks coherence, essence and life of its own.
> It is an arena of frustrated dreams and shattered visions.[33]

Toyin Falola says, "It is hard to come across an African intellectual who does
not accept the idea of neocolonialism."[34] He says that neocolonial structures
have become so "entrenched" at the turn of the twenty-first century that "many
parts of Africa have actually declined to a pre-1961 level and are begging
former imperialist masters to do whatever they like with them as long as they
offer assistance."[35] The language of neocolonialism has been openly used at
Pan-African gatherings, including the 2001 World Conference against Racism
in Durban, South Africa, where "the effects and persistence of colonialism"
structured "lasting social economic inequalities" in the world.[36]

Just as formal colonization functioned through colonies, neocolonialism
functions through the particular form of political organization known as the
modern nation-state. These states are especially necessary to the mystification
of the operation of power so crucial to neocolonialism. Nation-states produce
confusion. They claim to be alternatives to formal colonization yet they are
typically built on the same irrational borders of the colonies they replace. They
claim to be founded on principles of freedom while building wealth through
racial capitalism, through human enslavement, incarceration, and other forms
of violence. They claim to be founded on a principle of equality in law while
ignoring treaty rights of Indigenous nations. Nation-states rely on the patriotism
of their dominant cultures, yet must sell their own citizens on a constructed
identity. The most important aspect of the mystification may be that this one
model of statehood is the only alternative. The contradictions between the stated

identity and the actual practices of a nation-state are presented as problems of progress, a better future always on the verge of becoming.

Mahmood Mamdani describes the mystification of the functioning of nation-states as "amnesia." To live in a modern state is to exist in a fog of disremembering. An essential feature of the model, he says, is its production of internal colonies, a "two-state solution to the problem of the native."[37] This is displayed in nation-states from Nazi Germany to South Africa and Israel/ Palestine. The nation-state model is most aggressively demonstrated in the case of the United States, he says, which claims to represent the world's moral authority from its founding on chattel slavery and native genocide. Nation-states rule inherently through violence, says Mamdani while claiming to rule through democratic processes. They normalize violence then blame their wars, rates of incarceration, militarized borders, and brutal treatment of minorities on what they claim to be inevitable processes of state formation. But the nation-state is already failing, collapsing under its own weight according to Hamid Dabashi. Its impending death is signaled by the broad uprising that has transformed the Western world known as the Arab Spring in 2011. In its wake of state collapse, he predicts, "the post-colonial subject becomes a defiant subject," and nations can once again coalesce.[38]

From a line of sight in Maasailand, states like Kenya exist as power brokers that facilitate the neocolonial transfer of wealth from African lands to the West. The role of the state is to maintain the powerlessness of Maasailand to enable its pillage. It produces land policy to destroy communal ownership, privatizes Maasai resources without consent of the community, and electoral politics to destroy the power of Maasai cultural leadership. The state then looks the other way as elections in Maasailand are rigged with impunity, and land is illegally grabbed with the help of its own installed leadership. Unlike under formal colonization, these means of theft are mystified by the rhetoric that Kenya is a democratic nation, and therefore the problems of inequality will be resolved through development over time.

From that point of view in Maasailand, it is not accidental that Kenya was founded as a democracy in name but not in reality through the years that the state was built. Through those critical years of state formation, Kenya ran on a one-party political system directed by the office of the president. Jomo Kenyatta governed the country through hand-picked provincial commissioners who personally oversaw all local police forces.[39] Kenya became the partner of the newly crafted institutions of global power, the World Bank and IMF, which defined the country to be backward and in need of intervention, of the ports, roads,

electric grids, and other infrastructure of "development." Kenyatta quickly began
modernizing urban parts of the country, establishing the face of an electoral
politics and courts and state bureaucracies, expanding the elite economic classes
that had been formed under the British, and producing a wealth gap mirroring
the scale, if not the breadth, of Western democracies. Kenyatta himself played
a personal role in these developments. Indeed, the face of neocolonial power
in Maasailand is the face of Jomo Kenyatta, and the other *ilashempa orok*
accomplices, the "Black/whites" or "Black colonialists," Central Kenyans, and
their allies who personally grabbed Maasailand back from retreating Europeans
at the dawn of Kenyan statehood.

At the time of Independence, even radical supporters of African anticolonial
movements in the West claimed that Western nation-states were the continent's
best future because "there were no African models" of statehood.[40] But in fact
many models of African states preceded colonization. African intellectuals had
built a body of theory through the colonial era known as Nationalism to articulate
their evolving ideas about post-colonial futures. In Toyin Falola's account, some
Nationalists rejected all influence of European cultures as "corrupt and decadent,
its society too alienating, and its technology too degrading of human values."[41]
Others sought to draw from what was useful. But collectively they imagined an
eventual statehood that would coexist in some way with African nations, in other
words not the complete conversion of identity required by citizenship in Western
nation-states. Nationalists expressed that their own "African personality" need
not be "avoided, abandoned, or destroyed" in exchange for the "progress" of
statehood. This personality, common they said to African cultures, valued the
well-being of the community over the individual, leading to communal rights
and ownership, the belonging of "harvests to the many."[42] Nations might coexist
with different forms of states under African rule.

African leaders and intellectuals, "nationalist and Pan-Africanists," were
critical of features of the Western nation-state model. Many called for a rejection
of the colonial boundaries which had arbitrarily collectivized African societies
under the rule of particular European empires. Some Africans pursued models
that would build regional power. As early as 1958 an All African People's
Conference of Pan-Africanists outlined a "Commonwealth of Free African
States," which its architects reasoned would be strong and united enough to
withstand "the dangers of exposure to imperialist intrigues and of resurgence
of colonialism even after their attainment of independence." The conference
denounced the artificial frontiers drawn by the European powers "to divide the
peoples of Africa, particularly those which cut across ethnic groups and divide

people of the same stock," and it called for "the abolition or adjustment of such frontiers at an early date." Nationalists rejected plans to locate Western military bases within African states, and promoted regional economies and an African common market, "to avoid the hegemonic control of the West."[43] As these larger battles were lost, anticolonialists fought for less consolidated and more confederated government structures. These include *Majimboism* in Kenya, a proposed governance structure that would have devolved a share of state power and economic autonomy to African tribal communities. Majimboism was promoted by the KADU political coalition which posed the main opposition to the dominant KANU party. KADU represented the Maasai United Front (MUF) and other communities that would later identify as Indigenous.[44]

What Kenya got instead was a capitalist nation-state constructed through a constitution drafted in London by British colonial functionaries and KANU party leadership. The specifically Kikuyu leadership that emerged through this process retained the chief strategy of the British by limiting power to their own ethnic community and close relatives, thus politicizing cultural identity as "ethnicity."[45] President Kenyatta held power under these conditions by ousting and assassinating rival leaders, feeding his Kikuyu political base, and distributing Kikuyu people throughout the country through settlement schemes and "willing buyer, willing seller" land policies. Kenyatta personally engineered the distribution of British-occupied Maasailand while burying competing Maasai claims, and he handed out parcels of thousands of acres of land to his friends and family.[46] As wealth was consolidated the Kenyan people as a whole were impoverished, including the many Central Kenyans who are among the urban poor, and aid agencies of Western superpowers became the providers of basic services, later to be joined by the international non-profit sector.

As a neocolonial state, it is not surprising that Kenya produces its own version of the colonial racial caste system. The legal color bar and some aspects of the social fabric of the particular British colonial racism were dismantled at Independence. But the epistemological structure of racism was retained. Today there are two types of African Kenyans: the "civilized" Kenyan who live in cities, speak English, and drive Mercedes to their jobs in offices, and the "primitive" Maasai and other rural pastoral people, who have absorbed the dehumanizing stereotypes once directed against all Africans. Westernized Kikuyu identity functions in Kenya in some ways similar to "whiteness" in an American context, extending value to enhance and secure property, and advertised to sell consumption of Western lifestyles.[47] Maasai and other rural Kenyans with recognizable cultural identities are dispossessed from land and subject to police violence with a nonchalance familiar to Black, Xicano/a, and Indigenous peoples in the United States. Their impoverishment, poor health, and lack of education are taken for granted as a reflection of their inherent inferiority. To be Maasai is to be a people whose lands, knowledge, and culture can be bought cheaply, their value realized elsewhere by others, in other words, racialized. As Maasai and other Indigenous communities absorb the racist and primitivist stereotypes once directed against all African people, they are pressured to develop self-loathing and to recognize that they must abandon their cultural identity to achieve visibility in the present.

Kenya manifests other dynamics known in settler colonial societies, including the appropriation by the state of the cultures of displaced Indigenous peoples in their attempts to produce a common national past.[48] Maasai shields and shukas are displayed in important public spaces including the Kenyan flag to suggest that all Kenyan people share the richness of Maasai cultural heritage. Maasainess is appropriated in some of Kenya's most cited literature, that of icons like Ngugi wa Thiongo whose silent red-draped pastoralists move in and out of narratives centered on the agency of Kikuyu protagonists, written in the Kikuyu language, to represent the original Kenyans existing before modernity.[49] This approach to nation-building is a page out of the playbooks of settler colonial states. For example, Patrick Wolfe says that in Australia,

> settler society required the practical elimination of the natives in order to establish itself on their territory. On the symbolic level, however, settler society subsequently sought to recuperate indigeneity ... Australian public buildings and official symbolism, along with the national airlines, film industry, sports teams and the like, are distinguished by the ostentatious borrowing of Aboriginal motifs.[50]

Wolfe says that white Australians formed a national identity as citizens through their own process of "belonging" to the land they occupied by assuming the Indigenous peoples to be part of their shared (imagined) cultural past.[51]

The challenge in Kenya today is a lack of discursive space through which Maasai can be known on their own terms, as a community with a political identity. The word *tribe* was once used in this way, but it has been exiled as a conceptual frame for its association with colonial-era racism. Kenya defines its diversity instead through a leveling concept of *ethnicity*, a term that reflects the historical differences of the cultural groups said to be engaged in competition over state power, in a process of assimilation to the "one-nation" of the state. Just as the United States can maintain an illusion that racial violence results today, not from the structures of racial capitalism but rather from a long hangover of racist attitudes stemming from slavery, Kenya can mask structural violence through its own different story. In Kenya, the story goes, violence is fundamental to ethnic difference and peace is only possible through the depoliticization and muting of ethnic identity.[52] Thus, the only mention of Maasai people in histories of Kenya since statehood refers to conflict following elections. The source of the violence is presented as a problem of the ethnic identity, referred to in coded language by region. For example, according to Daniel Branch,

> The long history of ethnicity in Kenya (and East Africa more generally) is of accommodation, of open boundaries and movement, rather than of indigenous peoples. A dangerous myth of purity and autochthony has taken hold among the residents of the Rift Valley in particular, and must be demolished as a matter of urgency.[53]

Within a mere few years of Independence, the whole structure of African statehood had begun to collapse. Ghana and Nigeria underwent military coups, Congo region descended into chaos, and European settler colonialism was becoming more entrenched in places where it had survived independence era purges, such as South Africa.[54] The conflicts are labeled in written history as "civil wars" and blame is laid at the feet of a jumble of factors, especially the corruption of African leaders and "tribalism" of African people. It is suggested that Africans are incapable of overcoming hostility that predates colonialism. But according to Rudolph Ryser, these conflicts are more accurately described as military actions of states, and the ethnic communities that control state power, to dislodge culturally identified communities from land.[55] States began to use a variety of means including "eco-terrorism," the destruction of economies based on environments, "development," as well as direct military action. Ryser estimates that 17 million people died in these "wars of nationhood" between 1945 and 1991, 60 percent of whom died specifically in wars involving what would come to be identified as "Indigenous nations."[56] Western-style nation-states and their consolidated power cannot exist as such unless they vanquish Indigenous peoples, Ryser says, because they must destroy the identity of the original nations to break their historical relationships to particular lands and "non-productive" economies.[57]

It was in this context that Maasai were among the first African communities to identify as Indigenous and seek solidarity with Indigenous communities globally. By 1982 the United Nations had created the Working Group on Indigenous Peoples, and a whole infrastructure of ILO and NATO committees, to unify an approach to the "problem" of the local communities who resisted incorporation into post-colonial nation-states, by pulling the conflicts into conference rooms in Geneva and New York.⁵⁸ Their efforts may have been initiated "to preserve and promote state interests,"⁵⁹ but they met an already coalescing movement of Indigenous communities in settler societies in the West, who would draw the resources of the UN into their own agendas. Their work through the Declaration on the Rights of Indigenous Peoples brought about a shift in global consciousness. It produced a solidarity through the identity "Indigenous," itself a space of contest over power.⁶⁰ Maasai were especially active in the 1990s and early 2000s before UN funding diminished.⁶¹ They were initially represented by the Tanzanian Maasai Moringe Parkipuny. He argued in an address in 1989 that through "western economic hegemony" and the "polluted" environment produced by "neocolonial" African statehood, the pastoral and hunter-gatherer communities in East Africa were subject to loss of their rights and cultures. He said, "These minorities suffer from common problems which characterize the plight of indigenous peoples throughout the world."⁶² By 2002 Maasai worked closely with twenty-six African NGOs who regularly attended the UN Working Group and over a thousand total Indigenous participants.⁶³

Ryser says that "Fourth World Peoples" make up 1 billion of the earth's population and occupy territory that includes 80 percent of the world's remaining biodiversity. They practice knowledge of alternative economies and political structures while resisting removal from land.⁶⁴ In the zero-sum calculations of nation-state rationality, Indigenous peoples can be seen as *inherent* roadblocks to state power, their claims to their own *identities* a gauntlet thrown in the road.

The Power of History and the Production of Silences

Maasai history was first written in this transition from formal colonization to statehood, and it was framed as a question about the historical validity of Maasai's claimed identity. The narrative quickly established was that the people who know themselves as *Olosho le Maa* had only recently been loosely affiliated bands of *Maa*-speaking nomadic people. They had become *Maasai* through their segregation from other African people under British colonization. The story offered a means to erase Maasai *identity* in the historical imagination at the same time that Maasai *land* was undergoing a new and deeper hypercolonization under the Kenyan state.

History had served a different function in the era of formal colonization. History was a story Europeans produced about themselves to anchor their claim to be the "civilized," and their entitlement to the resources of the world. They used written history to contrast themselves to the people they conquered, especially Africans, who they said were too primitive to have a history. Hegel wrote shortly before his death in 1831:

> It is manifest that want of self control distinguishes the character of the Negroes. This condition is capable of no development or culture, and as we have seen them at this day, such have they always been. At this point we leave Africa, not even to mention it again. For it is no historical part of the world: it has no movement or development to exhibit.[65]

Hegel's words cannot be forgiven for reflecting an ignorance of "the times." Europe had centuries of experiential knowledge of African civilization recognizable to Europeans, beginning at least with Roman engagement with Carthage and the kingdoms of Egypt, the Ethiopian allies against Islam through the era of European crusades to the holy land, and extensive trade across the Mediterranean with West African city states. Africa was instead invented into non-existence in the West as Europe itself grew through colonization, as its own cities and universities established and expanded by wealth derived from African slavery and colonization. New knowledge was produced as the corollary to old knowledge silenced. Academic fields had been established by the late 1800s to study the colonized people, and new scientific concepts such as race invented. Specific knowledge was also produced about Maasai people as a strategy of war: the British left behind archives of intelligence reports on the political structure of Maasai age groups and territories of sections, with special focus on warrior training and culture.[66] But Maasai history was not written. The only African history taught in Europe told the story of Europeans in Africa, and it was housed in small and backwater Colonial Studies departments in imperial centers. That did not change throughout the colonial era.[67] As late as 1963, rejecting the demands of his students for courses in African history, Oxford's most senior professor of History, Hugh Trevor-Roper, said,

> The African past ... was nothing more than the "unrewarding gyrations of barbarous tribes in picturesque but irrelevant corners of the globe ... Perhaps, in the future, there will be some African history ... but at present there is none, there is only the history of the Europeans in Africa."[68]

The ideological power of this story told in the West was contested from the beginning by African intellectuals literate in European languages, and they began writing their own histories in defiance in the early nineteenth century.[69] They wrote town histories "in the fashion of chronicles." They also invented oral history a century before its invention by Western scholars, a method described by Toyin Falola as "an intellectual revolution" that "revealed a complex body and knowledge," framing history through African epistemologies, through "religion and philosophy … African rationality and science."[70] These historians were influenced by the works of Pan-Africanists in the Americas such as W.E.B. Du Bois. His 1946 book, *The World and Africa: An Inquiry into the Part Which Africa Has Played in World History*, traced the history of East African empires, in Egypt and Ethiopia, to argue for the success of the continent's "long experience of ruling themselves."[71] Melville Herskovits, a white founder of African Studies in the United States, began publishing research on African kingdoms like Dahomey. He argued that African institutions could be built on African, not Western, models. These works exposed the "multiple possibilities" for African models of statehood built on diverse African pasts.[72]

Western historians continued to claim that Africa had no history until the successful revolts of African people in the 1950s and 1960s left no doubt that formal colonization was coming to an end. The United States would ultimately engineer the West's response to these demands, as it had surged into global hegemonic power out of the crumbling of European empires through the Second World War. The United States was now poised to wrestle the former African colonies from Soviet influence. Its agenda for Africa was to replicate its own nation-state model on the borders of former colonies to produce these states into the sphere of the West, as "democracies."[73] Western policymakers claimed that only democracies would bring "economic prosperity" to the former colonies, thus "it was the duty of Western societies to increase their scientific and technical research to disseminate the results to poor societies," to create the conditions for world peace through development.[74] New production of and dissemination of knowledge were critical to the plan.

In Africa what that meant was a sudden expansion of knowledge production *about* Africa in the West, and dissemination of knowledge from the West *to* Africa through education. Thus, knowledge production was structured on the core/periphery model. African universities were established or expanded in the years leading up to Independence to educate African people in the theory and practice of development.[75] At the same time, the infrastructures of meaning production and interpretation—journals, publishers, academic conferences, funding for research—were based in the United States. There African studies "broke onto the scene virtually as a new discipline" at this time, growing overnight from a "cottage industry to a multi-national enterprise."[76] African history was one of many fields of knowledge about Africa, and it was funded[77] into a "golden age," beginning in the 1950s and lasting through the 1970s, transitioning from Europe to the United States by the late 1960s.[78] There had been less than half a dozen university jobs in the United States in African-centered history in 1959, but 350 historians were employed in the field by 1970.[79] "Many hundreds" of books had been published on African history in European languages by the end of this period, which closed by the 1980s.[80]

This is the context into which African history emerged overnight as a new field of Western study and its specific purpose was to provide identity to African nation-states. The famous words of the French historian Renan, frequently quoted by Africanists in this period, are that history is necessary to nation-state formation to produce amnesia of the past, as "the essence" of nation-states is that

> they have forgotten many things. No French citizen knows whether he is a Burgundian, an Alan, a Taifale, or a Visigoth, yet every French citizen has to have forgotten the massacre of Saint Bartholomew, or the massacre that took place in the South in the thirteenth century.[81]

The United States is the prime example of the use of this approach to history.[82] US history tells a progressive story that British colonization ended with "Independence" and the foundation of a nation-state of "immigrants" eventually forming a multicultural democracy, a story of a perpetual work in progress. The story is repeated so aggressively as to mystify its obvious contradictions: the vast majority of the land of what is now the United States was occupied— and Indigenous communities exterminated, denied treaty rights, and removed to reservations—under the rule of the United States, not the period of British colonization.[83] American History is a masterful deception that rationalizes the hegemonic power within the United States, still centered in the white Anglo Protestant culture of the first British settlements and that has ruled the country since its founding. The main power of Western history is in its claim to universal truth, that one coherent story of a diverse people can be told in the words of Linda Tuhiwai Smith, through "one coherent narrative."[84] The narrative reifies the invented borders of the nation-state, producing it in the imagination as a thing of nature. The power of Western history of nation-states is that the "one coherent narrative" is a fantasy that produces false consciousness, disorientation, identity produced ideologically without clear sight on the white supremacy inherent to it.

US history has seen many challenges to its totalizing narrative. For example, intellectuals of the African diaspora have used history with great dexterity over the past century to challenge the white Anglo consensus. Du Bois used history to reframe public discourse through an Afrocentric perspective, through lectures and articles. He argued, for example, that the First World War was a response to the European colonization of Africa. His most important historical work, *Black Reconstruction in America*, was published in 1935 and it reframed the narrative of the Reconstruction era following the US Civil War and the structural production of racism through labor. C.L.R. James's *The Black Jacobins*, published in 1938, similarly reframed the most successful slave revolt in the West, the Haitian Revolution, in the context of the French and other movements of the Age of Revolution, bringing it into the Western narrative history of civilization.[85] These histories eventually moved forcefully into the academy beginning in the 1960s and 1970s, and they formed the basis of the development of radical new fields, of Black Studies and Black History. They ushered in decades of work that explore the structural reproduction of race—in banking, real estate, education, welfare—history that in turn is used by movements for racial justice. Thus, history is also an arena of contest over power in Western nation-states, and a potential weapon in the hands of minoritized peoples silenced in dominant narratives.[86]

Born into the same historical moment of the 1960s and 1970s, the field of African history was established in the Western academy as a contest over competing stories of Africa by Western and African historians. In some cases, Western funding to expand African universities landed into the hands of the small class of African scholars who had achieved PhDs through the waning years of colonization.[87] These included some historians whose history was grounded in anticolonial activism and the century of African nationalisms that sought African-centered futures, including Cheikh Anta Diop, Joseph Ki-Zerbo, and Adu Boahen.[88] In Kenya, history was initially crafted by Bethwell Allan Ogot, a Western Kenyan historian who had spent the years of Kenyan anticolonial activism in Scotland earning a PhD in history, and was hired in 1964 into the faculty of the University College of Nairobi.[89] Ogot soon replaced a white predecessor as chair of the History Department and was empowered to overhaul a Eurocentric curriculum, one he said would be "not shackled to the old Western civilization paradigm."[90] He and his colleagues hosted the first professional conference of East African historians, built archives and libraries, and hired as diverse an African faculty as was possible, including a Maasai historian in 1969, Ben Ole Kantai. Insisting that all students be taught to think critically, he created a new history syllabus in 1967 that introduced international economics, African-centered history of colonization, of Russia and the United

States and the Cold War, to prepare students to participate in a world in motion, "restructuring itself" in the "push and tug of transnational forces." Enrollment in history, he says, "expanded rapidly."[91]

This generation of Kenyan historians initially approached their task by reconstructing the diverse, contradictory multiple lines of sight of the many Kenyan communities. This approach opposed the nation-state history model, which sought to build a unified story of the past. But the approach of Ogot and others made sense, because the state of Kenya contains profoundly diverse communities each with their own histories. Muslim Somalis in the northeast are oriented to histories of the Middle East and the crisis of their separation by the Kenya/Somali border through colonization and statehood. Coastal communities have been oriented for centuries to the Indian Ocean littoral and its literate world of Arabic trade and island plantation slavery, while many Western Kenyan communities originate in shared cultural landscape with the Nile River littoral, some like the Maasai and Luo speaking different versions of Nilotic languages. Central Kenyans descend from Bantu migrants dispersed throughout the continent originally from the Congo region. Many Kenyan communities have origin stories of arriving from the earth or sky into specific homeland in East Africa. More recent immigrants include Indian Kenyans descended from British intra-colony movements of laborers, and a thin but extremely wealthy class of descendants of European settlers. A history of Kenya founded in these multiple narratives, diffused lines of sight, would expose the vastly different experiences of Independence among different Kenyan peoples, and the origins of the Kikuyu inheritance of state power.[92] The ability of the historians to see the value of such a decentered history undoubtedly reflected their positioning; several key historians were of Ogot's own Luo community, which has formed the core of government opposition since they were driven from power sharing with the assassination of the young Luo politician Tom Mboya in 1969.[93]

Ogot began to build local histories with his students by sending them home to their own communities on breaks between terms to gather oral histories, as apparently no funding could be obtained for this project.[94] He described this approach as a means to "decolonize" history by centering it in African places, because "the African, like other people, must start with his own little world, and then try to interpret this as part of a larger world."[95] African people, he said, were more capable to do this work than more highly trained Western historians, and that his students "working in their home areas amongst people to whom they were familiar" produced more valuable work than the "team of experts furnished with land rovers and tape-recorders."[96] History built this way, he said, would also build a state of the diverse people encompassed by Kenya, as "Surely unity is more likely to emerge when those who read history books do not see their own kind ignored or neglected."[97]

The approach, if allowed to continue, would undoubtedly have built a different Kenyan state as history would be a site for African people to wrestle out what it might mean to be Kenyan and face the challenges directly. The conversation would not be contained in an ivory tower, as Ogot said all Kenyan people would be invited because, "every individual should have access to his or her history."[98] Nairobi College faculty founded a public history institute in 1967, the Historical Society of Kenya, and opened branches throughout the country; this was open, they said, to farmers, trade unionists, and "housewives." The historians undertook a project to reconstruct the history taught in public schools, and they organized a conference in the mid-1960s to "interrogate" primary education by reviewing every "history syllabus and textbooks from primary level to university" to scrub them of racist content, and also of the assumption that African children should not be expected to think critically about what they learned.[99]

The approach to producing a diverse Kenyan history from multiple points of entry was eclipsed however by another project, one with greater access to the resources of the Western academy and that more directly served the academy's needs. This project would envelop Kenyan and other local and state histories within a master narrative of African history that would mirror the basic structure of the histories of Western nation-states. Ironically this work would first be undertaken by a collective of European historians who saw themselves as academic outsiders and radical supporters of movements for decolonization in Africa. Their intentions ended up mattering less than their positioning and the depth of their power over the field of African history, as several members of this group recognized later.

The historians who framed African history were mostly affiliated with the University of Edinburgh, mostly young and not all professionals, some still graduate students. Some were born into academic families and never finished their own PhDs, and they used networks of personal relationships to position themselves to write this history through their support of African Independence.[100] They included the iconoclast Basil Davidson, who had traveled with guerrilla cells in the anticolonial wars in Angola and Guinea-Bissau, and "brought their struggle to the world's attention," described by Edward Said as among the very few Western intellectuals to have "crossed to the other side."[101] What is most striking about this group is the tremendous personal influence they had on the framing of African history. Davidson alone wrote more than thirty books on the subject and produced an eight-part documentary series that introduced African history to a wide audience in the West.[102] Together they believed that they educated an entire generation of African people through the textbooks they wrote.[103] In some cases, they worked with African scholars and shared resources, and typically they reflected on their own privilege coming from imperial cultures and sought to engage ethically with their roles.[104]

We learn two main things from their reflections later on this work. First, they saw African history as an activist project in a perilous historical moment, a front of the work of decolonial movements that required them to take risks. Second, even though they were subjects of imperial societies they believed themselves to be capable of representing African perspectives because of their commitment to African independence.[105] Carolyn Neale, a graduate student at the time, spoke for many others when she said later that this cohort approached African history as a "revisionist project" through which they sought to

> entail a fundamental change in the relationship of black nations to white nations, and of black to white in Africa … There had been a political statement that black and white were to be treated as equals; now there was needed a cultural demonstration that such a thing was possible.[106]

They looked to history to provide evidence of African equality with imperial societies. But says Neale, they were not yet conscious of their assumption that to be equal, Africans had to be like Europeans. The slippage seems to have occurred in the multiple and unexamined definitions of the meaning of "African Nationalism" current among Western supporters of anticolonialism. The historians later reflected that they had taken for granted that the Nationalism for which African movements fought would lead to universal adoption of the Western nation-state model, in Davidson's words, "the nation-state deriving from the English and French revolutions … the specific nationalism of the economy of capitalism and the cultural hegemony of the bourgeoisie."[107] Neale said later that they therefore built the frame of African history on a "Whig interpretation" of nation-states that embedded evolutionary thinking that "placed Europeans and their political works at the pinnacle of human development."[108]

This impacted both the framing of the history they constructed, as a search for the one-narrative history of "Africa," and their approach to sources, which they undertook as a search for evidence of the story they set out to build: that African societies had been, even before colonization, proto nation-state in formation. Neale explained,

As the successful management of nation-states was seen as the test of equality with whites, it seemed important to establish that this form of government was not a wholly alien one, handed down by the imperial powers, but in some sense the natural culmination of indigenous development ... which would have produced something like the modern nations all by itself, even if their growth had not been forced and their particular forms determined by colonial rule.[109]

As activists, they felt not only entitled but duty bound to take liberty with sources, to cherry pick evidence, Neale said, as "objectivity looked like cynicism." Thus, they tended to include in the histories they wrote any evidence they found that African societies had engaged in "centralization" and "territorial expansion," and especially efforts to create "multi-tribal nations." They "simply dropped from their agendas material which was felt to reflect badly on African societies," or they

> transformed it, so that internal slavery became a family affair; conquest, an offer of law, order, and wider markets; cannibalism, a form of social cement, and authoritarian terror, a means of introducing new grounds of loyalty to the state.[110]

This framing erased the historical existence of Maasai and other non-expansionist African societies. They called them the "stateless societies," those who were "historical blank spots on the map of Africa," in Philip Curtain's words. Neale said that such peoples were treated by historians with an "air of disappointment," as those who "missed their chance" to be part of history, including "Ogot's 'stateless societies,'" to which she said the historians gave "little attention."[111] As they were excluded from modern history, the stateless societies were produced into a permanent primitivism in Africa's past.[112] Neale said that historians

> took the great variety of ways of living and thinking which exist and have existed side by side in Africa, where herders have drifted through the capitals of kings for hundreds of years and are camping now on the pavements of cities, and assigned each one to its place in the different phases of man's development laid down by the scheme of Western history, so that some belonged to the past and some to the future, with which the present was identified.[113]

This she said was further accomplished through the language of the periodization of African history, through words like *modern, achievement, necessary, progress,* and *development.*[114]

Though the work of the Edinburgh historians would be heavily critiqued by later historians for its lack of evidential rigor, the basic framing it built would be retained: African history would be periodized primarily around the agency of

Europeans, precolonial to colonial to modern statehood, a history pivoting on Independence as an event of rupture and reinvention. This framing had been built through the early "Golden Years" of the field and it was fleshed out after its shift to US universities in the late 1960s and 1970s, after which time "interest in African studies began to wane."[115] Already by the late 1960s funding agencies had begun to focus on faster roads to development agendas—agricultural sciences and population planning, while resources to write African history shifted to the United States, evaporating from African universities.[116] Journals based in Africa began to perish as Western scholars "diverted their attention almost entirely to those in the United States and Europe," and the "Western Academy was enshrined as the unique source of validation for the African scholar."[117] African historians worked under conditions of extreme disadvantage, lacking funds for field work and access to conferences and current scholarship, as their own field was produced on the other side of the world, and this led to criticism of the "professionalism" of their work.[118] Falola says that African scholarship was assigned to play a subordinate part in "an international division of academic labor with Africans supplying raw data for their Western colleagues to process." Africa, he says, is used "as a testing ground for theories and paradigms that are not necessarily germane to the concerns of the continent."[119] According to Thandika Mkandawire,

> [T]he tedious basic data gathering is left to the Africans and the theoretical digestion and elaboration is left to "Africanists" ... On the one hand, it leads to a kind of mindless empiricism in which Africans are contracted to churn out meaningless data, while on the other hand, it leads the "Africanists" toward fashish theorization of the African reality and pursuit of often exclusively expatriate and ephemeral "debates" that vanish as mysteriously as they emerged.[120]

In Nairobi, historians experienced this withdrawal of resources, and also pressure from their own students concerned that their mentors were "fragmenting Kenyan history" through multiple origin points, that they "jeopardized the integrated vision and coherent national story line."[121] Historians John Lonsdale and Atieno Odhiambo understood the erasure inherent in their project of building a Kenyan history through the one narrative as the only alternative, as was the Western nation-state itself. It is, they said, "a mirage, an African socialist fantasy" that states can form through "Consensual agreement."

> All states that claim to be nations have skeletons in their cupboards, stained with fratricidal blood. A united nation has never yet, in history, taken counsel together to make itself a state ... New states are often declared in the name of

people not yet aware of their own collective existence. Their heroically unified past and manifest joint destiny have yet to be imagined for them. … After a new state's formation, its schools can teach a standard language, its sergeant-majors shout it to conscripts on parade grounds. Peasants can thus be turned into citizens. Invented common festivals and subsequent long histories of political compromise may together combine, but not always, to create a patriot culture with a past to be proud of. All these remarks are as true of Europe or America as of Africa.[122]

These historians built as complex and honest a Kenyan history possible within the frame, which nonetheless orients the narrative to the history of the dominant Kikuyu community, the first to come under Western influence, to learn English, become wages laborers, and then to form unions and political associations, to partake in and challenge colonial power in ways that could be made recognizable to Western history. The Kikuyu community had engineered the Mau Mau uprising, the most studied event in Kenyan history and the event reconstructed to create a story that Kenya was founded in a "moral enterprise."[123] As Odhiambo said later, theirs was a project of invention.

> Historical consciousness was to play a vital role in this quest for national identity. And historians of Kenya have, in the past thirty years, had to grapple with this ambiguity as the central agenda …. This history has had to be invented, assembled together, arranged around the metaphor of struggle. This metaphor entails seeing our history of the past fifty or so years as a moral enterprise.[124]

The Kenyan history they built said Ogot "had been elegant, linear, and unconfusing, precisely because it left out so much" deriving "its coherence from the groups it ignored or dismissed."[125] In fact Kenyan historians as a class have been described as being "deeply ill at ease with both national and nationalist history" as they watched it support a story that was revealed to be less in the service of decolonization and more "the capture of state power in 1963."[126] Yet in recent years these historians have tended to adopt a language of multiculturalism and advocated the use of history to build a vision of nationhood that would be a "melting pots for all ethnic differences and contradictions."[127]

A radical critique of US/Western hegemonic power over African universities did coalesce, next door to Kenya at the University of Dar es Salaam in Tanzania. Historian Ndeywel Nziem later explained,

> It is deplorable that [Africans] remain dependent on theories essentially of western origin; they remain "consumers" of ideas developed elsewhere and exporters of the field data needed in European and American universities to establish scholarly synthesis.[128]

African scholars were accused of being incapable of studying their own societies with "objectivity," as they were subject to being swayed by African cultural perspectives, of "mysticism," for example, and of confusing "mythical" with "scientific" time. African historians were told, according to Nziem, in a telling metaphor, that for them "it was dangerous to try to perform the functions of both 'beetle' and 'entomologist.'"[129] Arnold Temu and Bonaventure Swai said that historians had been "taught to ride the waves rather than swim in them, to be objective." But that goal of "objectivity" was actually, he said, a means of imposing Western epistemology as the "positivist methodology" is itself "ideological" especially as it was used to argue that Africans were not capable of undertaking the interpretive work of history.[130] The Dar historians studied Walter Rodney's work on dependency theory and the Afro-Marxisms produced by liberation movements in Angola, Mozambique, Ginea-Bissau, and Ethiopia.[131] They educated their students in "the evils of capitalism" through a lens of Third World Revolution, encouraging them to use their educations to "commit class suicide" and fight Western domination.[132] They critiqued the role of historians in imperial knowledge production. Nziem said that the Western historian "shares a similar class position to the nineteenth century administrator, in the middle or lower echelons of the bourgeoisie." His vocation as an historian places him above the *hoi polloi* whom he "surveys ... retrospectively as the agents—or subjects—of change. He may feel sympathy for the mass, but hardly solidarity."[133]

For a brief moment, historians of the Dar School found common ground with counterparts in the United States, mostly social historians who came into the field at a time when US universities were rapidly expanding and classrooms were sites of gestation of movements against US imperialism. Universities birthed the Black Panther Party, and radical edges of the feminist movement and Students for a Democratic Society.[134] Faculty drawn to African history at this time saw their work, according to Michael Adas, to be a "mission" to educate the "ignorant west" about the dynamics of Third World geopolitics, to dissuade "kneejerk military responses," and to empower African nations with information and to present a better face of African people to the West.[135] Some of these initially worked with the Dar School. But that potential was extinguished, as historians said later that they had been told to back off, that they were "going too far." African history shifted into a consensus to disengage the field from all activism, to undertake a more "professional" approach of US-based social sciences.[136] Thereafter, according to David Newbury,

> Proper independence for African countries was viewed within an extremely
> narrow range of acceptable political alternatives: in no way was "independence"

as perceived in the United States intended to challenge "dependence": still less, the status quo.[137]

Newbury says that historians thereafter rationalized that they could "serve both the US public and the African people" through a "convergence of interest between the two."[138] The Dar School was discredited and labeled "Pessimists," who were said to have lost the "optimism" of those in the West that continued to struggle on behalf of nation-statehood in Africa. The ultimate rejection of the Pessimists by the Western academy is cited in the historiography as proof that the field of African history "matured."[139] African history in the United States became isolated in its own conversations lodged within the US academy, and according to Michael Adas, historians were untouched by this critique emanating from East Africa thereafter.[140]

Africanist historians instead directed their field through an innovative edge in US history being cut at the time by new left historians who were reinventing narratives from the perspective of the "people without history": women, working classes, Xicano, Black, and Indigenous peoples. Africanist historians appear to have been swept up by the energy of this work, the new lines of inquiry it had cracked open, the opportunities it created to occupy niches in unwritten areas. As David Newbury described it later,

> the emergence of a new educational climate in the United States, bolstered by postwar intellectual influences from Europe, led to a remarkable growth in interest in a whole host of new conceptual and methodological approaches: the systematic analysis of oral tradition, a heightened appreciation of ethnographic and cultural materials as historical sources, various types of structuralist studies, a variety of *Annaliste* approaches, diverse theories of under-development and a growing interest in Marxist paradigms; all found direct application to Africa, the newest field of scholarly historical analysis.[141]

Africanists set out to find the people without history in Africa, the "stateless" rural societies. But unlike the US context, Africanists were not from the communities they studied, typically did not speak their languages, had no access to their oral and other cultural archives, and were not subject to any structural accountability for what they wrote.[142] Thus, they were critiqued for "finding" African people through their own epistemological lenses. Temu said that the "people without history historians"

> have been content with viewing the colonized as an amorphous mass, and people as simply aggregates of individuals. It is the complexity of African societies and their interactions, he says, that is not shown in the social history of Africa.[143]

The dense layers of African cultural identities were collapsed in writing through which they came to be known through broader collective identities recognizable in the West, as "African women," "the poor," "small farmers," "pastoralists," "African youth," etc., people knowable through the labor they performed and their anatomies, through individuated identities. There was no comparable Western category for "tribe," a word that had been vilified in Independence-era discourse, synonymous in the words of American Historical Association chair Joseph Miller, with the racist stereotype of the "time-defying, history-denying static logic" of the inherently unchanging African primitive of the colonial era history.[144] The "insider" Africanist, said Miller, avoided both the romantic "noble savage" and the "hostile" savage stereotypes of the Western imagination, and instead built for stateless societies identities as farmers, and pastoralists, categories that could be understood in an historical relationship to peasants, workers, and capitalists. Through this lens, Miller said, "Africans emerged as active historical agents, in ways recognizable to historians practiced in the politics and processes of European and American history."[145]

This pursuit of "people without history" in Africa had material consequences in local African places as it was interpreted as permission to move "into the village," the "blank spots" on the map and interrogate the identities of the "stateless societies."[146] Some of these histories explored questions framed by the bigger pursuits of African historians and dependency theory, of the transformations of local political economies and societies under colonialism for example. But the majority appear to have undertaken instead a line of questions into the meaning of identity in these rural African communities, especially whether their claimed identities were real and provable in history. Unlike the earlier generation of Africanists, they were typically based far from those communities and knew them through briefer field excursions, at a time when funding for African history was limited. Their most important access was to archives and to the innovations of the new social history methods. They thus explored the historical identities of African communities by using positivist methods to read those archival sources, the written observations of Europeans in Africa. Jan Vansina says that through these methods, they incorporated the "perceptions" of colonial observers— administrators, soldiers, missionaries, and settlers—"directly, uncritically" into the stories they constructed, accepting their words "as fact, as if they were similar to incontrovertible experimental observations of the structures of crystals."[147] The historians expressly excluded the memories of the people whose identities were being examined which they considered to be biased. As Miller said in his AHA address, speaking on behalf of these approaches, the scientific methods were "objective" and therefore advanced, leading to an "express[ion of] historical experience without conscious intent," which could therefore not be "falsified" by the community under study.[148]

The field of Maasai History was framed in this way in the 1960s and 1970s, using colonial observers as theoretically unbiased sources to draw conclusions about Maasai historical identity. A few early histories were approached outside of the search for identity; these tended to rely on interviews with Maasai people for the questions they pursue rather than a primary reliance on British sources. Robert Tignor's book, *The Colonial Transformation of Kenya*, is an example of this scholarship, as is Kenneth King's "The Kenyan Maasai and the Protest Phenomenon."[149] But this approach has been uncommon, and the fully developed field of Maasai history has pursued questions of interest in the West, through British colonial sources, especially of the meaning of Maasai identity. An early and influential article by historian Richard Waller initiated this exploration by arguing that Maasai achieved an identity as people after they were forced onto reservations by the British.[150] Many interesting pieces of history can be glimpsed in this article. But its conclusion fails to account for the entirety of Maasai historical knowledge into the longevity of Maasai culture and history. Another influential article by historian John Berntsen[151] introduced the use of social science methods to evidence the fluidity of Maasai identity. The article claims that Maasai of the nineteenth century saw themselves as "pure pastoralists," believing themselves to be people who therefore live exclusively on milk and meat, and that the "ideal was shared by almost all Maa-speakers." But its author argues that "in a strict sense no Maasai pastoralist was a 'pure pastoralist' in that he could not follow a completely pastoral diet of meat, milk, and other pastoral products," a claim supported by archeological and anthropological evidence that corn was eaten in early settlements in Maasailand. Therefore, the article suggests that that Maasai were confused about their identity, seeing themselves one way but living another.[152]

Less than two decades after it began, this basic narrative of Maasai History culminated in the publication of the book *Being Maasai: Ethnicity and Identity in East Africa*, which presents the work of historians, archeologists, linguists, and other scholars that together challenge the coherence of Maasai historical identity.[153] Through fifteen separately authored essays, the scholarship brings Maasai into modernity as fluid and fractured subjects.

"Maasai" and "pastoralism" have become so closely linked in the historical and ethnographic literature, not to mention in the thought of Maasai pastoralists themselves, that Maasai are commonly viewed as prototypical pastoralists, secure in their own exclusive ethnicity.[154]

A chapter in *Being Maasai* by Richard Waller, built on his earlier argument using the same body of colonial-era British sources, argues that the British arrived in Maasai land at a unique though temporary moment of cohesion when two Maasai subsections, *Purko* and *Kisongo*, had begun to develop an incipient identity, seeing themselves as "purely pastoral" people, whose wealth in cattle enabled them to live sustained by pastoralism alone. But this ability was short-lived in the article's account and had been made possible by an unprecedented expansion of *Purko* and *Kisongo* through an imperial-style conquest of other Maasai sections. The article says that in the last third of the nineteenth century the power of the *Purko* and *Kisongo* was in decline on its own, but the British happened to arrive at this time of cohesion and they mistakenly attributed a permanence to Maasai identity and built a reservation system based on that understanding.[155] It was British agency, the chapter concludes, that created Maasai identity.

> In Maasailand, the colonial administration was imposing its own definition of what it meant to be "Maasai" and energetically trying to enlist Maasai support for it, using the image of "the alien" both as a threat and as something against which "Maasainess" could be measured.[156]

We are told that the British *saw* "Maasai," created "Maasai," and brought them into *being* through their gaze. Maasai history is thereby brought into the larger story of African history, where in the words of Africanist John Iliffe (quoted in this book): "Europeans believed Africans belonged to tribes; Africans built tribes to belong to."[157] The book ends up suggesting that Maasai identity is used advantageously by Maasai to promote self-interest,[158] is a "powerful ideology," that is "manipulated in the service of one social goal or another" by Maasai people.[159]

Being Maasai has been universally loved by reviewers; it has been called "a triumphant unity," "the most accomplished and certainly the most comprehensive" look, not just at Maasai culture, but of "historical studies of ethnicity in Africa."[160] But while the authors demonstrate no ill intention toward Maasai, their book does not seek their approval, and Maasai are all but completely absent from its pages. The exception is a chapter built around an interview with a rural Maasai woman, listed as an author but under a fictional name, on the subject of her identity. The chapter, "The World of Telelia: Reflections of a Maasai Woman in Matapato," absorbed Maasai gender systems into the territory of interpretation claimed by Western scholarship. The author of the chapter acknowledged that this Maasai woman "evaded my attempts to draw her into discussion on movements among Maasai women asserting their temporary independence." But he pushed on, past her own story, what he describes as a "benign account" of a women's fertility dance, as well as her own expression of Maasai ways of ordering the roles and responsibilities of men and women. He concluded by finding what he sought anyway, accusing "Telelia" of "conspiring" with her husband and elders "in maintaining a regime" that oppresses women.[161]

In short, Maasai and other African history teaches us that we should see African identity as a constant process of mutation from the nineteenth century down to the present—and accept that identities continue to change today, implying that assimilation is the natural and desirable progression in the context of African statehood. That Maasai have no coherent historical identity is now referred to with the authority of an undisputable truth in many current works, which have also continued to engage with Maasai identity as a central question.[162] The reason this matters is that it maintains an impression of scholarly support for more aggressive challenges to Maasai and other Indigenous self-representation, feeding a widely expressed assumption that the conversation about Indigenous identity is the property of the "civilized" West.[163]

To claim the right to name a people's identity is to claim the right to control their lands, something recognized by critical scholars in other contexts.[164] Sankaran Krishna says,

> If identities such as the nation or ethnicity, or notions such as "traditional homelands" of native peoples, can be shown to be historical and social constructions and fictions, governments and elites can use such ideas to deny their responsibility for past crimes, or to oppress certain claims for reparation or redress.[165]

David Anderson says specifically that the histories of African pastoral people have been written to produce knowledge to further the agendas of African states and their development partners, the "politics of the present."[166] These histories, he says, support either the clearing or transformation of Indigenous pastoral land for other economic purposes. The historians have "invented" different versions of the pastoral people under study, he says, to support their positions on whether change should be gradual or rapid and thus have "propagated their own myths of the pastoralists' world, where the hard edge of 'progress' has confronted the romanticism of 'tradition.'"[167] Both versions rest on a shared claim that pastoralist identity is fractured in history, "that far from there being a single 'tribal' identity, most Africans moved in and out of multiple identities."[168] The identities of African pastoralists are presented as the product of the missteps (the agency) of imperial management of previously only loosely affiliated tribal peoples, the "immobilization of populations" onto reservations, which they say created ethnic identity, so a very recent process.[169]

Today, as Maasai people assert their own self-representation and seek a seat as a community at the table in Kenyan governance, this false narrative—that Maasai identity is not supported by history—can be seen to have undermined their efforts. One recent example is the Kenyan Building Bridges Initiative (BBI), a coalition formed after the 2017 broken Kenyan presidential election, to which Maasai were invited to participate and to bring their grievances about historical land injustice.[170] The Maasai community responded to the invitation by holding a series of meetings throughout Maasailand over many months, and thousands of Maasai people gathered in Narok town in late February of 2020 to demonstrate their support of the statement on land injustice drafted through this process, to be delivered to Kenya's president and opposition leader. Shortly after this gathering, the Kenyan *Saturday Nation* featured a piece by the historian Lotte Hughes titled "Why Maasai's BBI Demands Are Unworkable, Especially on Land."[171] That original letter is now difficult to find, and it is unclear whether Hughes or the newspaper chose the title, but Hughes did later elaborate her critique of the Maasai statement in a longer piece that is still freely available online. Here she questioned what a return of the land to the Maasai would mean in practical terms given the diverse ethnicities of modern-day Kenya, likening the BBI statement to a claim based on "racial purity" and comparing it to "the nativist, far-right racist narrative poisoning societies—including in the UK, where deluded Little Englanders are calling, post-Brexit, for illegal migrants to be expelled." She wrote,

> Even if the land were returned, to whom would it be returned? Individuals, communities, county governments dominated by the Maasai? How about the diaspora? Would everyone who is part-Maasai have to prove their blood quantum (a dangerous notion) in order to receive their cut?[172]

The Maasai BBI statement expressed the historical knowledge of an entire nation asserting its right to define its own identity, of what it means to *be* Maasai, an identity formed by culture and accountability not blood quantum. The statement demonstrates that Maasai land rights is not a campaign to violently expel non-Maasai people from Maasailand, not in any way politically aligned with the right-wing racist narratives produced by imperial societies. It instead expresses

Maasai land rights to be an assertion by an Indigenous people of the *right to exist* and receive impartial, nondiscriminatory treatment under Kenyan law. Instead of violent expulsion, it expresses a right to assert that all people, coexisting with the Maa Nation, on Maasailand, are accountable to their human and non-human relationships; this notion of community is framed through a Maasai, not a Western, understanding of identity, one we believe is resonant with other Indigenous peoples in other contexts but commonly misunderstood within the discourses of Western capitalism.

The world outside of Maasailand did not have access to the statement of the Maasai community, but it did have access to Hughes's critique of that statement. Unfortunately, the terms in which that critique is articulated resonate with broader Western biases based in colonization that see Africa's Indigenous peoples and their attachment to land as evidence of blood-and-soil tribalism. Just as the meaning of Maasai identity has been missed by historians of the past, it can be missed as Maasai assert their rights in the present.

The Western academy has achieved real power over Maasai self-representation. To move past this current reality, historians must be willing to step back and allow Maasai people to enter the scholarly conversation about Maasai history on their own terms, to find a ground of collaboration from a place of equal footing.

The colonization of Maasai History has been a process inseparable from the colonization of Maasailand and so to liberate the history is a project entwined with liberating the land itself. In the next chapter, we turn to the first question typically asked by Maasai people about history, which is "how specifically did we come to lose our land?"

Kenyamal Enkop: The History of Maasailand Occupation

Very little has been written about the question that animates Maasai interest in history today, which is *how specifically did we lose our land?* The currently published Maasai history provides broad strokes for the first part of an answer: the mass eviction of Maasai people during the era of British colonization for European settlement. But the critical second part of the story has not been written at all, that of the deeper and more permanent occupation of Maasailand in Kenya under the Kenyan state. Histories of the Kenyan state do not engage with Maasai land loss since Independence since it barely recognizes even the continued existence of Maasai society. Kenyan history tells the story only of its dominant Kikuyu community allowing that history to speak for all Kenyans. A more diverse history of Kenya has been curtailed by the claim that ethnicity is inherently dangerous to the stability of Kenya and so history must tell a unified story.

But while Maasai are not spoken of in Kenyan history, Maasai *lands* are essential to the telling of the story. The British colony was built primarily on occupied Maasailand, especially in Nairobi and the settled territory in Naivasha and Nakuru, the heart of *Purko* Maasai homeland. Together these lands were called "the White Highlands" by European settlers, and at Independence the name was retained by historians to refer to the lands of departing Europeans. Thus, the same lands from which Maasai had been removed mere decades before were erased of their historical identity in histories of the Kenyan state, imagined to be empty "white" land available to be returned to any African people. The White Highlands are essential to the story told of the origin of the Kenyan state in the Mau Mau Land and Freedom movement that went to war with the British Empire in the 1950s. The movement sparked among Kikuyu workers in

Translation of *Kenyamal Enkop*: "Despair is everywhere on the land."

Maasailand, at Olengururone, and its principal aim was to "take back" the White Highlands from Europeans, and in essence to transfer Maasailand to Kikuyu workers employed by Europeans. In this chapter, we tell the story of that land loss and settlement after Independence, which is a story that resonates with histories of "settler colonialism" in other contexts.

This chapter also presents an overview of the post-Independence cascade of land loss in southern Maasailand, which was designated the Masai Reserve in the era of formal colonization. It touches on the establishment of group ranches and subsequent privatization of Maasailand, and the impact of policies designed to destroy Maasai economies in favor of production for outside markets. Subdivision created space for an elite class of Maasai to form by grabbing land themselves, which has devastated the ability of the Maasai community to use electoral politics to pursue collective rights. These policies were initiated before Independence and have been a primary mechanism of the neocolonization of Maasailand since.

The main sourcing for this chapter is a body of work on the origin of the Kenyan state. These may not acknowledge the Maasai community, but they trace the history of the land from which Maasai were removed. They include especially a number of in-depth histories of the Mau Mau Land and Freedom anticolonial movement. One of their most significant findings, built on rigorous archival investigation, is that the wealth of the Kenyan colony was generated through a collaborative relationship between the colonial apparatus and leadership of the Kikuyu community and that they benefited together. Indeed, the story implies that it was the wealth built through this collaboration that positioned the Kikuyu to assume power from the British at Independence. This revelation is important but incomplete. The land that Kikuyu and British settled and then fought over was Maasailand, and it was only available for settlement through the forced removal of Maaail people. The Kenyan state could only be founded on the further seizure of that same land if Maasai themselves were vanquished from history. Adding Maasai back into this history exposes that the British and Kikuyu collaboration necessarily considered Maasai to be a common enemy. Only this revision of history can explain the current politics of erasure through which Maasai, and all other Indigenous and other minoritized peoples, are denied an existence in Kenyan history, and through which their identities are considered to be threatening to peace.

British colonization of Maasailand was similar in all of the broad strokes to British colonization of Indigenous lands throughout its empire. The British began to arrive in Maasailand in the late nineteenth century in response to increasing political competition among European governments for control of resources and local markets throughout Africa. This would lead to the Berlin Conference of 1884–5 and the European "scramble for Africa" at the end of the nineteenth century. Britain and Germany both set sights on East Africa, the British especially determined to occupy and expand an existing Arab trade network that connected the East African coast with Lake Victoria, the headwaters of the Nile River. This plan would lead British armies deeper into the lands of three primary peoples: the Kamba, a farming community partnered with the Arab traders living between the eastern edge of Maasailand and the coast; the Gikuyu (Kikuyu), also farmers whose homeland lay around Mt. Kenya just north of the desired route; and finally the Maasai.[1]

Maasailand was the vast savannah to the north and West and the land that had not been penetrated by Europeans, and so the Maasai people presented the greatest challenge. The ancestral homeland of the Maasai people stretched some 700 miles from what would become northern Kenya into central Tanzania, and as many as 400 miles from east to West, including Enkare Nairobi, the place that is now Kenya's capital city. Maasai people in the Kenyan colony alone, in the words of a British colonial administrator, "had practically half the Protectorate to roam over."[2] As a first strategy, competitors Britain and Germany sent emissaries to gather intelligence on Maasai society. In 1882, Dr. Fischer of the German Geographical Society set out from the coast with hundreds of soldiers to reach the *Purko* homeland of Nakurro (Nakuru) and Enaiposha (Naivasha) and a year later, Joseph Thomson of the British Royal Geographic Society crossed Maasailand and also wrote of his observations of Maasai society in a best-selling book, *Through Masai Land*.[3] Europeans were repelled in all of their early encounters with Maasai.[4] But the information gathered from these forays was sufficient to concretize a plan to build a railroad through Maasailand and to identify the areas most desirable for European settlement. British forts began to appear to the east, in Machakos in Kamba land, in 1894 and the forest belt, Nairobi, "the place of cool water" in the *Maa* language.

What followed was military engagement by British troops of all African communities that lived on the desired railway route, including Kamba, Kikuyu, Maasai, the "Nandi," or Kalenjin, and the Kisii. The eventual conquest of Maasailand is known primarily through British administrative sources who kept detailed records, published in George Sandford's *An Administrative History of the Masai Reserve* in 1919.[5] We explore that history further in Chapter 5, but in short, the British used military tactics honed through their wars in other colonies. By the end of the nineteenth century, Maasai society had been brought to a breaking point through an onslaught of smallpox and other British diseases, and through war involving massacres and perpetual engagement between British and Maasai soldiers, known as *ilmurran*, or warriors. Starving Maasai people were taken in by an expanding network of British forts and from that position were evicted from their homeland.

The dynamic in East Africa between settlers, colonial administrators, and native peoples was also similar to that of other British colonies: violent evictions of Maasai people from Maasailand were driven by the land hunger of European and white South African settlers and attempts by the colonial authority to maintain control over conflicts between settler and colonized peoples. Several wealthy settlers quickly laid claim to the watered parts of northern Maasailand, the highlands beginning in Nairobi and stretching West into the Rift Valley, a partially forested belt that was the lifeblood of the larger Maasai homeland and the headwaters of the river systems that water the dry savannah to the south. The belt was the most important drought reserve that made the sacrifice of Maasai life on otherwise impossibly dry land possible; the forest was shared at its edges with Kalenjin herders, was homeland to Ogiek hunters, and the source of medicine for all of these communities. The settlers named this land after themselves, the "White Highlands," which is the name adopted on maps and in history books. The colonial authority was beholden to this settler class and it undertook two waves of evictions, in 1904 and 1910, which they sought to legitimize through two "Agreements," documents that laid out borders and which the British claimed were thumb-printed by Maasai leadership. This process led to the establishment of the Masai Reserve on dry land south of the railroad line which had been completed in 1901.

Europeans believed that such violent conquest of colonized peoples was appropriate as long as they acted within the jurisdiction of their own law. This sometimes required a pretense of treaty making with those that they had broken militarily. Britain had created a legal framework to declare East Africa a "protectorate" of the Crown, but since 1833, protectorates were defined as foreign countries, thus as sovereign entities, and British law gave "the imperial power little more than *political jurisdiction* over the territory."[6] The land itself had to be "acquired by conquest or agreement, treaty or sale with the indigenous people." Treaties were problematic because in East Africa, land was typically owned communally. As one British administrator said about land in the Kenyan colony, "for treaties to be anything more than an empty mockery, it would be necessary that they should be signed by several thousand petty chiefs and headmen."[7] To solve the problem, the British Foreign Office abandoned its "legalistic approach" and assumed a new policy through the Indian Land Acquisition Act, passed in 1897, "despite severe doubts in the Foreign office as to the legality of such an action."[8] Through the Foreing Jurisdiction Act of 1890 the Crown assumed the right to dispose of "waste and unoccupied land in protectorates where there was no settled form of government and where land had not been appropriated either to the local sovereign or to individuals."[9]

The rationalization cleared the way for the British Government to draft the 1904 Anglo-Masai Agreement which justified the removal of an estimated 11,200 Maasai and their 2 million cows, goats, and sheep for settlement and resale by forty-eight Europeans. Though that Agreement was guaranteed to last "as long as the Maasai exist as a race," it was nullified in a second, 1911 Agreement, which was hastily constructed following the initial forced removal of 20,000 Maasai people and 2.5 million stock from their home in the north to an expanded but environmentally inferior Southern Reserve, the borders of which roughly coincide with current Maasai land.[10] Both Agreements appear to have been drawn from templates of treaties made with Indigenous peoples in North America, and the British reported that signers acted of their own free will.

In 1910 and 1911, whole sections of Maasai were removed at gunpoint from Laikipia, their villages burned, a removal in the words of later Maasai leadership, that "involved the giving up of good land by the Masai for their present poor land."[11] Maasai people challenged the legality of the 1911 Agreement in a 1912 lawsuit against the Crown "for the restoration of Laikipia and other land protected by 1904 British Agreement, and for damage and loss suffered during the various moves."[12] The suit was dismissed by a British court on the grounds that "the treaty of 1904, being a compact between two sovereign states, was not cognizable by any British Court."[13] Ironically defeated because of their supposed sovereignty, Maasai were rendered impotent in any further legal claims, and the colonial government then took a variety of steps to officially settle the land.

The first and most fundamental way that the British produced wealth in Kenya was not, yet, through the commodities grown or mined on the land. It was produced by transforming the land itself into commodity and by creating the infrastructure of speculation and resale, the procedures of surveying and titling. After the rebranding of northern Maasailand as the "White Highlands," the value of land "shot up by some *4000 percent* between 1908 and 1914" alone.[14] The colonial authority existed to provide legal and police protection for titles and to solicit buyers to whom they sold parcels in tens of thousands of acres. This first phase of European colonization—through which the meaning of land was reassembled as currency—is also typical of British colonies elsewhere, and it was the means through which an aristocratic settler class was established. These include the families of the "founding fathers" in Britain's north American colonies, who inherited or otherwise obtained huge tracts of land on the Eastern seaboard of what is now the United States. Settlers to Kenya included "aristocratic immigrants," large landowners who controlled the Kenyan Legislative Council, or Leg Co, "using political ties back in London—many fathers, brothers, and uncles sat in the House of Lords." They achieved low-interest loans, government crop subsidies, and land leases tailored to their desires.[15] Settlers were often at odds with colonial administrators. The colonial governor claimed in 1910 that "[a] large body of settlers takes the view that their rights in the country have been gradually won by pressure and struggle against a Government whose resistance has been professedly due to its position as guardian of native rights."[16]

The next phase of colonization was more difficult, that of attempting to turn a profit from economic activities on the land. Central Kenyans, Kikuyus and their neighbors, were farmers and so were not scheduled for removal as were the Maasai, whose pastoralism was deemed incompatible with commercial agriculture. Central Kenyans were ultimately removed from only a small portion of their lands and they were retained instead to provide the labor of an indentured settler class. They were forced into peonage as the British carved out a plantation economy in the fertile areas to the north and West of Nairobi. To manage laborers, the British enlisted the collaboration of an elite class among the Kikuyu in Kiambu—the Kenyattas, Njonjos, Koinanges—the same families that would assume power over the Kenyan state at Independence. In this way, the British transformed the broader Kikuyu homeland into a patron and client system that enabled a strata of Kikuyu chiefs to accumulate land and wealth and that transformed the majority into property-less wage laborers. This was the means through which Kikuyu people were brought into alignment with the British already in the beginning of the colonial era, as unequal partners in the colonial project.

To solidify the relationship, the British began to extend British culture to Kikuyu people, though in ways that maintained their inferiority. Schools and churches were built in Central Kenya and some parts of the community achieved literacy though they were banned from higher education. Kikuyu chiefs were given license to move into all available sectors of the emerging colonial economy. Historian David Anderson notes that "by the 1940s the district was renowned for the wealth of its farmers."[17] One chief, Waruhiu wa Kunga, who would be assassinated by Mau Mau revolutionaries in the 1950s, was "both a prominent landowner and a businessman. His farmlands in Kiambu were productive and prosperous, and from their Nairobi offices his family ran various haulage, wholesaling and retailing businesses." Because they controlled labor, Anderson says, "Such men as these were the gatekeepers of the colonial state."[18] The majority of Kikuyu people were forced into servitude as a landless peasant class, taxed and placed on formal labor contracts by a rapidly solidifying Kikuyu elite.

Maasailand would not go quite as easily. The 1911 evictions had technically removed people and pastoralism from northern Maasailand to create the "White Highlands," but as the next chapter on Mau Narok will demonstrate, many remained in the north. Settlers had staked claims to hundreds of thousands of acres each in some cases. To develop any portion of that land for agriculture required local labor. However, settler attempts to draw Maasai into service, as herders or guards, were not successful. The Crown wanted to see the land developed for agriculture and so the settlers needed to show progress toward that end, and the pressure increased as the First World War created extreme demand for food produced by the colonies. Farming was hard and dirty work, especially before mechanization, and European settlers were few and disbursed in hostile territory. Development of the land required labor, and that required the collaboration of a class of African settlers who would receive enough benefit from the system to support it.[19]

European settlers of occupied Maasailand therefore contracted with chiefs in Central Kenya to import Kikuyu laborers. There was a lot of wealth to go around as land values continued to rise, and "the thousands of unexploited acres under speculative ownership provided ... the means to attract a permanent labour force on to the settler manor." The settlers could not hold on to their tens of thousands of acres themselves, and they began to make it available to their workers. Kikuyu workers in the White Highlands thus "enjoyed an enormous access to exploitable land," that from which Maasai pastoralists had only recently been removed. They were also supplied with equipment to till the land. These Kikuyu workers thus formed a class of settlers in occupied Maasailand.[20]

The replacement of Maasai with Kikuyu people on European farms in Maasailand created a new identity for the land in the European imagination, as indigenous Kikuyuland. The Danish settler Karen Blixen bought 6,000 acres of land in Ngong southwest of Nairobi in 1913 to establish a coffee plantation. Coffee is a labor-intensive enterprise, and Blixen found that to put 600 acres into coffee cultivation, she needed to provide between 1,000 and 3,400 acres to Kikuyu workers for their own farms.[21] The plantation itself was not ultimately successful, and though not part of the official narrative, it is possible that she

hosted hunting tourism for a more stable income.[22] A museum stands on that
estate now which tells a mistaken version of the history in which the Kikuyu
workers were its local people. But that land was undisputedly the territory of
the *Purko* and *Keekonyokie* sections of the Maasai and home of the family of the
Maasai *oloiboni*, spiritual leader. The famous *oloiboni* Olonana had herded the
same land given to Kikuyu workers, and he lived in Ngong until his death in
1911, just two years before Blixen arrived in East Africa. The museum displays
a letter to Blixen from Jomo Kenyatta written in the 1930s, expressing gratitude
for an unspecified support for his (Kikuyu) people. As she left Kenya, Blixen
sold the whole of her 6,000-acre estate, and bought other land at Mbagathi
on which to settle her workers. Some of that land, also contested Maasailand,
was later transferred to the Kenyatta family. Blixen wrote many books after
returning to Europe later under the pen name Isak Dinesen, and Maasai
occasionally appear in her books as nameless nomads lurking on the edges of
her farm.

After the forced removal of Maasai from Laikipia beginning in 1910, a flood
of settlement took place. Vast farms of tens and even hundreds of thousands
of acres were claimed there and also in and around Nakuru. European settlers
sent labor recruiters to Central Kenya to bring tenant farmers to the Rift Valley
and that "heralded a wave of Kikuyu migration" of 70,000 people between 1904
and 1920. David Anderson says that migrants included "many Kikuyu who had
lost their land to white settlers in central Kenya." But others went West just to
find greater opportunity.

> [Kikuyu] Squatter families were permitted to reside on the farms and use
> grazing, and also cultivate small areas for themselves. In return, they gave a
> limited amount of labour to the European farmers, up to 180 days each year, for
> which they were paid at the prescribed rate. For younger men keen to acquire
> livestock and capital the move west seemed attractive. The lack of good grazing
> in central Kenya enhanced the appeal of the Rift Valley farms in particular, and
> many Kikuyu families in Kiambu and Nyeri even encouraged younger members
> to move west in order to gain access to the resources available.[23]

The lands just north of the Masai Reserve in particular became "frontiers of
opportunity" for Kikuyu settlers.[24] The borders were typically not marked on the
ground and could be manipulated to create opportunities to claim land beyond
the European farms. Towns were established in Nakuru and Naivasha, leading
to the further removal of Maasai from those places, and new classes of Kikuyu
migrants facilitated the flow of goods and the towns as "petty traders." The record
excavated by historians suggests that on whole, "In material terms the squatters

who went West did pretty well. Incomes were relatively high, compared with those realized within the Kikuyu reserves."[25] The descendants of these settlers from Central Kenya continue to occupy the same watered Maasailand today, in Nakuru, Naivasha, Kinangop, and Western Nairobi, on land their families obtained through colonization, while members of their ethnic community maintained control for decades of the government that protects their rights to this land.

Historians have characterized this generation of Kikuyu settlers as "adventurers and refugees," "whole households, with dependents," who set off on an "exodus … to colonize the Maasai pastures now under white ownership in the Rift Valley." They called the place they settled *ruguru*, "the west."[26] A dominant percentage migrated from southern Kiambu where chiefs invested in the settlers and tried to maintain control of the pace and extent of the migration through arrangement with Europeans. Meanwhile, European settlers were romanticizing their adventures as "pioneers" through books by Blixen and Elspeth Huxley, embellishing stories of rugged individualists like Lord Delamere and other men who called themselves the "Kenyan Cowboys." Those settlers lived like kings, overseeing vast rural estates and on weekends riding into Nairobi to meet their friends at the Norfolk Hotel, or going on shooting safaris in the Masai Reserve.[27] The Kikuyu "frontier" also developed its own culture. Kikuyu in the Rift Valley were typically not educated or Christianized as their families were becoming back in Central Kenya.[28] They were living in boom conditions where their labor was needed, away from the oppressive presence of British soldiers. Workers on European farms earned enough to build herds, and Nakuru could barely keep up with demands for goods and services, butchers, builders, and hotels. The above ground economy alone provided opportunity that could not be imagined back in Central Kenya—there were 150 licensed African shop keepers in Nakuru district by 1951, and many more unlicensed. Industries flourished that funneled the wealth of Maasailand out of the region, such as trade in livestock, wood, and charcoal.[29]

African people were technically prevented from buying and selling land under colonial policy, but the Kikuyu settlers, "in effect … were allowed to buy [land] in return for labour service" establishing claims on pieces of land both within and on the borders of the European estates. It was through this piecemeal occupation by thousands of small Kikuyu settlers that "Maasailand was being turned inside out," redefined, cleared, and transformed from pastureland into small farms and towns, as "African cultivators, the majority of them Kikuyu, now invaded the choicest areas of the pastoral plain, under the protection of its new overlords."[30] While the Europeans had largely failed as farmers themselves, the Kikuyu settler class was successful in turning a profit for the Crown.[31] The growth continued into the 1930s, at the end of which "the Kikuyu squatter community numbered more than 150,000." By the 1940s, one in eight Kikuyu was a tenant on a European-owned farm. The settlers "retained higher levels of illiteracy yet were on the whole wealthier than their brethren in the Kikuyu reserves."[32]

These were the conditions under which Kikuyu settlers began to see Maasailand as their home; according to John Lonsdale, they "did not know where Kikuyu was; they mistakenly believed it was where they lived, on a white farm."[33] The attachment they developed to this land resembles that of settler colonial societies that remove Indigenous peoples from land as a strategy of conquest, as the land is distributed to settlers to secure their loyalty to a colony, or later, a nation-state.[34] The ideological justification for the dispossession of Indigenous people is typically that "we" could use the land better than "they" have.[35] Displaced Indigenous peoples from other parts of the world describe the ideological transformation of the settlers who initially see themselves as pioneers on behalf of the society they were born into, to develop a colony for that other home.[36]

But then a shift tends to occur in settler colonial societies, in the identity of subsequent generations who experience a sense of belonging to the place settled. These children and grandchildren of the original settlers begin to see themselves not as a settler class, but as the founders of the nation-state. The land they occupy is cleansed in their imaginations of the people removed for settlement. Settlers justify their occupation of the land because they believe "it was the hard work and determination of these early migrants that developed the nation. Through their achievement … they brought us 'civilization' and 'gave' us democracy and the market economy." The settlers occlude the memory of the violence through which the people were removed from the land, and instead describe the war they waged on the "virgin territory" they brought under control and "civilized."[37] According to Aloysha Goldstein, speaking generally about settler colonialism:

> Settlement provided European colonizers with a sense of themselves as locals. "Settlement" as such already implied an entitled and possessive relation to place, as compared with the supposedly unsettled nature of indigenous populations. This worked in concert with colonial ideologies that subordinated indigenous peoples as primitive" and by divine right rendered the continent the property of those Europeans who would suitably cultivate the land.[38]

These perspectives help to explain the passionate entitlement expressed by spokespeople for the Kikuyu community in the Rift Valley such as Koigi Wa Wamwere, a long-serving member of Kenyan Parliament from Nakuru. Wamwere describes colonization as if Maasailand had no past before it was "whitened" through settlement. With Maasai removed from the picture, he can present Kikuyu people as the main victims of colonization. He has written, "My parents and other Gikuyu people did not march into the Rift Valley as robber barons, as some people claim today, but were driven there as impoverished and wandering slaves looking for a place to settle."[39] Once nation-states are formed around settler societies, and the Indigenous land is fully occupied, the cultures of the conquered Indigenous peoples are drawn on to give a sense of culture for the country, and in this way an "aura of indigeneity" is allowed to return to the land.[40]

But the expansion of Kikuyu settlers into seemingly free land was very short-lived through changes in both Central Kenyan and the Rift Valley farms. Fewer opportunities existed back in Central Kenya as land there had become more consolidated in fewer hands.

> from the 1930s the hardening of the boundaries between settler farms and African lands, combined with African population increase, brought the first real evidence of land hunger and emerging landlessness in central Kenya. For the Kikuyu especially, the land question had by the 1930s become *the* crucial political grievance.[41]

The chiefs in Central began to question their arrangement with the British when even they began to be denied entitlement. Koinange Wa Mbiyu broke with the British not over an ideological rejection of colonialism, but over the refusal of the Kenya Land Commission of 1933–4 to restore his personal property. In the Rift Valley, tension did not emerge until after the Second World War. The war itself brought a surge in "untold prosperity to settlers and squatters alike," raising expectations.[42] But those profits only enabled the Europeans to finally mechanize their farms, which unbalanced the power relations with Kikuyu settlers. Europeans began to impose new limits on grazing and cultivating through new worker contracts. The workers refused to sign these and organized strikes and boycotts which eventually collapsed. The option for many was either to move to Nairobi and try to survive there or return to their family's home in Central Kenya.

Though the settlers had living relatives back home in Central Kenya, there was no welcome for them there. Competition had developed within the Kikuyu community as land scarcity increased and became a volatile issue. "Neighbors and relatives took one another to court to protect their access to the scarce and valuable commodity of land" and these conflicts strained Kikuyu traditional relationships of obligation between poor and wealthy, of leaders to community members. Daniel Branch continues, land formed "the very stuff of Central Kenya's political debates over the previous five decades at least."[43] European farmers in Central Kenya had also become nervous in the face of land scarcity and tried to assert control by imposing more restrictive contracts on their workers. Chiefs in Kiambu were appalled by attempts by the Rift Valley settlers to return as they threatened a delicate balance with the white farmlands. As John Lonsdale said, "erosion in the reserves raised the specter of hordes of famished peasants trampling down the white highland fences in search of land."[44] But the Kikuyu settlers needed to go somewhere.

> By early 1946, "a steady trickle of families was to be seen on the escarpment road up to Kijabe, or herded like livestock into the third-class carriages of steam trains at Nakuru, Gilgil and Naivasha, bound for central Kenya. Between 1946 and 1952 the trickle would turn into a torrent, as more than 100,000 Kikuyu squatters were forcibly 'repatriated.'"

The colonial administration had tried to relieve some of the pressure with a failed attempt to place some of the workers on settlement schemes in the Rift Valley. A total of 11,000 workers, mostly from southern Kiambu, were relocated to *Oleng'uruoni* in 1941. *Oleng'ururoni* was a "high, scrubby piece of land on the edge of the bamboo forest above Nakuru," whose Maasai name means, "the place of ashes." The settlers cleared and tilled that soil for nine years, growing subsistence crops in defiance of government plans to turn the land for profit. But they were evicted in 1948 and lost a court battle to reverse the order.[45]

It was at this point that the different interests among Kikuyu classes ground to a breaking point, leading to the movement known to itself as the Kenya Land and Freedom Army, known internationally as Mau Mau. Mau Mau was both an anticolonial movement against British occupation and a war among Kikuyu people over land. Its radical base was of those workers on European plantations in occupied Maasailand who had been evicted and then rejected back in Central Kenya. A class of "organic intellectuals" emerged to lead these displaced Kikuyu people to assert their land rights to Maasailand in *kuna*, "first clearance." They argued that it was the Kikuyu who had "nourished the white highlands with their sweat ... Dynastic history, sweat and ritual sway over the land all told squatters that they ... were earning property rights."[46] Their consciousness as laborers who were owed compensation led them to greater affinity with landless and exploited workers in Nairobi who had campaigned for unions since the 1920s to achieve better pay and working conditions. They began to experience greater affinity with these urban workers than with the chiefs that facilitated their move West but then had prevented them from returning home to Central Kenya.[47]

The educated Kiambu elite had organized the Kikuyu Central Association (KCA) as an organ of negotiation with the British, and they revived a traditional practice of oathing to unify Kikuyu people behind their leadership. Oathing had historically been used in Kikuyu society to solidify land deals; in the KCA version, oath takers swore allegiance to the Kikuyu community and the recovery of broader Kikuyuland.[48] They were considered too tame in their demands among the Kikuyu settlers in occupied Maasailand and were ineffective in attempts to recruit among them. But the settlers developed their own oath by 1948 which rejected the bible used by the KCA and clarified that killing was "a matter of duty." Mau Mau leadership established a headquarters in the "outcast" city of Nairobi, where refugees from the colonial system lived in slums and tried to survive "on the edge of criminality" as middlemen. They built the infrastructure of the Mau Mau movement there, and "linkages with the Kikuyu countryside were forged as young men carried arms" and the trade union movement "ran a protection racket, through which it got funds from Asian and African businessmen." As this volatile movement formed in Nairobi and on Rift Valley farms, back in Central Kenya and the Kikuyu reserves, "a group of missionary Kikuyu literati, landowners and businessmen closely tied to the colonial system constituted the basis for a class of collaborators." Mau Mau formally broke with the KCA in 1950, two years before the Emergency was declared.[49]

The symbolic birth of the Mau Mau movement had begun in occupied Maasailand, in *Oleng'uruoni*, among these Kikuyu workers who were driven out of the Maasai Highlands and Nakuru and Naivasha. The birth in blood happened several years later. Beginning in November 1952, Kikuyu workers on European farms went on coordinated killing sprees that involved shocking violence: a small child butchered in his bed by a house servant who had saved his life only days earlier after he had been thrown by a horse.[50] Kikuyu chiefs were slaughtered in the open. The colonial government responded swiftly and imposed a State of Emergency that lasted eight years. The British waged an air war in the forests of the Aberdare and Mount Kenya, where Mau Mau operated as a guerilla army fed by surrounding Kikuyu farmers and through networks in Nairobi. One hundred and eighty suspected Mau Mau leaders were immediately detained. While those detained included Jomo Kenyatta and other leaders of the

KCA, the Kenya Land and Freedom Army was actually led by Dedan Kimathi of Nyeri in Central Kenya. In recent years historians have shifted the gaze from the handful of Mau Mau atrocities committed against Europeans to the thousands of acts of brutality by the British through mass incarceration at rural and urban detention camps where suspected rebels were forced to work, were tortured, and "rehabilitated." Nearly the entire population of Nairobi was put into detention for "screening," at one point. Though other communities had faced extreme British violence, such brutality may have been unprecedented in Central Kenya[51] and the horror had lasting impact there. Roughly equal numbers of Kikuyu people supported Mau Mau and the Homeguard British collaborators who staffed the detention camps, and the dynamics were even more complex.[52]

Mau Mau expressed itself as a movement to *reclaim* land from Europeans. But it was not a movement to restore the homelands of all of the colonized peoples, or even specifically to restore Kikuyu land. Kikuyu people had only been removed from an estimated 6 percent of their land, all of which was returned to the Kikuyu community at Independence.[53] What Mau Mau sought was to make permanent the transfer of northern Maasailand to Kikuyu settlement. As the story of Mau Mau was positioned to be the moral origin of the nation of Kenya, Kikuyu entitlement to Maasailand became fused with Kenyan Nationalism at that point.[54] John Lonsdale found that Kikuyu people experienced their removal from Maasailand to be "a tragedy for Kikuyu, later hymned as martyrdom."[55] The sons of Kiambu ejected from *Oleng'uruoni*, unwanted in Central Kenya, dispersed to the forests to wage war against the British colonists in the White Highlands and take "back" Maasailand. But to claim that the movement they created was only an *anticolonial* movement, a movement to destroy and replace colonization, one must vanquish Maasai from history. That story must also collude with the colonial pretense that the "White Highlands" had in fact been made "white" through a few decades of European occupation, and to side in that way with the British against the Maasai.

Regarding Kenyan history, by far the biggest resources of the Western academy have gone into reconstructing the story of Mau Mau to provide a moral center to the national identity.[56] But instead of unity, that work has exposed contradictions. The deeper historians have dug, the more they found Mau Mau to be not a story of national unity, but "a lightening conductor of disagreement."[57] Mau Mau has been multiply interpreted over the past fifty years; some histories sought to show the integrity and intelligence of the movement, that "militants were neither savages nor madmen," and capable of democracy. That reading of Mau Mau captured the minds of anti-racist movements and Black intellectuals in other parts of the world, as well as youth in diasporic communities in Jamaica, London, and Harlem, New York.[58] But that truth is also complicated by the movement's relationship to land and the use of colonial power to access land in the Rift Valley. Despite evidence that some small number of non-Kikuyu people joined Mau Mau, including some Maasai,[59] Mau Mau was essentially a Kikuyu movement, requiring an oath of allegiance, not to an imagined "Kenyan" state, but to the Kikuyu House of Mumbi. Historians say that Mau Mau serves as a battleground over who deserves to inherit Kenya,[60] in Daniel Branch's words, "as a crude ideological justification for this regionalization of power" in Central Kenya. Branch says that he has learned through "countless conversations" about the debt many Kikuyu people feel that they are owed for having liberated Kenya from the British.[61]

As the historians have demonstrated a commitment to "contextual fidelity" they have exposed the contradictions in Kenyan history.[62] Some have even called for a new history of anticolonial resistance that happened in many places, on the Coast, among the Nandi and Pokot,[63] to write about what E.S. Atieno Odhiambo refers to as a plethora of nationalist movements, including Maasai "with their national centre at *Sanya Chini* in Tanzania."[64]

Mau Mau shared a core objective with both the British and the emerging Kikuyu elite, to use Maasailand to build the wealth and political power of the Kenyan state and its dominant class. Even before the Mau Mau Emergency, the British colonial authority developed plans for an eventual transfer of power to Kikuyu leadership. The plan maintained the critical features of the colonial infrastructure and economic and financial ties to the West. Northern Maasailand was key to this plan. As early as 1946 the British government began funneling large sums of money into Kenyan development "to transform African cultivators into peasants and European farmers into capitalists."[65] The skeleton of neocolonialism in Kenya was embodied by the "Swynnerton Plan," produced in the 1950s as a roadmap for the World Bank-funded development of Kenyan land for global markets, protection of land value, and creation of settlement schemes for landless Central Kenyans in the Rift Valley. British and Kenyan policymakers together planned to settle the "White Highlands" with "the better kind of African," those from Central Kenya.[66] The land policy explicitly sought to maintain some large farms but to replace Europeans with elite Kenyans.[67] R.J.M. Swynnerton, Kenya's Assistant Director of Agriculture, said that through his plan, "former Government policy will be reversed and able, energetic or rich Africans will be able to acquire more land, and bad or poor farmers less, creating a landed and landless class." This, he said, was "a normal step in the evolution of a country."[68] These plans were incorporated into the design of the government of the Kenyan state and embodied in the country's constitution drafted in London between 1960 and 1963.

Parceling out Maasailand was the means to achieving a united Kikuyu electoral base. Kenyatta endeared himself to Kikuyu people beyond Kiambu by securing Rift Valley Maasailand for the broader Kikuyu community.[69] According to Lonsdale and Odhiambo,

> From 1970 to his death in 1978, Kenyatta established a kind of monarchical court from which he promoted Kikuyu nationalism and entrenched Kikuyu dominance. The other Kenyan peoples reacted by further consolidating imagined communities that they had established before 1952. Kenyan nationalism died and politics became ethnicized.[70]

But Kikuyu people were not united. Once in office, Kenya's first president Kenyatta turned his back on Mau Mau, and it was the pro-British Homeguard collaborators who were rewarded instead with settlement in the Rift Valley.

In the Highlands, this included the many thousand-acre farms taken by Kenyatta himself and distributed to his family members and political allies, and the government resettlement schemes through which individual plots in Maasailand were transferred to small Kikuyu farmers. The One Million Acre Settlement Scheme was established by the Land Development Settlement Board (LDSB) in 1963, and later moved to the Ministry of Agriculture, headed by that former colonial administrator Bruce McKenzie. Through the scheme, settlers returning to Europe were compensated for their vacated land and paid market value. Kenya had to take out loans from the British government and the World Bank to "buy" land from British settlers which alone amounted to nearly £12.5 million. The plan was to settle 35,000 landless families on small plots of farmland under individual titles to grow crops for agricultural markets. These families were explicitly defined as Kikuyu, the "better kind of African" mentioned above. Most of this land did not end up benefiting these small farmers as it was bought and resold to the growing elite classes of Kenyans and European investors.[71] While the One Million Acre Settlement Scheme was intended on paper to settle people within their own ethnic regions, the largest single settlement area was taken from Maasailand in the Rift Valley to settle Kikuyu people. Bruce McKenzie working closely with the Kenyatta government actively undermined various plans for Maasai people to be trained in agriculture, which would have created grounds for Maasai people to be settled on their land instead.[72]

The transfer of Maasailand to Kikuyu ownership was facilitated by Kikuyu land-buying companies. These included Ngwataniro, Nyakinyua, Ndeffo,

Mutukanio, Mbo-i-Kamitit, and Nyagacho, and GEMA the Gikuyu, Embu, and Meru Association of Central Kenya which had been created to protect Central Kenyan Interests, and Njenge Karume was the chairman. Between 1974 and 1980, one of these companies alone, Ngwataniro, owned by Kihika Kimani, settled over 50,000 Central Kenyan families in Laikipia and Nakuru, the heart of *Purko* Maasai homeland. By 1978, 95 percent of the farms that had been occupied by Europeans had been bought and sold this way, a quarter taken over as large farms of thousands of acres, and another half for formal settlement schemes. The transfer continued to be funded by the British government. By the time that frenzied buying ended in 1979, 1,400 farms covering 3.5 million acres had been transferred from Europeans to Central Kenyans and 225 settlement schemes had been established for small farmers in the "White Highlands." The urgent nature of the buying and selling reflected an awareness that Jomo Kenyatta would not live forever and the national "policy over land distribution and ownership could change drastically."[73]

The "frontier" of Maasailand was closed by the time of Kenyatta's death in 1978 but subdivision accelerated into the 1980s as large farms continued to be broken up and ownership of Rift Valley land was distributed to greater numbers of Central Kenyans.[74] As Michela Wrong put it, Kenyatta ensured at the Lancaster House conference that Kikuyu be allowed the land in the Rift Valley.

> Borrowing money from Kikuyu banks and Kikuyu businessmen, tapping into the expertise of Kikuyu lawyers, the president's fellow tribespeople rushed to buy the land of departing whites under a million-acre resettlement scheme subsidized by London. Descending from the escarpment, they flooded in their hundreds of thousands into the previously off-limits Rift Valley.[75]

According to Bethwell Ogot, except for two brief periods, Jomo Kenyatta was devoted, not to a national vision, but to the development of "The Greater Kikuyu Society," and Kikuyu diaspora across Kenya. As president, he was active on behalf of Kikuyu settlers, on the coast and the "former White Highlands," and GEMA, to expand Kikuyland into an even greater "imagined community."[76]

The land grabbing continued under Kenyatta's successor, though on a much smaller scale, limited to land that had not yet been distributed. This included the Maasai Mau Forest. President Daniel Arap Moi, Vice President under Kenyatta and a close ally, favored his own Kalenjin community for land distribution. Following "numerous" legal cases against Kikuyu land-buying companies, in 1986, Moi demanded the shutdown of all the remaining 1,000 of these and the subdivision of the farms they had bought, claiming they had cheated the public. More grants of government lands were made to well-connected individuals and speculators, although now the beneficiaries were more directly affiliated with Moi who, like Kenyatta, used land to build a loyal inner circle and broader political base.

> Settlement schemes were often used to settle parachuted outsiders, while local officials, ministers and civil servants allocated some plots to themselves or their families. The result was often violent disputes, legal cases and land left idle as a result. Local politicians faced a difficult choice, trying to placate their constituents while not upsetting a patronage system of which they themselves were often the beneficiaries.[77]

The Mau Forest was among the most valuable land that was privatized and distributed under Moi. Mau Forest is the critical watershed that feeds an entire region of East Africa that includes the Serengeti ecosystem and the Western Masai Reserve, and it had been held in trust for the use of the Maasai community in recognition of its importance. Moi was given a personal gift of thousands of acres of the forest through corruption among Maasai administrators of the Mau Forest land trust to plant tea, thus beginning the cascade of land grabbing in the forest through the following three decades. Maasai community interests were not protected at this time as traditional leadership had been disempowered in favor of elected members of County Councils and government chiefs. The personal interest of Kalenjin and Maasai elite in profiting from the Mau Forest has since presented the greatest challenge to restoring it as a critical lifeline to the whole ecosystem of Maasailand. This elite class of Maasai formed under Moi and while they are small in size they exert a tremendous negative power over efforts to restore the forest. As they have in many cases shifted loyalty from the community to the class of landed elites and lacking other forms of access to power, may be even more threatened by Maasai assertion of land justice than those from Kiambu.

While northern and watered Maasailand was undergoing settlement, the dry reservation land to which Maasai people had been removed under the 1911 treaty was retained. But its borders were eroded through illegal grabbing and the interior opened to privatization and individual sale. The descent of private interests on Maasailand at this time mirrors the story of the plunder of Indigenous land in North America through allotment, what US President Theodore Roosevelt called "a mighty pulverizing engine to break up a tribal mass."[78] Soda ash and gold continued to be mined in Magadi and Lolgorian[79] by the same companies protected behind the same barbed wire built by British military. New and expanded tourism industries annexed the main watered areas within the reserve for parks and wildlife reserves. The British, Kenyan, and US governments used the opportunity of statehood to fully infiltrate Maasailand through schemes developed in the colonial era to make even this remaining dry land profitable through commercial agriculture and ranching. They claimed that Maasai required development, which could only happen through privatization, which would allow "unused" land to be sold, and the cattle industry to be managed through Western science and population control. The Swynnerton plan of the 1950s that had paved the path for settlement schemes also outlined policies that would be necessary to break up communal ownership of Maasailand on the Reserve. These were adopted as the Land Registration Ordinance of 1959 and the Registered Land Act of 1963.[80]

A first step was to reinvent communal Maasai land as "Group Ranches," which divided the land into sections titled to identified voting members, all only "male" heads of households. The World Bank funded the establishment of Group Ranches through loans to the Kenyan Livestock Development Program, which granted individual residency rights to areas designated "common" land. Group ranches covering nearly a million acres were adjudicated in Kajiado and Narok between 1969 and 1971, and the watered areas around Mt. Kilimanjaro were demarcated and sold for agriculture. Group ranch membership was limited to the Maasai community in theory. In reality, outsiders took advantage of the opportunity to grab land and non-Maasais with no claim to group land were illegitimately registered and later given private parcels as a result.[81] According to historian Esther Mwangi, "the Maasai nevertheless accepted the idea of group ranches mainly because they needed to secure their land against incursion by government, by non-Maasai cultivators and by the elite Maasai."[82] Donkol Ole Keiwa says: "The Maasai as a people did not want privatization of land. So, the government convinced the educated Maasai to support subdivision because it protected their own rights to greater tracts of land."[83]

Maasai pastoralism was also undermined by Group Ranches, as they served to infuse Maasai culture with Western approaches to development. Following some of the science of grazing produced in the United States at this time, which found cattle to be destructive to ecology in the US West, government administrators sought to "modernize" and "improve" Maasai grazing. Members could be swayed to vote for a reduction in herd size and breeding schemes that later failed. The government initiated schemes to breed the Maasai Zebu cattle, small and resistant to drought, with larger animals with greater capacity to produce milk. That led to greater loss of cattle during dry seasons and the need to create dipping stations, as the newly bred cows were less resistant to ticks.[84] Maasai were promised permanent land security in exchange for their agreement to the next step in development, the complete subdivision and privatization of Maasai land. President Moi was one of the most ardent advocates for Maasai land subdivision, and in 1996 twenty-two group ranches were fully subdivided.[85] Maasai land has been checker-boarded through this process as "Kikuyu, Luo and Kamba moved in large numbers into Kajiado District, and by 1989 the Maasai were a bare 57% of the District's population in Kajiado and less than 50% in Narok."[86] A handful of Maasai families became rich by acquiring large portions of community land through the privatization process that began with the establishment of group ranches, through gifts made by the Kenyan government to silence opposition to the general theft of Maasailand.

The question "how did we lose the land?" is not settled. Kenya's constitution was written on Kenyan soil for the first time and actualized in 2010, and a question remains about its ultimate impact on Maasai land rights. The constitution has provisions to support Indigenous cultural survival that have potential for land rights claims. It has also been used to punish "tribalism," in ways that evoke the logic of termination policies in the other Indigenous contexts. The same year that the constitution was anointed by the Kenyan people, Maasai at Mau Narok brought the first legal challenge to their removal from land in almost a century and the movement ignited by that case continues to feed cultural resurgence and a claim to Indigenous sovereignty, an opposing direction from assimilation. So, the future of Maasai lands is also in the hands of the Maasai people.

The next chapter presents the history of Mau Narok, which sparked the land rights movement beginning in 2008, and which has led to a return of several thousand acres thus far. The history of Mau Narok shows that the occupation of Mau Narok is not a story of the past, but an active production in the present, one that is far from permanently settled.

Melo Enkop: The Story of Mau Narok

This chapter presents the research that ignited a movement for land rights in Mau Narok in 2008. The research into Mau Narok began with a tragedy and a gift: in 2005, Elija Sempeta, a Maasai lawyer, left Meitamei a packet of photocopied archival documents following his presumed assassination in the driveway of his home in Ngong outside of Nairobi. Sempeta was a leading Maasai land rights activist at the time of his death as still a young man. He had been involved in a challenge to continued European settler occupation of Laikipia, and another investigation into the occupation by an international corporation of a soda ash mine at Lake Magadi. Sempeta's death temporarily quieted the land rights work in Laikipia and Magadi. But the documents he left behind were a rich trove and we began to dig.

We were most captivated by those that formed a picture of a period of Maasai land rights activism in the early 1960s. This work was led by the Maasai United Front (MUF), a rare footnote in published histories. The MUF had gathered evidence of over a dozen specific violations of Maasai treaty rights that included Laikipia, Magadi, and also Mau Narok. We learned from the documents that members of the MUF had traveled to London to confront the committee that was drafting Kenya's constitution. The British government could not legally deny their claims and so instead kept them in the dark and buried their work. The defeat of the MUF was the first step in what would spiral into a totalizing crush of Maasai activism for an entire generation. In the fray, the collective memory of the MUF was scattered and lost. Only literate Maasai had access to the written record that contained much of this history, and so ours became a project of knitting the archival history to the community memory. We gathered together with many hundreds of community members over the years to present and discuss what the

Translation of *Melo Enkop*: "The land of our forefathers will not go."

Thank you to Kaitlin Noss for her work on the research presented in this chapter, which also informed Kaitlin Noss, "Common Ground: Territorial Racial Capital and Revolutionary Solidarity Between the United States and Kenya," Doctoral Dissertation, Department of Social and Cultural Analysis, New York University, August, 2019.

archives revealed. Through this process a new narrative emerged of a long history of anticolonial resistance extending backward and forward in time.

Of the dozen land rights demands made by the MUF, we zeroed in on Mau Narok to feed an effort of recovery already underway on the ground. A Maasai manager of one of the ranches, Moses Mpoe, had stumbled onto information that the family of Peter Mbiyu Koinange that occupied 5,000 acres at Mau Narok had no actual legal ownership. The title was held by a German citizen living in Europe, G. Class. A brother-in-law to Jomo Kenyatta, Koinange had been Kenya's powerful Minister of Internal Security in 1976 when Class says that he was rousted in the night and deported by the Kenyan government because he had refused to sell his land to Koinange directly. Class had attempted instead to transfer the land, with Mpoe's help, to a Maasai land trust, Olmaroroi Trust Ltd., and its members had occupied the land for two years until they were removed by the Kenyan government in 2005.

The archival search began with a place name, Mau Narok: thus, it did not begin in the usual way, with a question drawn from a gap in existing published scholarship of Maasai or Kenyan history. Neither author of this book were Africanist historians when we began so we built the broader context of Kenyan and African history outward from Mau Narok. It eventually became clear that the history of Mau Narok could not be written to align with the story that colonization ended with statehood in Kenya, and that led us to a broader engagement with that history and the rest of the book.

Mau Narok is the name given to 30,000 acres that form the shape of a boot dipping down into the former Masai Reserve, now Narok County. That border was excised from the Masai Reserve and placed in Nakuru County to the north following Independence. Mau Narok was once a necessary drought reserve for an entire section of the Maasai community. Today it has been cleared of forests and converted into large commercial wheat and barley farms, as "some of the best agricultural land in Kenya."[1] Because of its rich soil, flowing rivers, and frequent rainfall, Mau Narok was part of the larger stretch of northern Maasailand most coveted by settlers for speculation and development. The story of its occupation begins in 1904 which saw the first removals of Maasai people from the broader region for resale and settlement. The British drafted two "Agreements" in 1904 and 1911 to rationalize their claim that Maasai gave up this land willingly.

On a map Mau Narok looks like a quintessentially jerrymandered border, and that is accurate. It is the highly valuable watered land torn out of the northern rim of the dry southern Masai Reserve in violation of the border agreed to by the British in their 1911 Agreement. A single British settler, Edward Powys Cobb, petitioned the crown for undefined land at Mau Narok before he arrived in the

Kenyan colony in 1907. The land he sought was subject to the 1904 Agreement created to rationalize the forced removal of Maasai from the deepest homeland of the *Purko* section, present-day Naivasha and Nakuru. Maasai were moved onto two reserves at that time, one further north in Laikipia and the other south of Nairobi and the railroad connecting the Kenyan coast at Mombasa with Lake Victoria to the West.

By 1907 British plans were already underway to abrogate the 1904 treaty as settlers now wanted Laikipia as well. The colonial administration knew that to force all Maasai from the north to the dry southern reserve would require borders to be carefully drawn: Laikipia had lacked sufficient water and grazing, and every year after adjustments had to be made to the border to prevent mass starvation.[2] According to Normal Leys, the colonial administration understood that drought reserves, the "best and favorite grazing grounds,"[3] must be included in the Reserve to avoid the previous mistake. According to British records, in May 1910, the British called a conference with Maasai leaderships to discuss the proposed move from Laikipia to the southern reserve. At that time, they recorded, the *Purko* Maasai age-group leader Ole Gilisho, a respected traditional leader and anticolonial activist in oral history, expressed dissatisfaction with the land initially allocated for them in the south. Ole Gilisho was commissioned by the British to assemble a group to inspect the new area. The other person named and known in the British record is Ole Masikonte, also an age-group leader. Together, according to British records, they walked the length of the first proposed border, and reported back that the southern reserve as demarcated lacked sufficient water, a report that threatened the potential for a second move. The record suggests that the British were convinced that chaos would ensue if they attempted to confine the entire Maa nation on the dry southern reserve without sufficient headwaters and drought reserves on the northern border.[4] For their part, Maasai leadership had no choice but to negotiate from a powerless position. As will be discussed in Chapter 5, the Maasai people were subjected to extreme violence in the evictions, and their removals were uncontrolled by any rational due process.

The 1911 Agreement appears to have been worded to reflect this border negotiated with Maasai leadership that left the watered land of Mau Narok inside the reserve. The northern border of the Masai Reserve would be drawn, it said,

> to the south-western boundary of the land set aside for Mr. E. Powys Cobb, and by a straight line drawn from the north-eastern boundary of the said land to the highest point of Mount Suswa.[5]

The language was ambiguous, as Cobb had in fact petitioned the government for two different pieces of land. This history is published in the 1919 *An*

Administrative and Political History of the Masai Reserve by George Sandford, known as "the Blue Book."[6] It says:

> No definition has as yet been finally arrived at of the boundary of the Masai Reserve with Mr. Powys Cobb's land as far as the south-eastern corner of farm No. 548.

The intention apparently was for the northern border of the Masai Reserve to include Mau Narok. Again, from the Blue Book:

> Historical data of the localities occupied by the Masai showed that an equitable continuation of the boundary from the source of the Mbagathi was in a direction approximately due west, while the fence that had been erected in fact ran due south. In order to come to a final settlement of the matter, officers representing both sides were instructed to make investigation on the spot. As a result of this inspection the Governor decided that the boundary as fenced must be altered to conform with that described in the treaties.[7]

Cobb did not receive any kind of official title to the land until 1922.[8] But he had staked a claim on the ground, gradually, to land inside the Reserve rather than north of it. In 1916 Cobb directed surveyors to draw the borders of his farm deep into the area designated the Masai Reserve. The Narok District Annual Report of 1916–1917 stated:

> During the year the land on Mau Narok promised to Mr. Cobb was surveyed, and the masai [*sic*] were again told that it was to be a farm and excluded from the reserve. This caused a good deal of dissatisfaction, Masikondi and other elders maintening [*sic*] that they had been promised the whole of Mau Narok at the time of the move and making allegations against the government of a breach of faith.[9]

The government recognized the Maasai claims at this time. They stopped the surveying and beacons were left to rust in the grass, and Maasai were not evicted from any land. Ten years passed and Cobb tried again to further his encroachment into the Reserve, as the District Commissioner for Narok wrote of Mau Narok in 1926:

> [T]he profusion of beacons actual and alleged which appear[ed] to be dotted indiscriminately over a large area rendered impossible for one who is not a qualified surveyor o[r] armed with the impedimenta of his office, to say where the boundary line between the Masai Province and Mr. Cobbs farm runs.[10]

The colonial government did not issue any formal statement, and Maasai communities continued to herd the land confident that the border they had negotiated was upheld. Cobb, who did not have the means to develop the land beyond his small homestead, bided his time. He kept his claim alive by refusing to acknowledge the Maasai border and continually pushing his own reach further into the Reserve. One example demonstrates his strategy. The 1911 Agreement signed by the British includes a promise that *Purko* Maasai "control of at least 5 square miles" of land at *Kinopop* (Kinangop) for *Enkipaata*, the ceremony through which Maasai boys enter warriorhood.[11] In 1911 it was reiterated:

> that nothing in this agreement contained shall be deemed to deprive the Masai tribe of the rights reserved to it under the agreement of August ninth one thousand nine hundred and four aforesaid to the land on the slopes of Kinopop [sic] whereon the circumcision rites and ceremonies may be held.[12]

However, Maasai were forcibly evicted from *Kinopop* shortly after the move from Laikipia in 1910 and the British faced an uprising. Cobb was asked to allow the coming ceremony to take place on "his land" at Mau Narok, to help the administration justify the seizure of *Kinopop*. Cobb agreed, but on the condition that in exchange he would charge what he called "a nominal rent" forcing the administration to provide documentation that the land fell within his farm.[13]

Initially when conflicts between Cobb and the Maasai community reached local courts, the courts upheld Maasai claims to the borders they claimed had been identified in 1911. For example, in 1926, several of Cobb's Lumbwa (Kalinjen) employees were caught trespassing on land well within the borders of the Masai Reserve, which Cobb's personal survey map from 1916 identified as part of his farm. Colonial police arrested Cobb's employees. When informed, "Mr. Cobb assured [administrators] that the Manyatta in which the Lumbwa (who were employees of his) were found was on his land."[14] Asking to see the land in question, the administrators "went to the boundary of Mr. Cobb's farm, when Mr. Cobb admitted that the Manyatta was not on his farm."[15] But Cobb continued to direct his employees to use the reserve as an extension of his farm. In doing so, he created conflict to force the courts into a continuous renegotiation of the borders. Later in 1926, Cobb had six Maasai people arrested for trespassing on his farm.[16] The defendants claimed that they were on Masai Reserve land on which they had been grazing for years with no complaint from Cobb. In that case the Maasai were convicted of trespass based on the testimonies of one of Cobb's employees and a European Police Constable. Neither of these men had knowledge of the situation beyond what they had been told by Cobb.

However, District Commissioner Bader said that the ruling was injustice and he called for an appeal. Unlike the Maasai community, Bader had access to administrative files, and he used them to argue that the border of the Masai

Reserve existed well north of the boot outlined in Cobb's claim. Bader showed that in 1923 the southern border of Mau Narok was defined by a colonial administrator, Mr. Storrs-Fox. He claimed that at that time Cobb and the surrounding Maasai communities agreed to this border. Bader also drew a map of the location of "Storrs-Fox line" which bisects the "boot" and locates almost half of the land currently known as Mau Narok within the Masai Reserve. Bader noted that, for three years, "Mr. P. Cobb did not dispute the boundary as indicated to the Maasai by Mr. Storrs-Fox."[17] The six Maasai were acquitted based on a judge's ruling that in the initial case there had been "illegal and incompetent evidence" and that "the best evidence was not before the Learned Magistrate concerning the Boundary line between Mr. Powys Cobb's farm and the Masai Reserve."[18]

Despite this ruling, the "Storrs-Fox line" does not appear in the documented record after 1926 and it was not thereafter treated as a legal ruling on borders created in the 1911 Agreement. Cobb was able to build a sawmill in an area clearly demarcated as part of the Masai Reserve,[19] he was given permission to cut wood from "the Masai forest,"[20] and he was granted remission from his rent for two years after claiming that Maasai communities were occupying up to four-fifths of "his farm" during a drought.[21] In an attempt to bolster his claims to Mau Narok, Cobb encouraged the 1928 O'Farrell Survey of his farm, which "placed intervisible iron beacons along the entire length of the farm boundaries with the Masai Reserve."[22] As that boundary differed from the one apparently negotiated by Ole Gilisho, and the second one upheld in court, the surveyed border quickly fell back into disarray. Throughout the decades after the placement of these beacons, officials in the Narok region acknowledged that "the boundary is a purely artificial one—an undemarcated line with beacons hidden by the grass—it is not surprising that trespass at least takes place."[23] As late as 1953, in a discussion between the colonial administrators and local Maasai leadership, the Director of Surveys, while looking at the boundary between the Masai Reserve and Powys Cobb's land, admitted, "the boundary with the Masai Land Unit is badly overgrown and consequently not readily visible on the ground."[24] In response, District Commissioner Hosking agreed that "there is nothing to indicate the exact position of the boundary."[25] Cobb continued to claim use of more and more land within the Reserve which led to escalating conflict. Maasai communities were forced by colonial administrators to move their villages away from the border at Cobb's land, deeper within the Reserve, a policy that was acknowledged by the Provincial and District Commissioners to be illegal.[26]

Individual colonial administrators may have shown sympathy to Maasai communities. But that ended in the early 1950s, the era of Mau Mau and the chaotic scramble for land leading to Kenyan Independence. A new breed of administrators took control and they uniformly supported Edward Powys Cobb regardless of the bare-faced illegality of his claims. They independently changed the legal definition of trespass by Maasai, or their stock, on settlers' land and levied heavy fines against the Maasai.[27] In 1957 and 1958 alone, Maasai community members had paid in fines 12,860Ksh and 17,930Ksh, respectively.[28] These fines were known to be illegal under colonial law, as the Superintendent of Police in Ngong acknowledged in a letter to his Commissioner:

> It should be noted that these payments made by the Masai are purely voluntary, and do not have the backing of the law and to antagonize the Masai unduly or unfairly would almost certainly "kill the goose that lays the golden eggs."[29]

The new attitude increased both settler depredations against the Maasai and police violence in response: Maasai lost cattle to theft, arrests of Maasai at Mau Narok were more frequent, and resistors were shot and killed.[30] *Ilmurran*, warriors, in particular, became such a common scapegoat that other cattle thieves began to take advantage of their negative reputation. In one proven case among several cited, a farmer's non-Maasai employees "had bought red ochre and smeared it about the place in such a way that it [was] inevitable that both the police and farmers would automatically blame the Moran Masai of the District for [the] theft."[31] Maasai *Ilmurran* were soon viewed as the perpetrators of all criminal activity, and the colonial administration issued Pass Laws,[32] patrolled the buffer zone between farms and the reserve with attack dogs,[33] and gave settlers, including Powys Cobb, the right to shoot Maasai at will.[34]

Eventually, the colonial administration sought to entirely abolish the institution of *Ilmurran*, the main structured system of Maasai cultural education. The Narok district commissioner described warriorhood as "organized crime which includes murder, assault, theft, disobedience of orders of administration and elders and general indiscipline."[35] The administration devised training schools and forced labor camps for young Maasai men in an attempt to destroy warrior training and in the process also undermine local resistance to colonial acquisition of land. A commissioner at the time explained that once warriorhood had been eradicated and the Maasai community was fractured that "[the Maasai] will become men of property and responsibility; thus falling into a class more easy to control and 'sanction.'"[36] It was at this time that Maasai people were finally driven off of Mau Narok, long after the deaths of Ole Gilisho and Ole Masikonte and the elders who had known first-hand any borders negotiated in 1911.

Mau Narok underwent transformation heading into Independence as its role in the emerging capitalist postwar world became clear: Mau Narok would be "the archetype of dependent peripheral capitalism" that enabled a continued flow outward of wealth from African soil through agricultural development schemes.[37] The context for this change was a British agenda coming out of the Second World War to mitigate its own postwar economic crisis by building on Kenya's wartime growth and developing its export market economy.[38] The Crown created the European Agricultural Settlement Board (EASB) in 1946 to encourage settlement in Kenya of war veterans of "British or Dominion Nationality" by offering them loans and sale of "unproductive farms" in the Kenyan White Highlands.[39] Then the Mau Mau attacks on European settlers began in 1952 leading to a frenzy of land sales, and abandoned farms and equipment caused a plunge in land values. Outgoing European settlers led by the "Kenya Coalition" demanded that they be compensated for their farms, and threatened to run the economy into the ground if their farms were not bought in full by the Crown.[40] In fact, after colonial rule officially ended in 1963, the Kenyan government incurred 12.5 million pounds in loans from the British government to buy land from the departing settlers at market value.[41]

Despite significant assistance from the colonial government, Cobb, like other European farmers, had struggled in the 1920s and 1930s with limited crop yields. He described this failure as "dismal" and "heartbreaking."[42] In 1952 Cobb retired and sold all but 5,000 acres of Mau Narok to the EASB, which set about dividing the 25,000 acres of land into twenty-nine separate farms for sale to other Europeans.[43] Most of the remaining land was retained for Cobb's wife Ethel, who continued to live at Mau Narok for the next twelve years.[44]

With Independence on the horizon, the structures of neocolonial land use were hastily created, primarily through a 1953 plan developed by R.J.M. Swynnerton, the colony's Assistant Director of Agriculture. This "Swynnerton Plan" was a broad scheme to make Kenyan rural land productive for export markets. It was the blueprint specifically for restructuring captured Maasailand in both the northern "White Highlands" and the Masai Reserve. The plan would lead to the creation of the group ranch system and individualization of land tenure in Maasailand. These were steps in a dual agenda to reorganize Maasai society for a commercial cattle industry and to enable the sale of land to outside speculation.[45] In the land known as the White Highlands, the Swynnerton Plan promoted a consolidation of land into large-scale farms, which would be developed by the World Bank and European and US governments. These would subsidize the Kenyan land market to protect land values and distribute plots to Central Kenyans through settlement schemes.[46] Loans were provided, in theory, to support landless small farmers, creating an illusion that Kenyan land would be "returned" to Kenyans. However, they instead enabled the purchase of large commercial farms, typically of thousands of acres.[47] The Swynnerton Plan was the means through which Kenya, in the words of East African historians, was "captured ... for the World Bank and the capitalist world system."[48] This plan would inevitably create an economy of rich land owners and produce economic insecurity for the rest, and this was not accidental. Swynnerton himself said that through his plan:

> [F]ormer Government policy will be reversed and able, energetic or rich Africans will be able to acquire more land, and bad or poor farmers less, creating a landed and landless class.

This, he said, was "a normal step in the evolution of a country."[49]

By identifying the European settled areas as the "White" Highlands, the colony had been able to attract settlers. Now that same racialized identity also gave the land its special power to generate the extreme wealth realized by many of those settlers through exploding land valuation. In 1955, in the full wake of Independence, the new colonial land policy reconfirmed this strategy through new discourse. Kenyan land was designated to be "Scheduled" or "Non-scheduled," categories which nonetheless "roughly correspond with the European and African areas of Kenya."[50] In 1960, "European" was dropped from the EASB, renamed as the "Land Development and Settlement Board (LDSB)," without "destroying the existing structure" with the directive that its authority was to be "so clearly above distinction of race that it would be secure against possible attacks in the future."[51] However, the work of the LDSB was to develop Kenya along segregated lines. "Native lands" such as the Masai Reserve were to be streamlined for development, while the high-potential areas of the White Highlands were to be settled by tenant farmers[52] of "the better kind of African,"[53] selected through an application process based on "full tribal particularities" and other "details."[54] The most likely candidates, according to the plan, were Africans who already owned or managed farms.

> "The Kikuyu are the tribe most likely to come forward for settlement but some Luo, Abaluhya, Nandi and Kipsigis may do so as well" and the plan noted, "in Kikuyuland ... some might cash in on this."[55]

Segregation of land under Independent Kenya would no longer be overtly racial: it would be tribal instead. Kikuyu politicians would use Maasailand to consolidate their tribally based political power by opening up the areas of Maasailand that had been "whitened" by the British to nearly exclusively Kikuyu settlement.[56]

This was the context into which Maasai leadership organized as the Maasai United Front (MUF). The MUF challenged the British government to honor the terms articulated in the Agreements and return the land they were vacating to the Maasai people. The Agreements bound the British to their recognition of Maasai as a sovereign people and to the borders defined in the Agreements themselves. Maasai could defensibly argue that they had never relinquished their right to Laikipia, Magadi, or to Mau Narok and many of the other lands encroached upon across the northern border of the Reserve. The MUF argued that occupied lands of all other Kenyan communities were being returned specifically to those communities: to deny such a return to the Maasai people would constitute discrimination. Led by Justus Ole Tipis, the MUF traveled across Maasailand to gather information about local violations of the treaty borders, and produced a report citing all current claims.

The MUF makes a first appearance in British records at a meeting in Nairobi in 1961 between African leaders and Secretary of State for the Colonies Ronald Maudling.[57] At that meeting, Chairman Ole Tipis demanded the return of land to unify all Maa-speaking people in one shared home, "governed by one local Masai authority." He said that the "scattering" of sections of *Olosho le Maa*[58] and the severing of Kenyan and "Tanganyika" Maasai were "classic example of divide and rule" that had left the Maasai people minute minorities everywhere "cleverly excluded from statistical reports which give a false impression of the tribe."[59] Ole Tipis claimed that Maasailand had been "grossly ignored" through the joint agenda of the British and emerging Kenyan government, saying that together they had "relentlessly pursued a policy of extraction towards what was left of the Masai lands" through the parceling out of land and "legal tricks."[60]

But Maudling had already been briefed on how best to reject these arguments.[61] "The basic problem presented by the Maasai," he was told,

> is similar to that presented by the other minority tribes and groups as independence approaches, namely how to meet their fears of being dominated by the majority tribes, particularly the Kikuyu, and in particular, losing their land.[62]

He was told that indeed "the Kikuyu covet the areas of Maasailand which are suitable for mixed farming," lands which were also the best grazing pastures.[63] But, he was told, that transfer of land to Kikuyu farmers was already underway as a key component of the plan for Kenya's postcolonial economy. This transfer would be cloaked in the language of equal rights and free markets, to make all land available to "all Kenyans." This approach would present "the basic tenet of the Kenyan Government's land policy" to be "non-racial and non-tribal." Land was to "be regarded as an economic asset," which could be redistributed by the government, unhindered by local community rights.[64]

The MUF recognized that a fight for the whole of the land stolen from the Maasai people under colonization would be futile. They focused instead on a seemingly more achievable goal, appealing that the British recognize the boundaries they themselves had committed to in the 1904 and 1911 Agreements. These had been breached in ways similar to what had happened at Mau Narok. These eleven land rights claims appear on maps today as a ring of scars and open wounds across the northern borders of Narok and Kajiado Counties.

The first five of these were "Land claimed by the Masai as falling within the Treaty area" including:

1. "Land in Ngong West of Mbagathi River";
2. "Land South of Athi River Railway Station";
3. "Land Between Mt. Suswa and Farm 1769";
4. "Kinangop";
5. "Mau Narok."

Other claims included "Land admittedly within the Treaty area which has been taken, or re-settled, in breach of the Treaties," including:

6. Olpusimoru in the Mau Forest "taken from the Masai about the year 1948";
7. Ukarih;
8. Olenkuruoni, which was set aside for "the Dorobo, a section of the Masai", but settled by Kikuyu people in the 1940s; and
9. areas of Kilgoris in the Trans Mara which had been leased to the Luo people for ten years ending 1959.

The two final claims were for land taken for mining:

10. Magadi, where a lake had been excised from the Reserve for lease to Tata Industries in the early twentieth century to produce soda ash, and
11. Lolgorian, a gold mine.

These claims were summarized in a document submitted to the Committee charged with drafting Kenya's constitution which met formally at Lancaster House, London, beginning in 1961.[65]

The claims of the MUF were not supported by the African delegation to Lancaster House. These were dominated by the KANU political party and led by Jomo Kenyatta, with Peter Mbiyu Koinange as his right hand. Both men ended up with large personal farms of thousands of acres at Mau Narok.[66] Tom Mboya, the most prominent Luo politician and secretary-general of KANU, was no more sympathetic to Maasai land rights than were his Kikuyu colleagues. Resettlement of Kikuyu farmers in Maasailand was a crucial component of his own vision to restructure Kenya's economy to participate in exporting agricultural crops to the global market.[67]

The MUF was barred from the conference at Lancaster House. But the leadership resolved to send its own delegation anyway to negotiate terms with the British as representatives of the "Maa nation." In preparation for the arrival of the MUF, the British devised a strategy. They would stonewall Maasai requests for a hearing, then when pushed, they would reject the claims and attempt to pacify MUF delegates with promises to negotiate an agreement between the Maasai and the KANU government after Independence. They recognized, though, that Maasai "would probably regard this as of little value to them."[68] The conferees would tell the MUF that Maasai land rights would be protected in a bill of rights which would prevent the Kenyan government from arbitrarily seizing land, though they knew that this offered no protection at all over "control of transfers of their land to non-Maasai." As to Maasai claims to their original lands in the Rift Valley, the briefing was clear: "Whatever the strength of their original claims to these lands, we do not admit that this present claim has any foundation."

> [I]t would be contrary to public policy for the Masai, who have not developed their own land, to be given the right to carry their primitive agricultural practices to other land in Kenya, which is urgently required for re-settlement and which ought in the general interest of Kenya to be utilized to the maximum possible extent.[69]

The Maasai delegates arrived in London and through their persistence they eventually undertook three separate meetings with the Constitutional Conference Committee.[70] Ole Tipis argued for return of the drought reserves during the first meeting: Kilimanjaro, Mau Forest, and Ngong, the only "high potential" areas in the whole of Maasailand.[71] Ole Konchellah pointed out that, regarding the settlement schemes, other communities were being resettled on their traditional lands including the Kikuyu, Nandi, Nyeri, and Kericho. "This was clearly right and the Maasai would never complain about this or claim lands belonging to other [sic] tribespeople. But, by the same principle, no African who was not a member of the Maasai should be resettled on lands traditionally belonging to the Maasai."[72]

After the second meeting, the MUF pushed the Kenyan delegates to the conference to identify where they stood on the issue of Maasai rights. Mr. Ngala of the minority KADU political party showed some support, admitting that "[i]t would be quite wrong for Masai land to come under the jurisdiction of other tribal authorities or the central Government or Central Land Board."[73] Kenyatta, however, speaking for KANU "made it clear that [KANU] recognized the rights of the Masai in their Reserve, but felt that they could not be expected to go beyond this until Her Majesty's Government had stated their own position clearly." Tom Mboya said that KANU certainly supported "development" in Maasailand, but suggested that funding would have to come from the British. Ole Tipis said that KANU's position was not acceptable.[74] As Maasai had not been officially invited to the constitutional conference they had to raise money for their travel and stay in London, and at this time the funds were running low.[75] Ole Tipis sent a telegram to the colonial secretary expressing frustration, writing, "Masai were coerced into making suicidal treaties with British Government stop Now they suffer famine disaster as result stop We will fight by all possible means any unjust decision by government regarding our lands."[76]

Meanwhile, the British government set to work developing legal briefs to discredit the treaty status of the Maasai Agreements. Two British government lawyers supported the Crown's position that while the 1904 and 1911 Agreements were ruled to be "treaties" in a British court in 1913, they were instead merely "agreements of a political nature."[77] They reasoned that "the annexation of Masailand in 1920, with the rest of the Colony, destroyed the Protectorate basis on which the Agreements rested. Her Majesty cannot have treaty relations with Her subjects." They continued, "In any case, there are some grounds for contesting the 1913 decision; it is probably [*sic*] that in the Agreements the Masai ceded so much of whatever sovereignty they originally held as to destroy their legal personality in international law." The lawyers did not address questions about how a treaty might be nullified through the determinations of only one party.[78]

At the third meeting at Lancaster House, the worst fears of the Maasai delegation were realized. The Secretary of State said that the British government "regarded the 1904 and 1911 Agreements as binding both on Her Majesty's Government and on the Masai people. There could be no doubt regarding their authenticity,"[79] but that the British would only recognize the current boundaries of the Masai Reserve, and would not help Maasai recover even the lands stolen through the colonial era in defiance of "treaty" borders. The KANU party representatives supported this decision. John Keen walked out of the meeting at the end of the Secretary's statement. Ole Tipis said that the Secretary's decision "was a complete betrayal." He said, "The Maasai are only claiming their own land."[80] Ole Konchellah reminded the Secretary that "the land originally occupied by other tribes was to be returned to those tribes," but that Maasai land "was to be placed in a common pool and to be distributed by the Central Land Board." He said, "The Masai would never agree to this and would fight for their rights to such land and would refuse to be dominated or enslaved" and that "the Masai would never forget their right to such land."[81]

Having decided that it was free of legal obligation, the Crown admitted that it might have had a "moral" obligation to advocate on their behalf with the Kenyan government to recognize Maasai rights to the existing Reserve.[82] It was a hollow promise. The official policy read:

> For the time being, Maasailand would "likely remain for some time communally owned and under customary law and not registered to individuals," and that some protection would be afforded through "the Special Trust Land Ordinance and the Control Boards which may eventually be set up."

But, the Crown concluded, "[I]t is difficult to see how this position can be legally prolonged after Independence."[83]

Evidence abounded at the time that Maasai were also willing "to come forward" and settle the vacated European farms and to become farmers themselves. But they were barred from every attempt by the Kenyan government. For example, the Kenyan government rejected requests by departing European settlers to divide up their farms into small holdings and selling them to their Maasai and Kalenjin employees. Those attempts were vetoed by the LDSB and its later incarnation, the Central Land Board (CLB), was used to block those sales.[84] One of these departing Europeans was Ethyl Powys Cobb, who decided to return to England in 1964 and to transfer 4,200 acres left by her husband Edward to the Maasai community through a plan negotiated with Ole Tipis. The plan involved giving land to six Maasai families who would be provided modern farming techniques and equipment to cultivate the land, while a portion of the farm would also be set aside for an Agricultural and Animal Husbandry Institute that would train Maasai people in modern agricultural practices. Ole Tipis said that he had "the names of six Maasai leaders who would immediately take up this farm. The six gentlemen are on their part prepared to contribute their share of financial requirement."[85] Ethyl Cobb asked to meet with the Secretary of Agriculture, Bruce McKenzie, to work out the details, and she offered to provide 10,000 British pounds as startup capital, and to remain financially involved with the Institute if it were built on her land.[86] McKenzie dismissed the plan, saying only that the "Masai in Mau … [were] lacking in a progressive attitude to land development."[87] Several years later the Kenyan government found a more "suitable" buyer: G. Class, a German citizen. On July 13, 1967, through Kenya Farming Limited, Class bought 4,296 acres of Mau Narok for a quarter of a million Kenyan shillings.[88]

The reason for McKenzie's rejection was that Mau Narok had been slated for low-density, large-scale commercial wheat production, to develop the land as large blocks of farms owned by absentee Europeans or wealthy African Kenyans. Wheat had emerged to be the centerpiece of government agricultural policy for the region by the mid- to late 1960s and promoted by British investors as much as the Kenyan government,[89] and by 1967 Mau Narok had produced a large enough surplus to begin exporting wheat to Uganda and Tanzania.[90] The wheat boom of 1967 owed in part to an encroachment of wheat farming into the Masai Reserve through sharecropping which had begun in the mid-1950s and steadily increased thereafter.

The same Maasai who had been pushed off of Mau Narok, and then denied the possibility of inheriting Powys Cobb land, now were asked to make their reserve land available for sharecropping. The Mau Narok wheat farmers would provide machinery, seeds, and training to Maasai to turn reserve land to wheat, and Maasai sharecroppers would receive two bags of wheat per acre farmed or 20 percent of the total crop.[91] By the late 1960s, non-Maasai sharecroppers also moved in and began contracting with Maasai people to use their land. Wheat cultivation rapidly expanded at this point, and without literacy and other means to represent their interests in contract negotiations, Maasai sharecroppers experienced mounting exploitation. By 1967, 25,000 acres of the Masai Land Unit, the reserve land, was growing wheat through sharecropping. That year saw a surplus of wheat, but also serious conflict, as Maasai were swindled, and government investigations found it "abundantly clear that the charges of bribery and corruption amongst [non-Maasai] sharecroppers were well founded."[92]

The government tried to ease conflict and maintain the growth of the industry by regulating sharecropper contracts and subsidizing machinery through the Tractor Hire Service. This created more problems as conflict erupted between Maasai sharecroppers and the predominantly Kikuyu tractor drivers. In 1967, demanding back payment and citing other grievances, Maasai community members at Mau Narok rose up in protest and virtually shut down wheat production there. In October 1967, Ole Tipis and other MUF leadership, Ole Lemien and Ole Konchellah, called on Bruce McKenzie and demanded an end to sharecropping in Maasailand. McKenzie instructed the Kenyan Farmers

Association to freeze 75 percent of the value of the 1967 crop boom until a settlement was reached between the sharecroppers and the farmers.[93]

At this point the World Bank stepped in to change course in former White Highlands and teach Maasai people to farm. Their intention was not to contribute to a mixed economy that would include pastoralism. That would have been the goal of Ole Tipis and Ethyl Powys Cobb. Instead, in the words of a Ministry of Agriculture report, they intended to enable "the early and complete conversion of the Maasai peoples and their traditional territorial holdings to optimum economic usefulness within the Nation."[94] The Maasai Agricultural Development Organization (MADO) was created for this purpose. It was housed under the umbrella of the Central Agricultural Board and the general management of Andrew Mercer of the World Bank. Mercer was committed to the plan to fully convert Maasailand to agriculture. Where he differed from the Kenyatta administration was that instead of Kikuyu settlers, he sought to build an agricultural base in Maasailand of Maasai people. His first priority was to harvest the 1968 crop held up by the Maasai protests. Beyond that he sought to expand infrastructure, establish a "Farmers Training Center" for Maasai people, and streamline privatized land titles in the Maasai Land Unit. His goal was to add 33,000 acres to wheat growing every year until all 1.5 million acres of "good wheat potential land in Narok district" was cultivated. The estimated cost of this plan was 600 million Kenyan shillings to be provided by the World Bank.[95] MADO would supersede all other government agencies and be "entirely responsible for Agricultural development in the Masailand."[96] But unlike the logic behind the settlement schemes, Mercer assured the Narok District Agricultural Committee that the aim of his organization "was to help the Masai and that no cent from MADO would go out of the district." All profits generated would be used for development in Maasailand.[97] By July, 1968, fifty-six Maasai farmers were signed up to produce wheat on farms ranging from 50 to over 700 acres in size.[98]

In spite of this energetic start, MADO was terminated after five short months by the Provincial Commissioner for the Rift Valley, Simeon Nyachae. Nyachae, from Kiisi in Western Kenya, was a key lieutenant in the administration of President Kenyatta. Like Kenyatta himself, Nyachae had been brought back from his then-permanent home in London. In 1964 he was appointed one of a handful of powerful Provincial Commissioners, first in Central Kenya and then in the Rift Valley. Nyachae was part of the "iron frame upon which [Kenyatta] built his political control of the country" as PCs were Kenyatta's "effective proconsuls, supervising and controlling regional developments in much the same way as their colonial predecessors had done."[99] Though Nyachae had "no direct responsibility for administering the settlement schemes," he oversaw law enforcement and the adjudication of land disputes, and he was empowered to determine which Maasai families "had traditional occupancy rights to the land," those who might and would not benefit from any settlement.[100]

Nyachae promoted himself as a defender of the Maasai community. He claimed that the community did not support MADO as Maasai were not being consulted nor given loans.[101] He used that pretended insider knowledge to attack MADO until he was able to justify closing it. In June, 1968, Nyachae complained to Permanent Secretary of Agriculture and Animal Husbandry, S.B. Ogembo, that MADO was failing because it was not including Maasai communities in wheat development schemes. Nyachae said, "To treat masailand as if it were State land and in effect to go ahead without consulting the land owners, will no doubt cause political and social repercussions from the masai people."[102] His advice was to work through him, as the "man on the ground" who knew how to navigate local acceptance. If the Ministry wanted to "open up new areas for [wheat] development" in Maasailand, it had to "seek opinion of field officers, who are more conversant with ground problems, instead of assuming that people in remote areas could be directed in the manner some official in Nairobi may theoretically consider to be sound."[103] Mercer, the person most directly under attack, claimed that Nyachae had "deliberately distorted" the situation.[104] Mercer said that Nyachae had been in on the Ministry's decision to keep the Maasai community in the dark about the bigger agenda of MADO, and this was done for "certain political reasons."[105] The Ministry admitted later that it did not inform Maasai farmers about MADO to delay giving them the opportunity to reject it until the 1968 crop was planted.[106]

The main issue on which Mercer and Nyachae seemed to have disagreed was whether to allow Maasai to continue to own land communally, a concession that had been negotiated by MUF leadership in Narok. The wheat schemes envisioned by MADO would depend on Maasai farmers obtaining loans to develop their land, but for that they would need private titles as collateral. Mercer advocated a proposal of Maasai leadership to secure titles by *"Enkutoto,"*[107] or group land ownership, which would empower communities to be responsible together for loan repayment while also empowering traditional Maasai leadership. He said that "such divisions already [have] traditional councils" that would manage wheat development locally. But Nyachae privately supported allotting Maasai land by individual title.[108] Mercer had influenced others in the administration, such as the Agricultural Commissioner of Lands, F.E. Charnley, who expressed support for *Enkutoto* as it would prevent "a land grab by the wealthier and more sophisticated Masai." When land was allotted, he said that "the full rights and interests of all the people must be taken into account." He came to this conclusion he said after "several meetings with the Narok County Council and prominent Masai leaders from Narok district."[109] *Enkutoto* would make it harder for the profits of wheat growing on Maasailand to be grabbed by outsiders, which would be made much easier through individual titling.

Nyachae deliberately set fire to MADO through a duplicitous attack on the Ministry of Land and Agriculture, projecting onto them his own agenda to conspire to "set apart" land inside the Masai Land Unit for growing wheat without the consent of Maasai communities.[110] Secretary Mlamba suggested that Nyachae be disciplined for his unfounded accusation, and counter-charged that Nyachae had deliberately undermined the Ministry's work in Maasailand, that he did not "sell" MADO to Maasai communities.[111] Nyachae accused Mlambo of a "mental sickness" reiterating that he was the protector of his Maasai constituents.[112] Though it was not under his jurisdiction, Nyachae nevertheless effectively put a stop to MADO within a month of his letter to Charnley.[113] Kenyatta's Ministry of Agriculture ceded control over development in Maasailand personally to Simeon Nyachae.[114]

With MADO out of the way, Nyachae turned his attention to land privatization. The Ministry of Agriculture continued to warn that agricultural policy in Mau Narok was no longer to create large absentee farms, and that the intention of privatization of Maasai land was to prevent personal grabbing of large acreages and to promote the development of Narok as per the "people's wish."[115] Nyachae was aware of the competing agendas and of a "noticeable change of attitude among the Masai on the ownership and value of land" in the recent past. He knew that "the more enlightened Masai" had become opposed to the settlement of Kikuyu and other "acceptees" who hoped to benefit from Maasai land disbursal. There were also "clashes" among Maasai clans and families. Nyachae pursued an amendment to the Group Representative Act to give himself "power to make binding decision whenever he deemed it appropriate and particularly in cases connected with section, clan and family interest."[116] He personally arbitrated between Maasai land owners and Kikuyu tractor contractors over terms of leases and other Maasai grievances. He claimed to seek to protect Maasai from exploitation, but in the end the Tractor Hire Service continued to operate in Maasailand and to receive government subsidy without any requirement for change in operations.[117]

In 1969, just months after MADO's demise, Simeon Nyachae began acquiring huge sections of Mau Narok for his own private wheat and barley farms, deals that his biographer claims were personally arranged by President Kenyatta.[118]

After this first acquisition known as Sansora Farm, Nyachae obtained two additional farms at Mau Narok, and today his family owns a total of 10,000 acres. Nyachae's biographer also notes that Nyachae, as a Kisii man, could never have acquired this much land in other circumstances. He says, "Nyachae never acquired any property or businesses in Central Province, despite his long stay there as provincial commissioner" as he "believed that to do so would create conflict because of the intense Kikuyu interest in both land and commerce."[119]

The 30,000 acres of Mau Narok continued through the 1980s, 1990s, and early 2000s to be organized into farms of thousands of acres apiece governed mainly by the families of Nyanchea, Koinange, Kenyatta, and other absentee landlords. Maasai people living at the borders of this land did indeed learn to farm. Some of these have maintained their own small parcels and others lease their lands to commercial agriculture, but in both cases, farming is fraught, expensive, and barely enables survival for the majority.

The history presented above was originally researched and drafted through a Prescott College summer program in Kenya in August 2008. It was then presented to several hundred people in a packed room of the Seasons Hotel in Narok, windows darkened by shukas, casting a red glow. Maasai people poured over the details of MADO, maps and memos marked "CONFIDENTIAL," and especially lists of names of MUF members, projected onto a bedsheet hung at one end of the room. Ole Tipis in particular had been so vilified in the press in the years after the collapse of the MUF that the community had no idea of his efforts in London, of the integrity with which the words of the community had been repeated verbatim at Lancaster House and recorded on official memoranda. The clarity of the argument for specific land claims, made by the parents and grandparents of people in the room, was brought back to life. Tears were followed by expressions of sadness and then outrage, and then by heated conversations lasting into the night. The group adjourned after blessings were received by those commissioned to take the next steps. Three days later, hundreds of Maasai people moved back onto portions of the land, while others organized a media campaign and contacted lawyers to begin work on a High Court lawsuit case that was filed twenty months later.

The power of this history to reignite land rights activism lay in its excavation of the insight of the MUF who saw what was coming, knew that Independence was to be old wine in new skins. They knew this because they knew Maasai history and saw their current moment in historical context. The MUF fight for Maa nationhood has been restored to the memory of the community with a commitment that it will never be lost again.

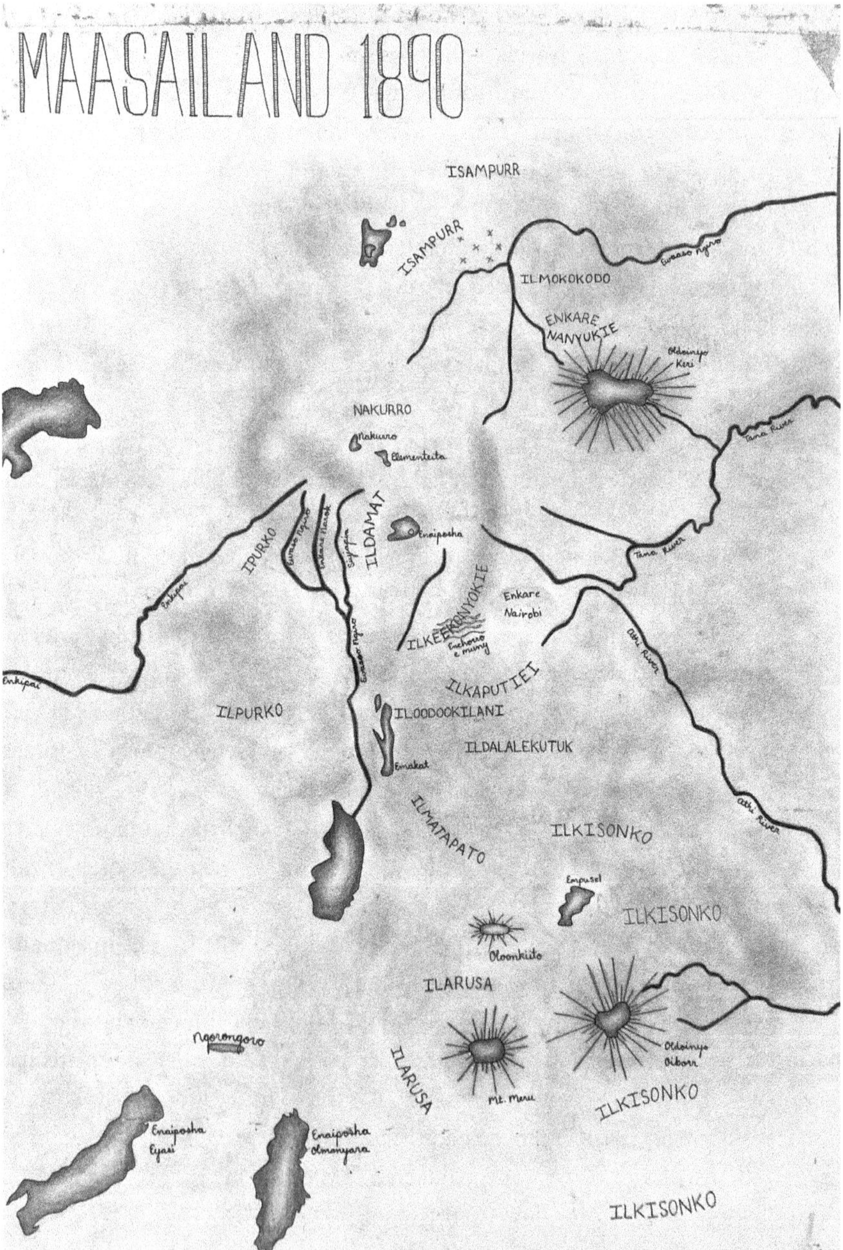

Figure 1 Map of Maasailand 1890: Before colonization, Maasailand was comprised of roughly a dozen subsections each with recognized specific homeland, and section membership continues to constitute important parts of Maasai identity today.

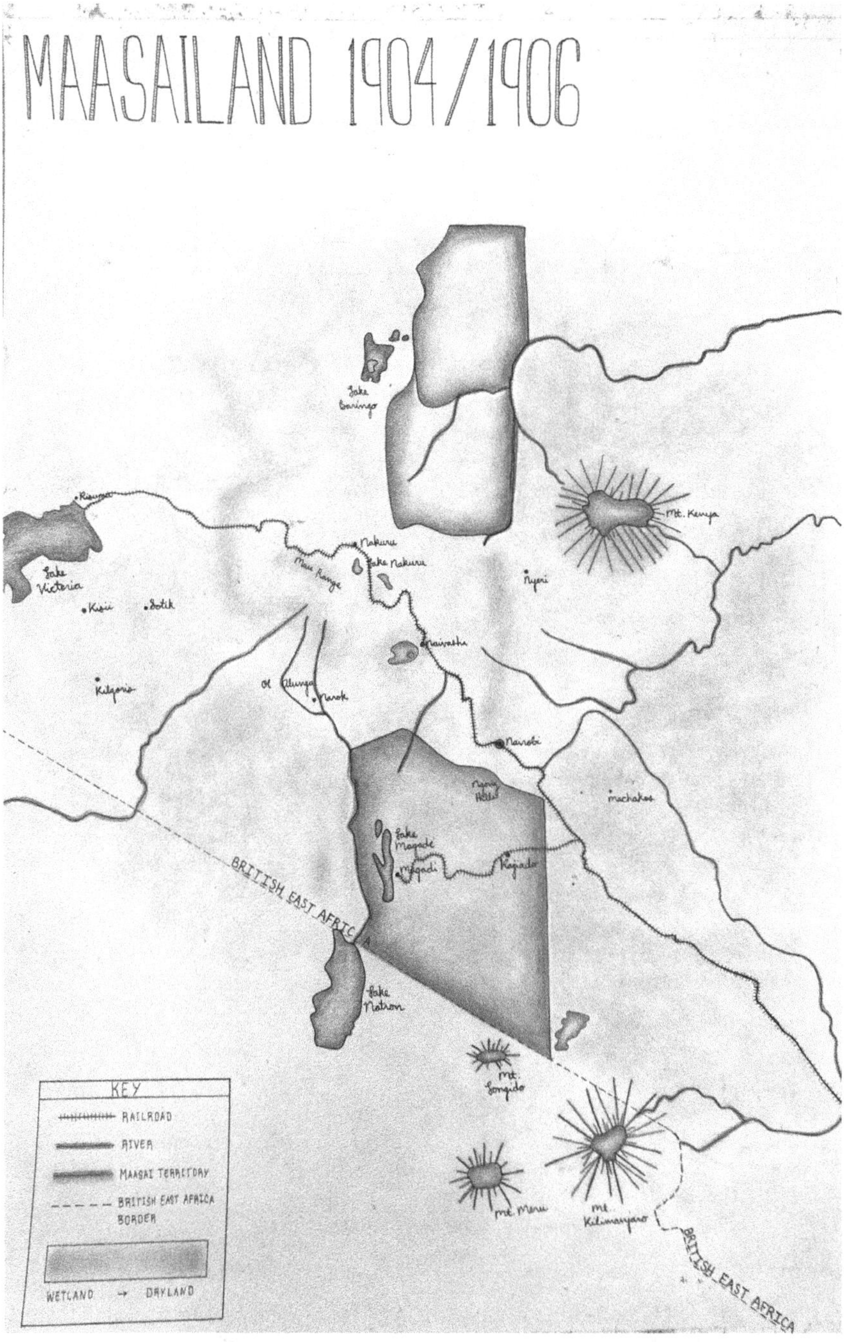

Figure 2 Map of Maasailand 1904/1906: The British intended to remove Maasai from the land most coveted for European settlement, the heart of *Purko* Maasai homeland in what is now Naivasha and Nakuru. This map expresses their intention to create two Masai Reserves north and south, expressed in the British "1904 Agreement."

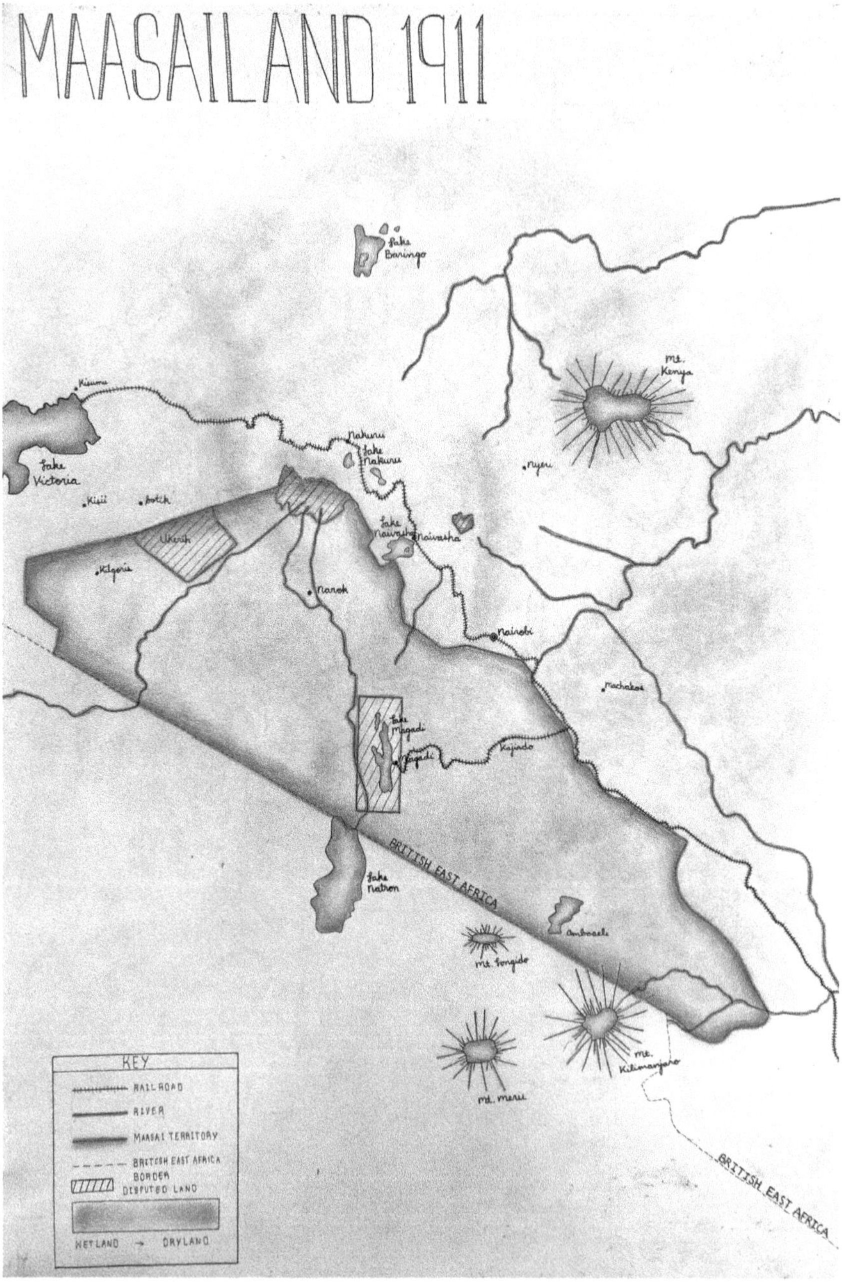

MAASAILAND 1911

KEY

RAILROAD
RIVER
MAASAI TERRITORY
BRITISH EAST AFRICA
BORDER
DISPUTED LAND

WETLAND → DRYLAND

Figure 3 Map of Maasailand 1911: As settlers and investors quickly expanded their reach throughout all of Northern Maasailand, a second series of evictions forced northern Maasai onto an expanded southern Masai Reserve, which was rationalized through a second British "Agreement" in 1911.

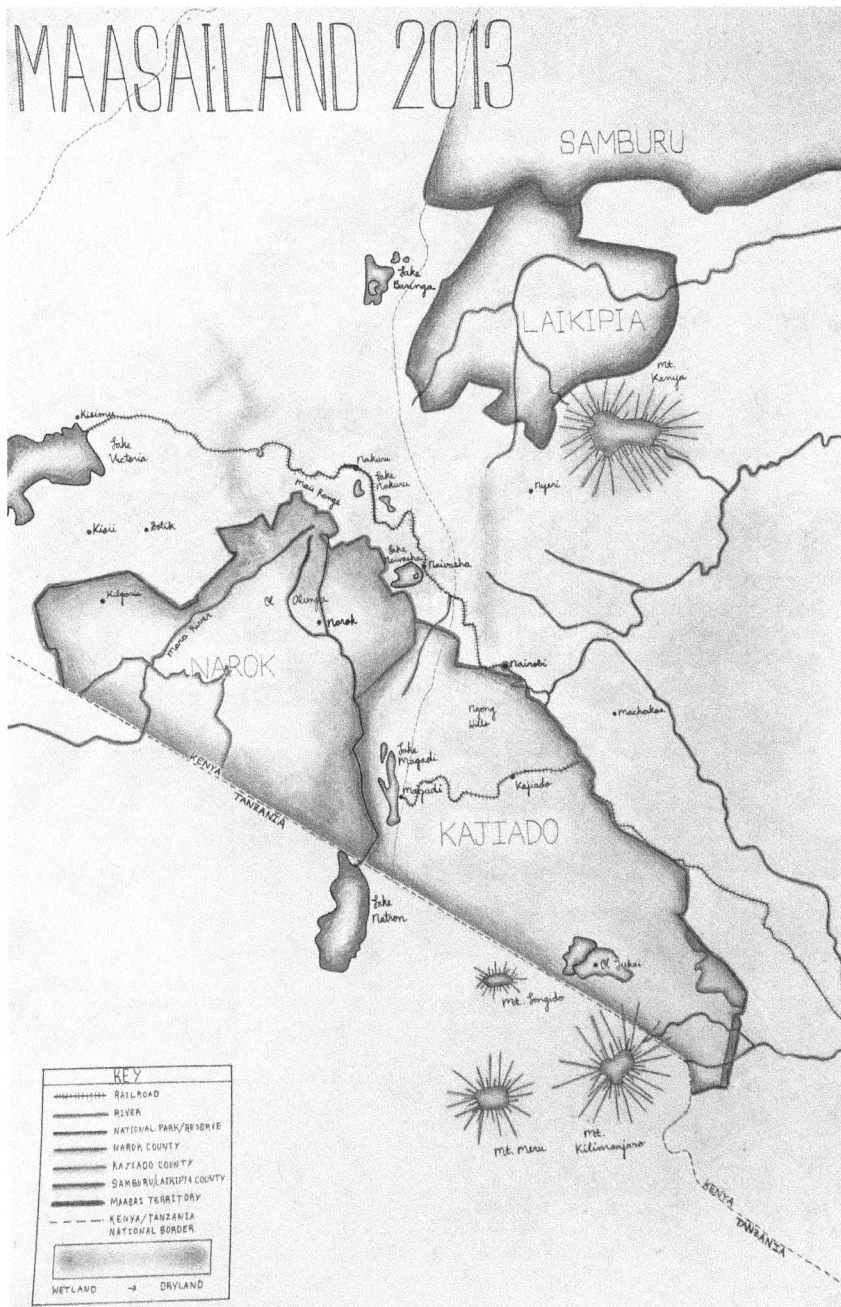

Figure 4 Map of Maasailand 2013: With the implementation of Kenya's 2010 new constitution, political power has been devolved to counties which are typically ethnically defined, creating the opportunity for *Olosho le Maa* to assert again a collective identity that includes the northern homeland of Samburu and Laikipia.

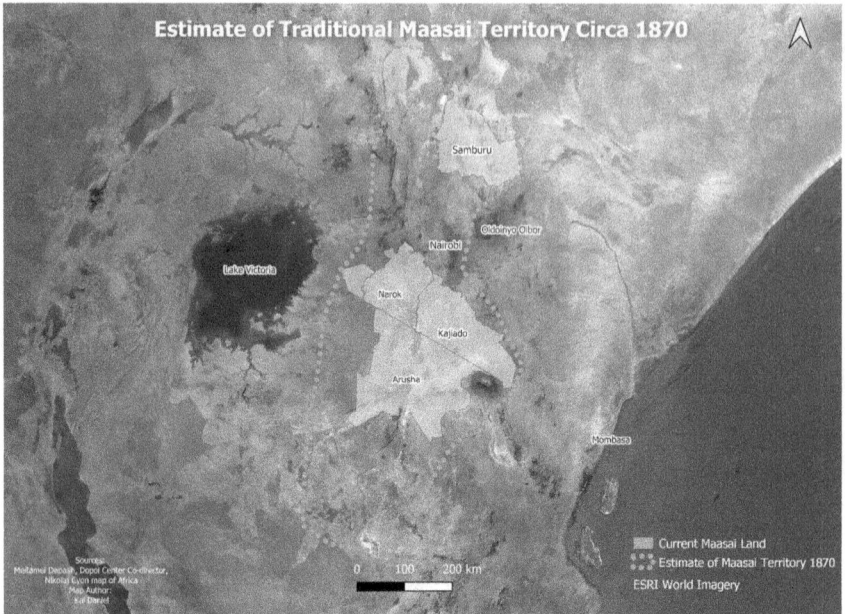

Figure 5 Satellite map of traditional Maasailand: Maasailand once extended 700 miles north to south across the border that now divides Kenya and Tanzania.

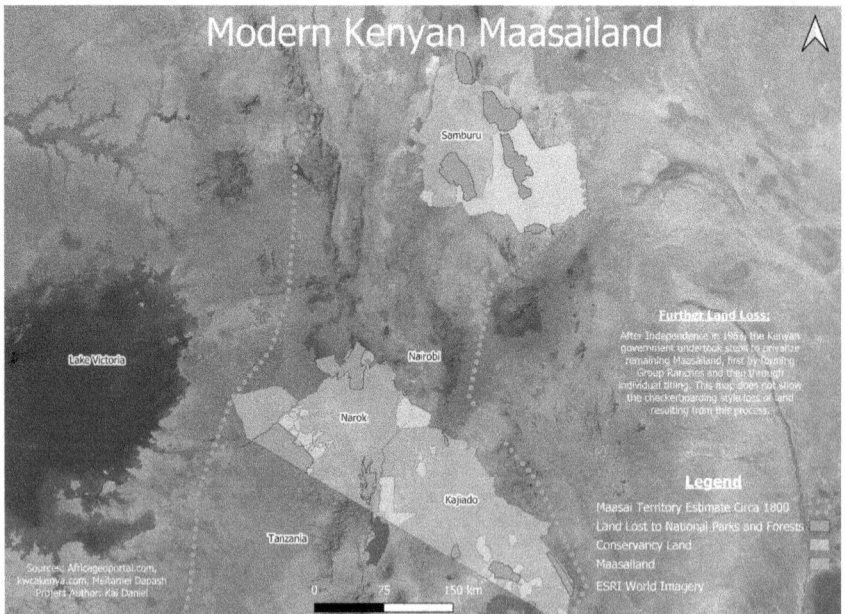

Figure 6 Satellite map of modern Maasailand: Remaining Maasailand is internally divided and subdivided into private land, conservancies, game reserves, parks, and a few remaining trust lands.

Figure 7 Olonana and British officers: British authorities claimed that the *oloiboni* Olonana was a friend and collaborator of the colonial regime; the Maasai community maintains that much evidence challenges that claim, including the suspicious timing of Olonana's early death while in British custody."

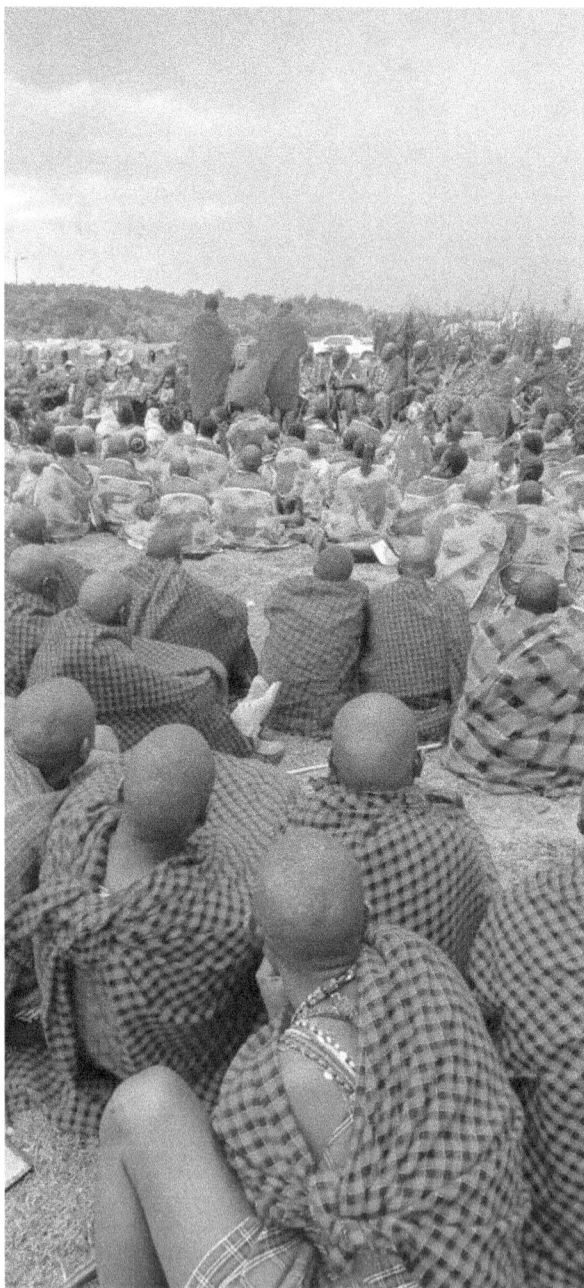

Figure 8 *Olng'esherr: Olosho le Maa* gathered in 2020 for *Olng'esherr*, what was likely the largest ceremonial gathering in Maasailand in the twentieth or twenty-first century, to celebrate the graduation of the *Ilmeirishi* age group into senior elderhood.

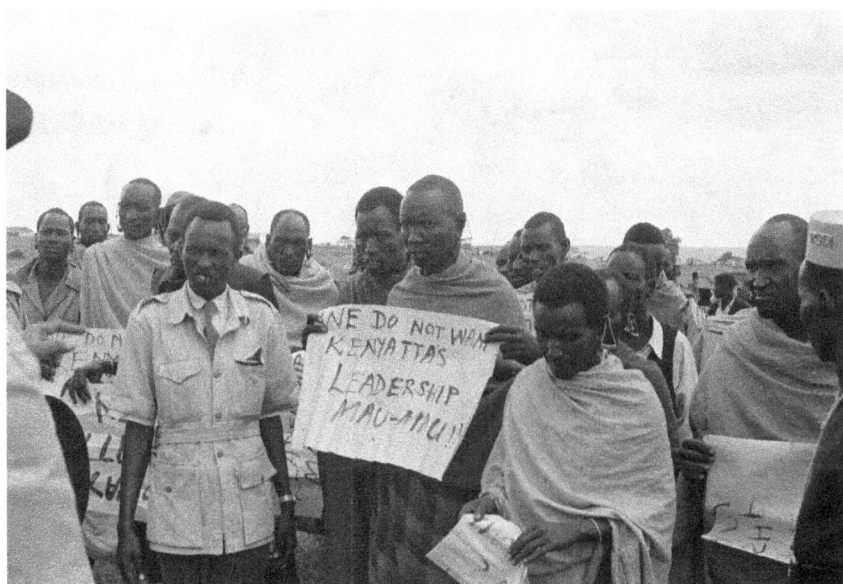

Figure 9 Protest at Independence in 1962: The Maasai community, led by the Maasai United Front, expressed a unified resistance to loss of sovereignty to Kenya in the Independence era. This photo is from a protest in Kajiado in 1962.

4

Amboseli: The Past and Future of Conservation in Maasailand

In 2005, Kenyan President Mwai Kibaki announced his intention to move the management of Amboseli National Park from the national government to the local Maasai-run County Council. This move would have had profound impact. The Park borders encompassed the swamps which provide the only drought reserve in the larger landscape which is extremely dry. Maasai are excluded from grazing in the Park, and they exist in extreme poverty outside. To reclassify Amboseli as a Game Reserve would have given the community the opportunity to explore integration of cattle and wildlife and other management strategies. The County Council might have built a management plan that drew on Indigenous ecological knowledge about human–wildlife coexistence in this place. Kibaki's intended move would seem to have answered the call of the international conservation movement for "community-based conservation."[1] Conservationists throughout the world have expressed awareness that the future of African wildlife depends on partnership with the Indigenous peoples with whom they typically share the land. In fact, the very term "community-based conservation" was coined by David Western, a Kenyan conservationist whose own work takes place in Maasailand. One might have expected Kibaki's declaration to be met with support. But instead, two powerful conservation organizations, the African Conservation Centre (ACC) and the Born Free Foundation, filed suit in Kenyan court to stop the transfer.[2] To that end they raised millions of US dollars for their ultimately successful court and public relations battle to retain management by the national Kenya Wildlife Service.

As this book entered the final stage of production, the Kenyan government announced that Amboseli was to be converted from a National Park to a Game Reserve, restoring Maasai involvement in management of the land. The research provided in this chapter contributed to this victory; it was first presented to the Olkejuado County Council, Kajiado, Kenya, in August 2006, by Prescott College students and community members.

Their campaign portrayed Maasai as incompetent and corrupt managers of wildlife ecosystems.[3]

In this chapter, we reconstruct the history of Amboseli to pursue a broader question: Why do conservation organizations working in Maasailand not recognize Maasai as obvious and natural partners in the protection and care of African wildlife? That was a question raised by Maasai people in the 1990s when they first reached out to develop such partnerships with Western conservationists. Maasai had assumed that the value of their historical stewardship of wildlife ecology would be taken for granted, evidenced by the fact that wildlife in Kenya only thrives outside of protected areas in Maasailand having been hunted to extinction elsewhere. Amboseli—*Empusel* in the *Maa* language, is itself both a former drought reserve of the *Kisongo* Maasai and dry season habitat for thousands of elephants, rhinos, giraffes, zebras, and scores of other wildlife. Together these shared water and grasses through centuries of the negotiated terms of coexistence for which Maasai culture is famous. Yet barring Maasai stewardship has led to disaster. The segregation of people and wildlife has seen impoverishment and insecurity of both. That reality begs a corollary question: How might Maasai communities gain this deserved recognition from global conservation communities and recover their historical role as stewards of Maasailands and the wildlife it supports?

What the history of Amboseli exposes is that Maasai demands to be included in conservation are indeed threatening, but not to the goal of wildlife conservation. Instead Maasai empowerment threatens the structures through which profit is generated from wildlife and those outside entities who benefit. These include the colonial and then Kenyan government, the international tourism industry, and also big international conservation organizations. These structures exist in a contradiction: they market a tourist experience through a fantasy that authentic wildlife exists only in a state of separation from human culture and activity, such as Maasai herding. This branding has led to the forced removal of Maasai people from wildlife areas.[4] However, the industry also relies on Maasai to continue to practice pastoralism outside of the Park as wet season habitat for the wildlife to sustain the density of wildlife required by tourism. It relies on Maasai to remain in a state of anemic poverty to prevent them from developing their land in ways that would destroy wildlife habitat. The cultural coexistence that enables wildlife to thrive continues to be practiced, but is shuttled out of view of tourists who pay the Park but not the community. International conservation organizations have a particularly checkered role in this history. They emerged into the early twentieth century with an agenda to commodify wildlife, not to protect the integrity and rights of wildlife communities or the deep socio-ecological relationships through which their habitat was created.

"African conservation" as it is advertised in the West is typically unrecognizable to Maasai people who see it function on the ground. The millions of people who write checks to conservation organizations to save the elephant from slaughter for ivory would be surprised, for example, to know that African conservation and big game hunting and ivory sale have until recently been intertwined. The first Western "conservationists" in Africa were big game hunters who responded to a fear that within a few years of European colonization they might have already decimated species in their African colonies to near extinction.[5] Unlike the U.S. conservation movement born under the influence of John Muir and the Sierra Club,[6] British conservation in Africa has been a movement through the twentieth century to protect certain species for their commercial value and to meet the desires of primarily white men in Europe and the United States, to hunt African wildlife.[7] The roots of the industry are found in British culture. Game hunting in Britain was an aristocratic sport since the time that common land was closed and all wildlife claimed to be the property of the Crown. Through African colonization British men of even middling classes could taste the royal pleasure of killing big game with little restriction. As a result, safari hunting was undertaken with abandon and included other Europeans and Americans.[8] The exploits of US President Teddy Roosevelt were not unique. On safari in 1909, with his son Kermit, Roosevelt killed "more than five hundred animals of over seventy different species," nine of which were white rhino, "including four cows and a calf," in spite of his knowledge that the animal was nearly extinct.[9] Elephants and rhinos were especially endangered as the market for ivory exploded through sudden increased supply. At a Berlin style conference in London in 1900, the Convention for the Preservation of Animals, Birds and Fish in Africa was signed by ministers representing the European colonial powers. Its mission was

> saving from indiscriminate slaughter, and of insuring the preservation throughout their possessions in Africa of the various forms of animal life existing in a wild state which are either useful to man or are harmless.[10]

Safari hunting was concentrated in Maasailand as many communities in East Africa had little or no wildlife on their lands when the British arrived because they hunted bush meat as supplemental food or for ivory and skins. But Maasailand was rich with rhinos, elephants, and other grazers with whom they continue to share the land, as well as lions and other predators whom they also did not kill without cause.[11] The Kamba people living northeast of Maasailand were involved with a preexisting trade in ivory facilitated by Arab caravans inland from Mombasa. Before colonization, that trade could not penetrate Maasailand where the elephants flourished. The caravans also traded in slavery and the Maasai warrior class prevented both slave raiding and hunting for ivory. This will be described in more detail in the next chapter. But colonization brought the *emutai*, the colonial war that nearly destroyed Maasai society at the end of the nineteenth century and with it their historical protection of wildlife. Weakened, Maasai territory could no longer prevent the activities of the caravans. Elephants and rhinos were quickly diminished in large numbers. In 1906, Deputy Commissioner of the E.A.P. Fredrick Jackson said that the Kamba people took advantage and organized large parties to hunt in Maasai the Southern Reserve, that

> it is only within the last 10 years or so that the Wakamba have dared to leave the confines of their own districts and enter the adjoining game country, owing to the dread of the Masai. Maasai no longer molest them.[12]

Quarterly field reports on wildlife numbers in Kenya revealed that rhino in particular were declining at alarming rates; hunters could find no suitable specimens, and elephants were being killed without regard to age or sex. As Maasai lost their northern land through the early 1900s, wildlife was nearly completely eradicated on settler land there, in Naivasha, Nakuru, and Laikipia, where no regulation could be enforced on private ranches.[13]

The 1900 Convention for the Preservation of Animals, Birds and Fish in Africa was the first colonial game policy, and it created a hierarchy of value for African wildlife. This hierarchy was built into colonial policy in Kenya. The Convention encouraged the killing to extermination of "harmful" species including lions, leopards, and wild dogs, considered "vermin" by settlers. It "conserved" instead those most desired for hunting. No Africans were present at the convention. Delegates were typically incapable of differentiating between African communities, between the pastoralists who coexisted with wildlife, the subsistence hunter/gatherers, and the African people who hunted for the international trade in animal products. In their ignorance they constructed all African hunting as "poaching," which criminalized subsistence forest hunters and ivory profiteers alike. Legitimate "hunting" was reserved for white settlers and tourists.[14] Their next step was to carve out "game reserves" to preserve hunting. The lands identified for hunting were "place[s] where the whites did not settle, either because of lack of good soil or enough water, or because of the presence of the tsetse fly." The Maasai Southern Reserve was especially valued for its density of wildlife.[15] In 1903 the first international conservation organization was founded in Britain,[16] and African conservation would be dominated through most of the twentieth century by champion hunters who defined "conservation" as the protection of their own access to "game."[17]

Thus, from the beginning, "conservation" was intertwined with killing wildlife for profit. Indeed, this put conservationists and Maasai communities at odds. Maasai experienced incompetent and destructive "conservation" under colonial management. For example, the colonial administration considered zebra and wildebeest to be a reserve food source especially in times of war. They slaughtered 6,000 of these animals in Maasailand alone to produce food for prisoners of war during the Second World War. The slaughter was a dangerous operation that unleashed bands of heavily armed and untrained volunteers on shooting sprees into a landscape where Maasai people grazed livestock. These "rangers" recalled later that they routinely used poison to solve wildlife "problems." In one case, their attempt to control hyenas who were hassling settlers led to the inadvertent killing of over fifty lions.[18] A postwar mass poisoning of locusts led to "enormous losses among birds" including the apparently permanent destruction of some species, especially around Lake Nakuru.[19] Wardens were typically not trained, were far too few to monitor any limits on hunting imposed by colonial-era policy. They said that they had no choice but to look the other way as white settlers and safari hunters slaughtered elephants and rhinos in exchange for the local intelligence they needed to do their work.[20]

In their drive to extract value from wildlife, "conservationists" only rarely admitted that wildlife they hunted had thrived because of a social and environmental ecology built by Maasai culture. We do not need to look to history to see examples of this cultural coexistence which is created anew today throughout Maasailand and is core to all Maasai land management. Maasai pay attention to the behavior of wildlife, assume that it is not random, and adjust their own resource needs where possible. In the whole of the Maasai Mara region today, Maasai know that cows are vulnerable to a virus passed by wildebeest giving birth, and they move all cattle from migratory routes when the annual wildebeest migration crosses the border into Kenya. Cows and many species of grazing wildlife create the dense diversity of grasses through differential selection. Zebras huddle outside Maasai villages at night as lions are wary of coming too close. Birds nest in trees within the thorn fences surrounding villages knowing that their eggs will not be eaten. Hyenas move at night into some spaces occupied by people during the day, where they find discarded bones but through practice understand that they must leave before sunrise. Individual lions or elephants who kill human beings will themselves be found and killed. Groups of Maasai warriors of the past would kill a lion as a part of their training. But wildlife is considered in Maasailand to have rights as communities to live and share water and other resources. In the deepest times of drought Maasai have not hunted and eaten wildlife, even as they watch their cattle and their own children die from hunger. Coexistence requires sacrifice by Maasai people, and the miracle is that they continue to make the sacrifice.

Conservationists through the colonial era in Kenya did not see that Maasai culture was a necessary component of the habitat that enabled such density of wildlife. They claimed instead that Maasailand was empty of human activity. They imagined Maasailand to exist in the "Pleistocene Age," a time before human existence.[21] By 1930 they began to take steps to preserve the land in this state by establishing it as a National Park. At the 1930 Game Preservation Conference, Major Hingston[22] told conference participants that Maasai people would not interfere with their plans, as there were only "a certain number of wandering Masai … who would have to remain there but they would not be injurious."[23] At the conference, Amboseli was described as "probably the finest piece of game country in the world," whose loss would be deeply felt.[24] But Amboseli, deep within the Masai Reserve, had been designated Maasai territory through the British 1911 Agreement. "Therein," lamented a colonial administrator later, "lies the rub."[25] Achieving National Park status would be the solution. The National Park model had been invented in the US West in the 1870s as land set aside from all human activity.[26] Parks differed from Game Reserves because their management is mandated by governments of nation-states and are therefore bound by international agreement and thus theoretically existed beyond the reach of governments. This was necessary to the goal of conservation because as Hingston said, "we have no idea what kind of administration may exist [in Africa] in 20, 50 or 100 years time."[27] The concern was that Maasai would regain their treaty-protected land at the end of British occupation. In spite of their claim that Maasai were too primitive to be considered, conferees tipped their hand as they passed a unanimous motion to prevent Maasai, those they claimed were merely "wandering," from developing their own plans for the reserve for twenty-five years. They would use this time to lock Amboseli into a National Park legal status.[28]

The Maasai "plans" that the British sought to block referred to the insipient tourism industry that had begun to establish a permanent infrastructure in Amboseli. In the 1930s, nearly all tourists to Africa were hunters; the tourism industry was established to provide them accommodation.[29] By 1937 the first Amboseli tourist enterprise, Rhino Camp, offered grass huts and then sleeping bandas to tourists. This arrangement was established, according to a local park ranger, between an entrepreneur, P. Gethin, and Maasai Chief Ole Mberre and Muna "a petty chief."[30] Maasai leadership had the apparent authority at that time to limit the development to only "temporary" construction. It was obvious that tourism would be very lucrative if fully developed with permanent lodges, but the 1911 British Agreement gave Maasai the advantage in their negotiations. As the Agreement prevented the colonial government from pursuing National Park status at the time, the conservation coalition first sought to have Amboseli designated a Reserve which the colonial government could achieve on its own. This step was accomplished in 1948. The Amboseli Reserve continued to allow hunting and it also took the step of removing Maasai people and preventing their use of the Ol Tukai swamps, the drought reserve. Some evidence of Maasai protest survives in the colonial-era documents. For example, a "certain young educated moran" from Loitokitok named Lemeki was vocal in his opposition to the removal of Maasai people from the watered areas in 1948. He was accused of having a deeper "ulterior motive" and was organizing the community "to get the Maasai to oppose the creation of the National Reserve."[31]

The excuse offered for the removal of Maasai from Ol Tukai was not based in competition between cows and wildlife for water and grass. Instead, the mere appearance of Maasai themselves would "ruin their safari experience" because "no one comes hundreds of miles over dry and dusty roads to see herds of cattle."[32] The incipient tourist industry sought to brand Amboseli as a place where travelers could experience life in the "Pleistocene." Beyond that, Maasai had been impoverished by colonial occupation, having been moved from a vast landscape together onto a small dry reserve without sufficient grasses and water. Indeed, the picture of emaciated cows, children with visible diseases, wrapped in old blankets, would have communicated to tourists the broader dynamics through which their safari experience had been constructed.

With the establishment of Amboseli as a Reserve, the tourism industry became more organized and the movement to see Amboseli designated a National Park broadened. In 1955, the East African Tourist Travel Association (EATTA), Ker and Downey, and the East African Hunter's Association waged a joint media campaign to pressure the Kenyan government to designate Amboseli a National Park. The true goal of the campaign, according to the Provincial Commissioner, was "to drive the Masai from the area,"[33] but they claimed instead that the issue was environmental, the "wanton destruction of the vegetation and the monopolization of water supplies" by Maasai cattle. Letters from American tourists began appearing in the *East African Standard* in October 1955 criticizing the government for "allowing" Maasai herders to graze on their own land. A letter from Mrs. Harold Ebinger of Aurora, Illinois, just returned from safari, asked:

> What are you people doing to your Africa? Are you willing to lose the characteristics which make Africa unique, the only country [*sic*] of its kind?

Mirroring the words of other writers, she asked Kenya to site boreholes for the watering of cattle outside of the Reserve and expressed distain for "inevitable flies" caused by "thousands of head of maasai cattle," whose existence destroyed the "sight of magnificent Kilimanjaro" and "God's wild creatures in their natural habitat."[34] The timing of the campaign took advantage of an unusually harsh drought year and the subsequent dust. The industry convinced the governor of Kenya, Evelyn Baring, to lobby on its behalf.[35]

Everyone at this point could see the profitability of tourism on Maasailand. M.H. Cowie, the Director of Parks, agreed that "[e]ach wild animal, whether large or small, has a very definite earning capacity measured in terms of revenue paid by tourist visitors to the colony. This can hardly be said of each Maasai cow."[36] The press campaign created tension in the administration, and led to the formation of the 1956 Game Policy Committee. The Committee was charged to create a permanent policy.[37] Again, glimpses remain in the archives of Maasai rejection of this plan for their land, which was protected still at this time by the 1911 Agreement. An unidentified Maasai person said in a letter to the Game Committee, "[W]e, the Masai, have lived in the Ol Tukai area, for many years and it is perhaps true to say that the tribe makes some contribution towards the popularity of the Amboseli National Reserve." They continued, "the Masai have their own grazing control measures which are closely related to the seasons of the year," and emphasized that they showed good faith by cooperating with the government on the Ilkisongo grazing control scheme, even putting up 10,000 pounds of their own funds for the project. The author concluded:

> [T]he Maasai have lived happily with the (wildlife) game for many years .... I feel that authorities should consider very seriously allowing the Maasai and the game to continue living together in Ol Tukai area, provided there are resources to safeguard the interests of both.[38]

The British 1911 Agreement remained in the way of further tourism development; it had been rearticulated in the 1938 Native Lands Trust Ordinance of the Masai Reserve that "unless the Treaties are to be deliberately broken, any alteration in status must be with the agreement of the Masai themselves."[39] However, in their confidential memos, policymakers built a case to extinguish Maasai treaty rights. Because the Maasai Native Reserve was created after the 1900 establishment of the Game Reserve on the same land, they reasoned, "there was, thus, an eleven year old game servitude on the land, at the time the masai agreed to accept the area offered."[40] The 1900 designation of game land had applied in theory to the African continent, not specifically to the Kenyan colony or to Amboseli. Nonetheless they suggested that perhaps the common good of the colony should be valued against the disadvantage it might entail to "a portion of the community," assuming that the determination of land rights lay with their discretion.[41]

Having rationalized severance of the land from any British obligation to the 1911 Agreement, they turned their attention to the question of fair compensation. Initially, administrators assumed that "there could be no question of converting Amboseli National Reserve into a Park unless an area of equal value to the Masai was added to the Native Land Unit," and that water would also have to be provided.[42] But the argument that only equal land could fairly compensate was quickly eroded as Royal Parks Director Cowie rejected that option. Cowie suggested instead paying Maasai in Amboseli "a reasonable rent" as in "any landlord and tenant arrangement." In the same breath, however, he took the next step, to suggesting that only water need be provided. He said, "I admit that money has little attraction for the Maasai, but if wisely converted into the facilities they most require, it would have a greater meaning, and they in turn would retain a share in one of the colony's greatest assets."[43]

The 1956 Game Policy Committee embedded this new language of "compensation" rather than "rights," into all future policy. They recommended that the National Park be created and the government "provide alternative water" to the swamp and to "enforce the use by Masai cattle of this alternative water supply only."[44] The Committee hired a geological survey to be done on Amboseli to determine where boreholes might be drilled. Regarding the water plan, the government acknowledged that the "agreement and willing cooperation of the masai … was neither forthcoming nor expected."[45]

Throughout this process—of debate about rights and compensation—Maasai communities in Amboseli were not informed about the plans being developed for their land. In June of 1956, with the Committee on the verge of releasing its interim report, the District Commissioner from Kajiado requested that it

> not be published till after the results of the water survey have been discussed.
> I consider it of vital importance that before anything appears in the press the

Masai are informed of the position by us. I do not consider it wise to tell them the long term proposal.

The Committee did consider briefly whether Maasai communities should be required to pay for this alternative water, however, but the idea was rejected because, according to the Commissioner, in a moment of candor,

> after all, the water is available and has been used free for years and I do not think it right to ask them to subscribe to a scheme which is primarily designed to keep the dust out of the visiting publics' hair.[46]

A month later, still kept in the dark, Maasai people were "definitely worried" at seeing surveying for water levels done in their land without explanation. The commissioner assured them that nothing would be done to change the Laitaiyek [*Ilaitayiok*] clan's use of the area until any plan was discussed with them. He added, however, that because of increased control to impose water and grazing routes, the community was "not at all convinced by my assurances." He gave instructions to "soft pedal the Ol Tukai drive" until the Provincial Commissioner arrived.[47]

While the Game Policy Committee worked through subterfuge, a new idea began to brew among them: they realized that their plan for a National Park at Amboseli actually relied on Maasai cooperation. While the wildlife and Maasai people had used the swamp at Ol Tukai as a dry season reserve, both spent more of their lives on the dry surrounding land. By carving out the Reserve for the exclusive use of wildlife, they also theoretically excluded the wildlife from the entirety of their wet season habitat, as that had been designated for cattle. For wildlife to survive, it would need free access to Maasai land and to continue to benefit from the historical coexistence there. At the same time, Maasai must be prevented from developing their land, turning it to agriculture, building roads, schools, and businesses, as the land must remain wildlife habitat.

It began to dawn on policymakers that Maasai would have to see some benefit from the wildlife, to "appreciate that game is not only a national asset, but also of benefit to the Masai people themselves." At this point, the Game Policy Committee considered soliciting proposals submitted by Maasai people "designed to preserve and control game in the best interests both of themselves and of the Colony."[48] The new strategy, according to Game Ranger Zaphiro and other proponents, would require "both courage and an entirely new attitude towards the Masai and the wild life that inhabits their Reserve than has hitherto been accorded by the responsible authorities."[49] The Committee recognized that the government would have to share some of the "direct financial interest in the economic aspect of such preservation."[50] This insight would lead to a brief moment of Maasai management of the Reserve. The moment was fleeting because it would occur in the first decade after Independence through agreement within the government that the arrangement was only temporary until National Park status could be achieved.

At Independence, as has been described in other chapters, Maasailand was subjected to an aggressive incursion to prepare for the full implementation of neocolonial development agendas. All of Maasailand was being carved up behind closed doors in London and Nairobi and assigned a purpose in the new economy, to be mined in various fashions for the benefit of the Kenyan state and the West. The resulting chaos caused breakdown in the community's ability to navigate survival for several decades, to hold its leadership accountable, and anger at the government mounted.

One example of this incursion and resulting breakdown was initiated through the Ilkisongo grazing scheme in 1955. The scheme was part of a broader plan to reconstruct much of the Masai Reserve as a profit-generating corporate cattle industry. Cows were to be removed from grazing land under the scheme and confined in crowded paddocks. It would involve breeding Maasai cattle to produce more milk and limiting the size of herds. The government first targeted the Matapatu and Loitokitok sections to implement the scheme and the Loitokitok were instructed to reduce their herds from 7,000 animals to 5,000 in a single year. The Maasai community understood that if they went along with herd reduction, according to Park Ranger David Smith, "that at some later date they may be excluded completely from the forest belt which will be become in effect a small National Park." They refused to reduce their herds and instead deliberately overpopulated them, "to swell their numbers" in Amboseli to hold onto the land. Smith continued:

> In August 1957 the situation was becoming desperate. More cattle than ever were in the area and the dry season was only just beginning. The Maasai were already losing many cattle daily through lack of grazing. They [Maasai] knew there were too many cattle in the area for their grazing to sustain the numbers, but they kept them there in order to reinforce their claim over the area.[51]

Conflict erupted. According to the new policy, lions and other wildlife were free to roam on community land but Maasai were legally prevented from killing any that attacked their herds. Maasai were becoming increasingly aware that the wildlife was more protected by the government than they themselves. At a *baraza*, an open-air meeting held by the governor of Kenya to address concerns,

Chief Kisimir said: "We realize that Ol Tukai brings wealth to the whole of Kenya by reason of the wild animals here which attract visitors from many distant lands. But we would ask that the interest of the human population of areas should not be forgotten or put second to those of the animals."[52]

As the government would not respond to wildlife attacks on cows, Maasai people took matters into their own hands. David Smith said that conflict erupted after the implementation of the Ilkisongo scheme, "soon the Rangers were bringing in daily reports of animals being found dead with spear wounds ... and I was constantly out investigating complaints for the herdsmen of cattle being killed by marauding lions or leopards."[53] Requests for government redress for lost cattle were repeatedly denied, as were human deaths. In 2006, Amboseli elder Wuala Ole Parsanka says that the issue has never been redressed and that the most compensation Maasai have been able to negotiate for the death of a person from a wildlife attack is 30,000 shillings,[54]

> for the death of a human being. It's embarrassing. You cannot buy a human being. And if that very same animal kills someone outside the park, you get nothing.[55]

Maasai have also sometimes killed wildlife in protest, to send a message to the government.[56] It has been an effective way to get the government's attention. Logela Olol Melita, a Maasai from Olgulului in Amboseli, explained:

> We are saying that we are the ones taking care of these animals, they are on our ranch land, and we know the animals better than the people who come here. We do this even when we do not see a benefit. But the government, these NGOs and Kenyan Wildlife Service claim to share the benefits of wildlife. They say "we employ Maasai people such and such." But we know that we get nothing compared to what they are earning. The benefits are a lie, so maybe we should go out and kill the wildlife that is more important to the government than people.[57]

At this same time, the transition to African statehood, African conservationists in Europe and the United States built a powerful new international infrastructure of big nongovernmental organizations to maintain control of African wildlife past Independence. The two most influential were founded in 1961: the African Wildlife Leadership Foundation (later AWF) and the World Wildlife Fund (WWF). Rather than leading the West in appreciation of wildlife, they have promoted the protection wildlife for sport and profit through much of their histories. They were originally composed of the same colonial-era conservationists, the big game hunters, and members of the "100 Pounders Club." According to reporting by Raymond Bonner published in 1993, these founders of African conservation were horrified by the prospect of wildlife managed by African states as they expressed behind closed doors a belief that Africans were "born poachers."[58] Therefore both organizations sought to dominate conservation from outside Africa. Of the two, the WWF achieved the most success. They did so by raising extreme levels of funding through a mass appeal to animal lovers in the West. They also, Bonner reports, raised money through networks of hunters and poachers. The WWF quietly offered access to European royalty to wealthy people who were considered enemies of conservation and human rights by the organizations base. These included ostracized white South Africans and other "criminal untouchables."[59] The WWF refused to support a ban on ivory until forced to do so, reflecting the gap between the organization and its small committed donor base who wanted to save the elephants. According to Bonner in his 1993 book, the WWF has been riven with internal conflict through its history over its lack of transparency, funding of brutal anti-poaching schemes, and over a racist structure and policy. WWF he says operated for thirty years without employing a single African, despite originating its work on the continent and even after thirty years in business, the Nairobi office of the US-based AWF employed only one African of nine senior associates. In 1987 AWF director Stanley Price had explained, "We're trying to run a Western type organization. It needs Western type skills."[60]

To establish Amboseli as a National Park was the agenda of international conservationists and they found a friend in Stanley Oloitiptip, a Maasai colonial government chief. After Independence, Oloitiptip became the representative of Kajiado South Constituency in Kenyan Parliament. As such he was afforded fairly unchecked power over a constituency that lacked literacy and the means to hold their representatives accountable. The local community reports that a power struggle emerged between Oloitiptip and Olkujuado County Council (OCC) Chairman Alex Legis.[61] Beginning in 1961 the OCC was granted temporary management authority over the Amboseli Reserve. Through those years, modest Reserve revenue was spent on community projects, especially education, and to a lesser degree on health care and roads. OCC records show that the Council built several dispensaries and cattle dips, supported schools, and developed plans to create adult literacy programs.[62] The OCC funded construction or maintenance on thirty-five minor roads in the district, and drilled boreholes with Council funds.[63] Philip Ngatia, a former non-Maasai headteacher of the Lenkisem Primary School in Amboseli, explained that the OCC "funded education very heavily before the Park." He pointed to a cinderblock school building and a generator for the school's borehole, all recently provided by the OCC "even without park money."[64]

The Council took a less structured approach to Reserve management than the one that would follow when Amboseli became a National Park. Amboseli today is crossed by roads built and monitored by the Kenyan government and tour drivers are expected to not travel "off road." In the earlier period of management by the OCC, the Council instead used a system more like the deferred grazing used by Maasai culture. The Council closed the Amboseli Reserve entirely to tourists for a month or two at a time, several times a year, to allow for the regeneration of grasses. This was done, apparently, with the knowledge of the grazing cycles of cattle and wildlife and also because "there was very little traffic going through at that time" in the Reserve.[65] Managing wildlife habitat for profit introduced a new relationship between Maasai and the land. As OCC Chairman Alex Legis remarked, the OCC was suddenly made "to look after the area," by the authority it was given in 1961. "But can I say," he continued, "that it was this area that had always looked after us."[66]

The OCC had only been awarded power to manage the Reserve and allocate the revenue until the plan to designate Amboseli a National Park was finalized. But this was never communicated to the OCC itself. Believing itself to be the permanent management authority in Amboseli, the OCC undertook to design a future for the development of the land and support of the surrounding community. In 1964 it completed a plan to establish a tourism industry at Amboseli, one that would keep the land as a Reserve, maintain it as a "community sanctuary" centered on the Ol Tukai swamp. The Reserve would be left free from Maasai grazing during specified times of the year, and tourist revenues would be put to use building schools and water projects and other necessary development. The plan would assume that during the wet season wildlife would continue to be welcomed on Maasai community land. During dry season, access to the water and grazing in the swamp would be negotiated every year to promote the health of both wildlife and cattle, goats and sheep. The plan would enable Maasai to remain invested in pastoralism while expanding into tourism. In 1964 the OCC report was presented to the Kenyan government. It was submitted specifically in response to the 1956 Game Committee request for proposals for local involvement in tourism.

This plan never came to light. It was buried by the Kenyan government for two years, ostensibly to work out the details of "water and other needs of the Masai people." But in fact, the OCC report was buried to give the government time to develop its own plan. The government's plan required Amboseli to be designated a National Park. It required the full removal of Maasai from Amboseli.[67] A document was prepared for the Ministry of Tourism, dated December 3, 1966, marked "Secret," which admitted:

[I]n April 1964, the Olkajiado County Council first resolved to set apart 200 square miles at Amboseli as a game sanctuary area, free of all livestock, if the government would ensure the provision of piped water for the Masai outside this area.[68]

The document commended the OCC plan but admitted that it would "compete" with the one the government itself had been developing. The report suggested that Maasai were not competent to manage tourism as "the scientific and technological management of such an area apart from administration and accounting inevitably places strain on the County Council resources."[69] Instead of working with the OCC and the local Maasai Council of Elders, the government developed their plan with Stanley Oloitiptip. There were two critical points of difference between the OCC and the government plans. The first already mentioned would be management policies. The second was revenue. The government's plan would see all National Park revenues flow to the national government and not the OCC for local development.

A first draft of the government's plan for Amboseli Park was presented in 1969 by two young men, David Western and Frank Mitchell. Both men were British Kenyans and recent graduates of the Institute for Development Studies at the University of Nairobi. Mitchell's work was to estimate the revenue that the OCC would realize under its plan. He found that in just fifteen years, the Reserve could generate a staggering 2.5 million pounds, or 50.3 million in today's USD. His projection was presented to the Kenyan public in Nairobi in a double-page ad in the *Daily Standard*. However, there is no evidence that any members of the OCC were given a copy of his report. David Western's task was to produce a draft proposal of the government's plan, which referenced Mitchell's revenue projections. Western said in his report that it was "essential" that Amboseli be designated a National Park. He recommended that Maasai not be directly compensated for the loss of land but instead through boreholes for water, and indirect revenue from tourism coming into the area including bed-night fees.[70] In 1971 the World Bank (WB) offered a $40 million loan for a livestock ranching scheme in the area, but was persuaded by Western and Mitchell to invest instead in wildlife tourism. The WB agreed, provided that the development of Amboseli Park benefit individual landholders and that additional funding be secured from the New York Zoological Society for boreholes to provide an alternative water source for the community outside of the Park. A new Olgulului/Olalarrashi Maasai Group Ranch was drawn around the Amboseli Reserve to streamline administrative issues between the government and the community. That year, President Kenyatta decreed that an unspecified 200 square miles of land would be set aside for a National Park in the region. When the deal was final Mitchell moved to a new job at the WB Headquarters in Washington, D.C., and Western and economist Philip Thresher were hired to write the final government plan for Amboseli National Park.

That final plan was completed in 1973. It contained the same admission made in earlier drafts that Maasai community "participation" would be necessary, as the wildlife that tourists would come to see at the swamps would need to spend the majority of its time on surrounding Maasai community land. The Park would not survive as an "ecological island."[71] Yet the proposal claimed that Maasai's pastoral lifestyle was "detrimental to the conservation" goal.[72] The plan designated cattle-free zones, including most of the swamps that the Maasai had relied on as livestock watering points especially during droughts. The Maasai were promised 400 acres in the Ol Tukai region, though that transfer has not happened, and allowed to retain some of their original petrol stations, and all Park revenue would be transferred from the OCC to the Kenyan government. Compensation to the Maasai community would come in the form of a "bed-tax" from local lodges, indirect revenue from jobs as "hotel employees," or through selling "cultural amenities" such as handicrafts, and water would be provided by the WB and the New York Zoological Society.

David Western has since said that the OCC was offered the opportunity to participate in designing the plan for the Amboseli National Park in 1969, at the urging of Stanley Oloitiptip. He said that the community rejected the offer, forcing the government to act instead.[73] In Western's account he worked closely with Oloitiptip, and together they defended Maasai rights against the opposing agenda of the government.[74] But OCC Chairman Legis says instead that Oloitiptip helped the government mislead the community and bury its opposition to the establishment of the Park. This ultimately led to the disempowerment of the OCC and allowed Oloitiptip to once again be the sole voice of the Maasai community in the Kenyan government. Logela Ole Melita was told by both of his grandparents Kasaine Ole Ntawuasa and Wambui, before their deaths, about a meeting convened by Oloitiptip near the Serena Lodge in 1969. The meeting they said was attended by "very many" Maasai people and by representatives of Kenyatta's government, to discuss the Park creation. Oloitiptip is remembered to have asked in the Maa language, "How many people here do not want the government to take the park?" When all hands shot into the air, Oloitiptip was said to have turned to the government representatives next to him and report that the raised hands reflected the people's support of the Park's creation.[75]

Western said that both the OCC and the Maasai Council of Elders rejected the proposal he drafted but also refused to participate in the process of refining it. But Chairman Legis says that they were never asked to be involved. Instead the Council was "blindsided" by the news that the Park would be created and the OCC's own plan discarded. According to OCC meeting minutes, as late as the winter of 1974, the Council still did not know that they would lose Park revenues in the transfer of Amboseli to the national government. The previous April, Chairman Legis said, "It has come to the notice of the Council that National Parks have posted a Park Warden to Amboseli without the knowledge of the council." But Legis said that [Perez Olindo,] the Director of National Parks, had assured him that "[t]he Government will not take over Amboseli till the whole machinery of negotiations between the Council and Government and local people have taken place." Legis reminded the Council that "[t]he [1971] takeover of Amboseli is to protect the Wildlife and to show the Maasai the benefits of Wildlife and not to take over finances accrued from Amboseli." But the Council remained anxious, and in the end it "resolved that if the Government is to takeover all finances from Amboseli Gates this council will collapse within a few days as there is no other source of finances to keep this council running."[76]

In September of that year, John Keen, a founder of the MUF and then current Kenyan Assistant Minister of Water, attended the OCC meeting to share information. He informed the Council that "[t]he Kenya National Parks is trying to take all the revenue from Amboseli." He continued, "You know very well that we do not have another source of revenue except from Amboseli" and he "appealed to Councilors to be united and defend our heritage."[77] Keen promised again, at the November meeting, that he would do his "lived best" to retain revenue for the Council. But he too was preparing for the worst. Afraid of the impact the withdrawal of revenue would have, "He appealed to the council to raise revenues from Natural Resources, i.e. Sand as to get revenue to build Primary Schools [and] Dispensaries."[78] Finally, on December 11, 1974, the OCC was informed of the government's plan to completely take over management and revenue from Amboseli, and an emergency meeting would be held on December 27. The Council unanimously resolved, "That all revenue remain Council property" but "should any agreement be reached there must be a matching grant equal to the loss of revenue to this Council."[79]

All potential opposition to the legality of the transfer of revenue was quickly arrested. By January, a working group had been assembled and began meeting on the logistical steps to transfer management from the OCC to the national government.[80] Chairman Legis expressed the unhappiness of the Council over the way the Parks Department had handled the matter "contrary to previous arrangements and promises" and that "no takeover of Amboseli National Park would take place until outstanding matters, such as water supply, grazing rights, Council assets and staff had been discussed and agreed on." He threatened that "patience was already wearing thin" due to the fact "that they had been let down so much" and that the Council had, until that moment, "been counting on the 1975 revenues." He said that the takeover of Amboseli had been "unilateral." The Minister of Local Government made a list of all points of controversy. The OCC agreed not to object to the takeover in exchange for continued grazing and water rights "until alternative water supply is established outside the park" and "some" continued revenue shared.[81]

By January 30, 1976, the Council was pleading to the Minister of Local Government for funds for the water projects, roads, and other projects the Council once paid for itself. As Council Member Wuantai explained at the January meeting, "the revenue was limited as a result of the takeover of the park."[82]

To this day, none of the government's promises for compensation have been honored. The government's plan included the assessment of a "bed-tax" of 40–60Ksh per guest to fund the work of the OCC. But that has yet to be implemented in the lodges around Amboseli. The plan promised that 400 acres of land would be transferred to the community in compensation for the loss of Amboseli. That also has yet to occur. The lodges built on the edges of the swamp hire very few local employees; in 2006 the few Maasai workers were hired to wear warrior costumes and chase away monkeys and were paid 100Ksh ($1.30) per day. Those Maasai who are hired for higher positions such a walking tour guide or bartender, even those with degrees, are put into lengthy "training programs" working without pay for up to two years.[83] Maasai-initiated projects have reportedly been co-opted by outside profiteers. For example, Daniel Leturesh, Chairman of the Olgulului/Olalarrashi group ranch, and Joseph Sayaialel, past member of the OCC, initiated a "cultural boma" program to bring tourists directly to Maasai villages. But the program became monopolized by tour operators from Nairobi who blacklist villages that do not allow them to take all but a fraction of what is paid. These operators warn tourists against buying jewelry directly from Maasai people, taking clients instead to curio shops where drivers receive commission.[84]

Research into the employment situation in Amboseli was undertaken in 2006 but community members report that little if any change has been achieved since then.

Most significantly, the promised compensation of water has never been delivered. The 1955 Ilkisongo Grazing Scheme promised boreholes in exchange for herd reduction, and Maasai of Loitokitok even borrowed 10,000 pounds, worth $196,000 today, to contribute to a water infrastructure.[85] But surveys undertaken at the time revealed just how expensive it would be to pipe water to the community. The biggest expense would not be incurred by the boreholes themselves. Instead, the expense stemmed from the distance that the water would have to be transported from the boreholes, which would necessarily be located next to the swamp, miles away into community land. The government's rationale was that it would be necessary to keep Maasai far away from the swamps so that they would not be seen by tourists. In fact surveyors had been directed to "find means to keep the Masai cattle as far away from the Ol Tukai area as possible."[86] A scheme by the African Land Development Board was also rejected for being too expensive for the same reason.[87] In December, 1957, the colonial governor took the advice of the Game Committee and declared that "the costly full scale scheme for providing water for Masai cattle in Amboseli, could not at present be justified."[88] The issue would be addressed when the National Park was established.[89] Maasai were assured through these years that they would always have the swamp to fall back on in emergencies, and the governor promised:

> The Government recognizes that the whole Amboseli area is within the Masai native land unit and belongs to the Masai whose rights to it are protected under the native lands Trust Ordinance. The Government will not take away any of this land from the Masai.[90]

Finally, after the establishment of the Park in 1974, the New York Zoological Society was to provide boreholes as part of the $40 million WB loan to Kenya and while some boreholes were dug, they all collapsed within a few years for lack of maintenance.[91]

None of the conservation organizations working in Amboseli have, at least publicly, lobbied on behalf of the promised water. Since 1995 this has included the African Conservation Centre, which was founded by the same David Western who drafted the government's plan for tourism at Amboseli in 1969 that eclipsed the proposal of the OCC.[92]

In Amboseli, Maasai continue to coexist with wildlife on community land in spite of the history described above. Maasai continue to care for wildlife that brings them no tangible benefit; they do this because their culture teaches that animals have a right to live on the land that they share. In this commitment, we see hope for the future of conservation. History demonstrates that Maasai have sought collaboration with outside partners for many decades. Those efforts continue today through various projects to train and unionize Maasai tour guides, facilitate beading cooperatives and Maasai-run cultural villages, and establish community land sanctuaries. Yet in July of 2022, security at Ol Tukai lodge blocked the leader of a local village of 600 Maasai people from attending a meeting at the lodge which had been organized in his honor.[93] Such discriminatory treatment of Maasai people, even respected elders and leadership, is typical. But as the history shows, it is not just ignorant prejudice that prevents conservationists from embracing Maasai knowledge. Those seeking to protect African wildlife must ask themselves who really profits from the tangled relationship that exists between tourism, conservation, and the Kenyan state. They must ask whether Maasai communities might make better partners in the effort to ensure that wildlife survives for future generations.

Olosho le Maa and the Long Century of Anticolonial Resistance

This chapter offers an outline of a new history of the Maasai people, one that aligns with the common sense, memory, and historical knowledge of *Olosho le Maa*. It is very incomplete and only a beginning, but written nonetheless, and with a sense of urgency. Maasai children no longer have the opportunity, to be fully educated in Maasai history and culture at home, as they spend many hours in formal education.[1] The Kenyan public school curriculum has recently undergone positive changes, yet it continues to present Maasai culture as a thing of the past, implying through omission that only assimilated Kenyan people have a future. In this chapter, we are led by this urgency, and by the questions raised in the community that give indications about Maasai futures. We have thus organized this new framing of Maasai history around this question: How has *Olosho le Maa* survived through the challenges it has faced through time, and what role has Maasai culture played in that survival?

Maasai have been aware of themselves as a people for many hundreds or thousands of years, stretching back in memory long before the expansion of *Olosho le Maa*, the Maasai community, in the Rift Valley of East Africa. Maasai knew themselves even before their journey south along the Nile River, in the region of Mt. Sinai in what is now Lebanon. The Maa language retains this memory in expressions spoken commonly today, such as *oi pasinai*, translated as "as it was in Sinai," to express periods of unrelenting hardship. There are many aspects of Maasai culture that are believed to have originated among the Israelites. These include the language and specific ceremonial components of

Donkol Ole Keiwa, historian of the Maasai community, made many valuable contributions to this chapter, which also benefitted from participants of a history conference held at the MERC/Prescott College Dopoi Center in 2017, and the Prescott College students and activists of the Maasai community who have presented research and facilitated discussion about history in many dozens of gatherings through the years.

the slaughter, "offering" of cows, goats, and sheep called *ilkipoketa*, the spiritual significance of the Olive tree, and the word for "those who are not us," *Ilmeek*, literally translated as "gentiles." *Olosho le Maa* emerged from a people who left the hard life in the north and migrated with cattle through the desert to find a new home. Elders say that the community was once literate, but on the long journey they saw that the heavy scrolls they carried would be unnecessary in their new life, and they abandoned them to desiccate in the desert.

Another origin story of *Olosho le Maa* begins with the creation of all human beings, and the first man and woman. *Naiterukop*, the first couple, who were given to the earth from the heavens arrived with cows. That Maasai people never existed before cows is considered to be essential to the story. *Naiterukop* had three children and one became a hunter, and another one a farmer; *Olosho le Maa* emerged from the third son, a herdsman who inherited the cattle. Maasai identity is thus so deeply embedded in this relationship with cattle that a person who does not have cows has no identity as Maasai. People know the individual members of their herds, their lineages and relationships with each other, and those many cows who have been received as gifts who wear the brand of the givers. As cows are exchanged in friendship, those who give and receive adopt new names for each other to reflect the event. While livestock are loved collectively and as individuals, they frequently die in drought, and are also slaughtered for food, and thus the relationship between human beings and cows and other domestic animals expresses that in Maasai culture death and life coexist. This is what Maasai mean when they say that they are the "people of the cow." These things are as true today as they have been in the past.

Maasai people migrated into the Rift Valley by moving south along the Nile River and settling in a valley within a valley, likely *Endikir-e-Kerio* (the scarp of Kerio), a "crater-like country" surrounded by a steep escarpment that was very dry.[2] Life there continued to be hard for people and cattle. After a "very, very long time," the people moved out of Kerio and into the highlands of the Rift Valley. They had made a discovery: birds returning from the top of the escarpment were seen carrying long green blades of grass.[3] A structure was built to move people and cattle up the escarpment, but only half of the community reached the top before the structure collapsed. Meetings were held by those at the top, and a painful consensus was finally reached: those who remained at the bottom would be left behind as *ilmeekurre kishulare*, "those who are no longer part of us." Today Maasai people refer to this separation as a beginning of a new era in Maasai history, as in "this has been happening since we ascended the cliff."[4]

This new era was one of a different life than had been known for many generations, as a time of expansion and prosperity, *Peyie eilepuni te ndikirr e Kerio*. During this period Maasai moved into their full homeland which came to extend 700 miles north to south and 200–400 miles east to west.[5] Roughly fifteen *iloshon*, sections, were formed as sovereign governing units as Maasai settled in different areas, each developing their own cultural expressions while remaining knitted through age groups and the ceremonies that bound generations. Some small number splintered into groups on the edges of Maasai society, speaking the Maa language but adopting new economies.[6] *Olosho le Maa* includes all of these, while "Maasai" solidified as those who strove to lead a fully pastoral life with the hardship that life implies. In that life, Maasai had to reckon with the wildlife that shared the land, the elephants, zebras, and antelopes that grazed the same grasses, and the lions, leopards, and hyenas that preyed on Maasai cattle, goats, sheep, and donkeys. The decision to coexist rather than drive out and destroy these animal communities would not have been a given but a decision made after serious debate, *aadung enkig'uena*. Coexistence was instilled through the culture which includes strict taboos against hunting and eating wild animals, and it is embedded in the structure of Maasai clans, each of which identifies with and is assigned the protection of specific wildlife. Wildlife thrived in Maasailand as herds grew through the expansion of Maasai culture into the broader ecosystem. Scholar Jim Igoe speculated that "Maasai herding regimes transformed East African landscapes … in favor of wildlife … through the exclusion of farms and permanent agricultural settlements" a change that likely took place over the course of "thousands of years."[7] It is easy to look at the density of wildlife in Maasailand as a feature of untouched "nature." But in fact, it is a built environment, nurtured over hundreds or thousands of years by the zebu cattle of the Maasai and "the typical Maasai economy" of pastoralism.[8]

The relationship of Maasai to wildlife is an extension of Maasai relationship to cattle, as the people are not whole in their identity apart from this coexistence. That means violence must be embraced as a part of life as people and animals do sometimes kill each other. Violence is ritualized in an extensive ceremonial life through which domestic animals are slaughtered for food. It is also ritualized through selective killing of certain wildlife, especially lions and some birds that were hunted in the course of the training of *ilmurran*, warriors. Violence is also employed to maintain borders with the wildlife, and individual animals are sometimes killed if they attack human beings or otherwise resist recognition of negotiated borders between them.

Violence was broadly incorporated into the political economy of Maasailand though *injorin*, raiding for cattle, which functioned similarly to versions of raiding among Indigenous peoples in the North American southwest. Like the British in Maasailand, Spanish settlers in what is now New Mexico, Arizona, and Texas saw raiding as undisciplined acts of savagery. But "raiding" among the Apache and Comanche functioned instead to maintain a balance of power between pastoral and farming communities, redistributing accumulated wealth in cattle and producing permeable yet clearly defined borders between them and Pueblo societies.[9] Today it is reported that raiding is remembered in the ritual life of the Pueblo communities as a kind of violence that was restorative to the land and people. Women and children taken in raids would be incorporated into captor societies, and through the violence of rupture from their original communities, they became the linguistic and cultural translators between farmers and herders that enabled them to share resources in times of food shortages and other crises.[10] Raiding became a most effective tactic of war against Spanish, and then later US armies, as it prevented settlement and outmaneuvered colonizing agendas.

Raiding functioned similarly in Maasai oral history. Before colonization raiding by both Maasai and neighboring farming communities maintained borders among them, to prevent an unsustainable concentration of cattle in agricultural areas that created competition for grazing land. Raiding was also used by Maasai to recover herds after disasters such as droughts. In oral history, *injorin* was practiced between Maasai and other pastoralists such as the Kalenjin, and also Kikuyu and other farming communities, who would raid when Maasai were seen to have become weakened. *Injorin* might not involve any bloodshed if the cows were relinquished willingly. But resistance could lead to casualties on both sides, and then also to larger conflict, in which many people might be killed. In that case, survivors would be absorbed into the community of the victors. Maasai oral history describes fully collaborative relationships with some non-Maasai peoples, especially the Ogiek, with whom they shared meat, honey for ceremonial brews, herbs, and knowledge of forests. But stricter borders were maintained with agricultural peoples, whose economies led them to constantly seek to expand into new territory. Maasai historian Naomi Kipury found that the oral histories of many communities in East Africa are "riddled with stories about their encounters with the Maasai" who were considered by many to be fierce and feared enemies.[11]

It is common knowledge in Maasailand that *injorin* was not undertaken to expand territory or acquire goods, or for any reason other than to gather livestock; in fact, the Maa word literally translates as "going to bring back cows."

In that way, *injorin* expressed the moral fabric of Maasai culture as even today Maasai consider themselves the rightful owners of all cows, and also those responsible to protect them. The Maasai motivation to increase the size of their herds through *injorin* was aligned with an equal desire and duty to liberate cows, especially those who are (disgracefully) yoked and put under the plow in farming communities. Liberating cows to graze on the open plains is remembered in song as an expression of the bravery of warriors. *Injorin* was thus part of a broader political economy that established cultural as well as economic borders among pastoral and farming communities, keeping all from becoming dominant. From all appearances farming, fishing, hunting, and pastoral communities in East Africa were thriving at the time of the British encounter, each in their own ecological habitats.[12] As the Maasai-built environment provided habitat not just for massive herds of wildlife but also for cattle, goats, and sheep, the British who first encountered Maasailand described Maasai as one of the richest tribes in the world.[13]

But that prosperity also threatened the balance of power in Maasailand, leading to a full-scale war among the *iloshon* just before the arrival of the British, in the middle of the nineteenth century. War, *enara*, is rare in Maasai history, and the *Laikipiak* war is the only one in memory. It happened in the time of *Ilaimer* in the mid-1800s, when one *olosho*, the *Laikipiak*, became "arrogant" and began to seek territorial control over the whole of the community. The *Laikipiak* gradually asserted exclusive ownership of land, rivers, and other resources, driving other *iloshon* and their cattle away, and "punishing" those who did not comply. After many failed efforts to restore negotiation, the other *iloshon* banded together to defeat into submission the *Laikipiak olosho* in a total war referred to by a rarely used Maa word, *iloikop*,[14] which refers to the murder of a Maasai person by a Maasai person. The word itself is a curse. Many men died in the *Laikipiak* war, as many as several hundred, though no women and children as their murder would be taboo under any circumstances. The last battle took place at *Oloorashat*, near Lake Elmenteita, by a rock formation said to be a warrior sleeping. The defeat of the *Laikipiak* people was not celebrated as it is remembered as "*Peyie eoro tolooshat*," a time when "we wiped out our own people."

Under normal circumstances, justice in Maasailand is meted out by courts assembled of community members. Those guilty of crimes as serious as murder are not incarcerated or physically punished in anyway; punishment is assigned to the clan of that person, and is paid in livestock to the clan of the victim or victims. The process is restorative in that the pain of loss is distributed to the whole clan who are held responsible for the behavior of an individual. When the *Laikipiak* war ended, there were too many deaths to process in this traditional way, and no way to assign blame to any parties. Instead, oral history remembers that the community was restored differently in the aftermath. Fighting stopped when *Laikipiak* men surrendered, and no survivors were punished at that point. They were allowed to retain their cattle and to join an *olosho* of their choosing where they would be accepted with the full rights of citizenship. Donkol ole Keiwa is a descendent of *Laikipiak* and his ancestors became *Purko* after the war. In his view, after the war ended, there was no bitterness, and that "as a Maasai person, when you go through some difficulty and survive, you don't have to be haunted by the past."[15]

When the British first encountered Maasailand at the conclusion of the war, they found a well-defended territory, a biodiverse landscape produced through grazing and some controlled burning to clear brush from tsetse flies. The prowess of Maasai warriors had prevented other attempts at infiltration of Maasai territory, especially the interregional trade in elephant and rhino tusks and human slavery which was facilitated through Arab caravans that crossed Maasailand from Mombasa to Lake Victoria.[16] Sources agree that Maasai may have extracted tribute from the caravans but otherwise treated them with disdain and did not allow them to make inroads among Maasai people, or to raid for slaves or hunt wildlife in Maasai territory.[17] Written history claims that the caravans worked in collaboration with Swahili, Kamba, and Kikuyu people who lived North and East of Maasailand. The caravans typically included hundreds of porters, who carried goods on foot, and many *askaris*, police. They were the means through which British reconnaissance came into Maasailand, in the mid-nineteenth century, and later British troops.[18]

Everything changed with the full arrival of the British in the 1870s, the time of *Iltalala*, when the many centuries of prosperity ended, and Maasai entered a protracted war that would last in various forms through the colonial era. Maasai were nearly destroyed in the first three decades of invasion. In English, that period of destruction is known as the "Triple Disasters" which are presented as serendipitous acts of God or nature that cleared a path for British settlement: in 1889 and 1893 two diseases transmitted from Europe—*Entidiyai* (Smallpox) and *Olodua* (Rhinderpest)—devastated the Maasai people and their cattle in unrelenting waves. A third disaster, an untimely drought, consumed the region. But the period is known differently in Maasailand as *Emutai*, the time of death, and *Enkidarroto*, "when the people were almost finished," a time of British conquest, when disease and violence worked in concert with warfare and other manipulations to destroy Maasai society.[19] In 1890, *Olosho le Maa* was further rocked by the death of the chief *oloiboni* Mbatiany, the spiritual leader of the whole community who had predicted the British invasion in a vision of a giant snake crossing Maasailand, dividing it in two, along the path of the eventual British railroad. The British declared Kenya to be a British protectorate in 1895.

The borders of the Kenyan and Tanganikan colonies had been drawn at the Berlin Conference in 1884–5, and they divided *Olosho le Maa* into those colonized by the British in the north and the Germans in the south. The colonial office in Tanganika was not established until after the turn of the twentieth century and it was located on the coast, in what is now the capital city of Dar es Salam. Tanganikan Maasai lived further from the headquarters of the colonial administration there than was the case in Kenya, and Germans tended to settle in the more fertile lands further south of the colony, not in Maasailand. Britain occupied Tanganika after its victory over the Germans in the First World War. But Maasailand continued to be governed after that time as part of two different colonies, with those on the southern side of the border possibly less interfered with than Kenyan Maasai in the early colonial period.

The most enduring story of the Maasai past, one taught in Kenyan schools and repeated as fact in many scholarly sources, is that Maasai did not defend themselves and their lands against colonial occupation and instead "collaborated" with the British. Both Maasai oral history and the historical record left by the British refute that claim. The British found *Olosho le Maa* to in fact be the one society that it could not break, and their conquest and occupation of Maasailand were undertaken through violence. This is the story told especially in *The Administrative History of the Masai Reserve*,[20] published in 1919, which was commissioned by the British crown in a period of escalating Maasai resistance and British war. The book was apparently written to rationalize the extent of British brutality in Maasailand, referred to as the "peculiar policy necessary in dealing with the Masai." The author, colonial secretary George Ritchie Sandford, claimed that in other ethnic communities in the Kenyan colony, British policies, especially the reservation system, had "produced a native so well under control" that they had not used force to contain them. But Maasai would not comply.

> The Masai were among the first tribes which came into contact with the administration but their conservatism has been so great, and their subservience to antiquated tribal custom and tradition has been so powerful that it has proved impossible as yet materially to alter and renovate their ideas. Why this peculiar policy is necessary.[21]

The British undertook the colonization of Maasailand through a multipronged strategy of extreme violence, attempts to incite conflict between warriors and elders, attempts to bribe some leaders, to invent others, to fabricate treaties to mask forced evictions, and by skewing their reports to the colonial administration back in London.

From a British line of sight, Maasailand stood in the way of their goal to outcompete other European powers for control of East Africa. They especially sought to supplant the Arab-run trade route between Mombasa and Lake Victoria, the headwaters of the Nile River. As they moved inland from the coast toward the Lake, the British encountered many tribal communities starting with the Indigenous coastal communities, then the Kamba, farmers closely involved with Arab trade, then the Kikuyu living around Mt. Kenya, north of Nairobi. But it was the Maasai who occupied the large stretch of previously unpenetrated territory to the west that stood between them and their full control of the route. The British first built forts; later they would create a bureaucratic infrastructure to redistribute and contain different tribal communities on reservations. The vast majority of land eventually seized by the British would be Maasai, and they laid claim to it through the garble of their own mispronunciations: *Enaiposha* became "Naivasha." *Emakat* became "Magadi." *Oltereet* became "Eldoret." *Kirtalu* became Kitale. In fact, many places in Rift Valley and Central Kenya today have names that are mutilated versions of the original *Maa*.[22]

It has been documented that the British Empire destroyed evidence of the atrocities through which they conquered subject peoples throughout the world, and Sandford's history suggests that punitive campaigns were initially waged widely against East African communities in the early years.[23] This question requires more research. The British claimed that they did not need to wage "punitive expeditions" against the Kikuyu and Kamba to bring them under control though this is likely false.[24] But nonetheless they reported that the period of "pacification" of the Kamba and Kikuyu was successful, and had

> to a large extent achieved the result ….of developing the native inhabitants of the Province into useful agricultural labourers fit for residential work on European farms and available for duty on works of public utility, and they have … a type of native … well under control.[25]

Maasai was the one "tribe" that would not submit, and so the British determined that the culture must be destroyed if colonization were to succeed. Commissioner Charles Eliot[26] said in a 1903 report,

> The customs of the Masai may be interesting to anthropologists, but morally and economically they seem to me to be all bad, and it is our duty, as it will also be to our advantage, to change them as soon as it is practicable … [Naivasha Maasai

must be made to settle,] instead of straying about with large herds of inferior cattle and sheep, which are reported to be of little use to the owners and of none at all to anyone else. It is also desirable to break up the tribes as far as possible, and discourage assemblies of warriors, circumcision, ceremonies, etc., which all conduce to raiding.[27]

Sandford's history includes detailed descriptions of one of the main tactics of British war against the Maasai, which was to leverage the caravan system to deepen slave raiding into Maasai territory.[28] In the early years of *Emutai*, Maasai had intensified raiding, to restore herds that had been destroyed in places by disease. Raids were undertaken against the British and the Arab traders and those they dealt with, Kikuyu and Kamba, as well as other tribes further west. *Injorin* was employed strategically against the British who found it to be very frustrating. Maasai mobility equalized to some extent the relative power of spears to guns. But raiding meant leaving Maasai territory. By 1897, Commissioner Arthur Hardinge explained that Maasai warriors had to "go long distances to raid for cattle, and thus leave their kraals almost undefended." He said,

> [T]he Wakamba and Wa-Kikuyu would be on the watch for these raiding expeditions, and, as soon as one was well on the way, would swoop down on the undefended or only partially defended kraal in overwhelming numbers, and the raiders would return with their spoil only to find their houses in ashes, and the women and children whom they left behind there carried off to be sold as slaves.[29]

The slave trade saw such a sudden increase in Maasai women and children in these years that it was reported that "[t]hese they are now selling at low rates, having more of them than they want, to local Arab or Swahili middlemen ... and to the natives throughout eastern Ukamba."[30]

At this time, in the wake of the US Civil War and abolition movements there and in Europe, the British had taken a public position against chattel slavery. They claimed that slave raiding had increased in the East African interior only because their own anti-slavery policies had driven the practice from the coast. They said that this interior slaving was done against their authority.[31] But the written record supports instead that the raiding happened under British protection, apparently through an alliance with the Kamba community. The British promised farms in Maasailand to Kamba people as a buffer between Maasai society and the planned Ugandan railroad line. The slave trade was facilitated out of Kitui, on the road between the British Fort Machakos in Kamba territory and the Mombasa port. Maasai kidnappings happened primarily in the vicinity of the fort, the land of *Ilkaputei* Maasai bordering Kamba territory.[32] British administrators celebrated the outcome of the expansion of the slave trade into Maasailand, Hardinge himself boasting in 1895 that Maasai

> have at last been defeated and broken up by the superior force of the Wakamba and Wa-Kikuyu, and, having had their old military organization utterly shattered, have accepted, and to a great extent are really controlled by the authority of the European district officers.[33]

While *Kaputei* Maasai were devastated by slave raiding, the trade was never able to penetrate beyond the escarpment west of the highlands of Nairobi into *Purko* territory. The expansion of the trade into western Maasailand was stopped by a fierce battle known as the Kedong massacre in the time of *Iltuati*, in 1895. The slave trade had peaked according to British accounts between 1892 and 1895, where "not a month passed without serious troubles in connection with slaving and slave-trading" in Maasailand. The Kedong massacre was an attempt by *Purko* Maasai to end the British use of slavery as a tactic of war by destroying the caravan. The battle did halt the advance of the trade further west and thus *Purko* Maasai "won" the battle. But the win came at a steep price.

Charles Ole Takai was told the story of Kedong by his grandmother. She remembered that a group of Maasai girls were captured by slave raiders while fetching water at a stream on a stretch of land between Mt. Longonot, *Oldoinyio Loonongot*, Mount Suswa, *Oldoinyio Onyokie*, and the Mau escarpment. This was a first such raid from a slaving caravan into the homeland of the *Purko* Maasai. As caravans also transported British soldiers and supplies, they were considered weapons of the British war in Maasailand. Two of the girls escaped capture and ran to warn a nearby *manyatta*, a warrior village. Warriors from the village ran to the top of Mt. Suswa to blow a horn signaling a call to battle while others ran as far as Kijabe and *Kinopop* (Kinangop) to gather as many *Purko* warriors as could be assembled. Many hundreds gathered at the *manyatta* over the next several days and they discussed and finally agreed that the caravan must be destroyed. They deliberately attacked in the low visibility of the hour before sunset, without warning, and they killed every man they found. Two "muzungus," the Swahili word for "white people," escaped and informed the British military, she said. A large contingent of soldiers arrived a week later and they retaliated by ambushing the *manyatta* that had organized the attack. In the account of Ole Takai's grandmother, British troops surrounded the *manyatta* in an organized fashion and began to fire on the men seeking shelter there. The warriors, with only spears, moved into the cattle kraal that forms the center ring of the village. Some hid from bullets behind cows, who were also slaughtered. The British continued to fire until no one was left alive.[34] Maasai warriors from as far away as Mt. Longonot and Aberedere were massacred there, possibly many hundreds.[35]

In Maasai oral history, the Kedong massacre changed the dynamics of the British war against the Maasai in several ways. It is known in oral history that an entire generation of warriors was scarred by the brutality of the massacre in the *manyatta*. Survivors of the age group, the *Iltuati* would assume leadership during the times of the British evictions beginning in 1904, and they would be more cautious in their dealing with the British than they might have been otherwise. However, the British use of slave raiding as a tactic of war in Maasailand was dealt an ultimately fatal blow at Kedong and slave raiding never again crossed the escarpment into *Purko* territory. The caravan was destroyed for a time, and that impacted the war as it had been necessary to supplying punitive expeditions in Maasailand, though it would be replaced by the Ugandan railroad on its completion in 1901.

Kedong also created a public relations problem for the local colonial administration. It might potentially expose the sanguine story of peaceful relations with the Maasai, what the local administration told to their superiors in London to be a lie. But it was an incident too large to be buried, and so it had to be explained. Sandford's official history, based on the reports of those local administrators, said that Swahili and Kikuyu traders had returned from Eldama Ravine in northern Maasailand after having carried out some "Government duty." As they camped at Kedong, some of the Swahilis snuck out and kidnapped two Maasai women from a kraal. In their escape, they fired in the village killing a cow. In this account, Maasai warriors spontaneously rose up and attacked the caravan in rage over the cow and the women. The story claims that a British "trader," Andrew Dick, happened to be in the area. He retaliated against the Maasai, presumably with employees of the caravan, and they killed "a considerable number of men," estimated by the British to have been at least one hundred. Dick is characterized in this story as having gone rogue, acting without British authority, and possibly motivated by a desire to steal Maasai cows. He was subsequently killed by a warrior while fleeing the scene up the escarpment with "a number of cattle."[36] Most difficult to accept in the official version is the claim that the British did not retaliate against the Maasai for destroying the caravan. Of 1,400 men traveling with the caravan, the British acknowledge that 456 were killed by Maasai warriors. But the official report claims Maasai had been justified in their attack because of the capture of the women. Sandford said, "As a result of the enquiry into these two incidents it was held that the Masai had been acting under such provocation that no great punishment was necessary."[37]

That Maasai had to be subdued through continuous force undercut the entire rationale for British presence in East Africa. The British claimed that their conquest of the land was driven by a "dual mandate" through which "savage" people like the Maasai would benefit from the example and tutelage provided by the rule of a "superior civilization." This rationalization was undermined by any evidence that the colonized peoples rejected British evictions and occupation. Events like the Kedong massacre threatened to expose Maasai as intelligent and skillful adversaries of war, not inferior supplicants. The British undertook other strategies to shore up their claims to a moral basis for conquest. They especially sought to compromise tribal leadership to recognize British colonial administration by appointing and paying a class of "government chiefs." That strategy was challenging because there were few if any existing chiefs authorized to speak on behalf of the different Indigenous nations in East Africa. Historian Robert Tignor found that "most of the Kenyan African peoples did not have individual rulers and were governed through councils of elders."[38] The British created their own "chiefs" by finding members of the tribes willing to be bought. They paid these willing men a small salary for their services collecting taxes and raising conscripts among their people for the British military.[39] But Tignor says that of the main East African communities colonized by the British, Maasai alone refused to comply. They "display[ed] no interest and even demonstrated ill-concealed hostility to [Kikuyu] type of colonial collaboration."[40] Tignor continues,

> Many of the Maasai chiefs were a different type of person from the Kikuyu collaborators. Although willing to hold office, they were distinctly not interested in active cooperation with the British. Proud and traditionally powerful men, they did not want to transform their society, but held office as a means of deflecting British pressure."[41]

Tignor's account was based on interviews conducted in the 1970s with Maasai, Kamba, and Kikuyu people, and is a rare direct written source about the experience of these communities in the colonial era. Tignor says that British records support his contention that of these communities, Maasai society maintained a unique degree of unity. He says that the majority of Maasai chiefs "shunned the organs of local government established by the British," and especially their pretense at criminal justice. He says that "Maasai settled their own disputes out of court"[42] and that in Maasailand, through the colonial era,

"No real collaborative administration arose. There was no para-administration, no commandeering of stock, and no corruption."[43] Tignor found that while other East African communities developed age-group structures, Maasai had "the most highly developed" of these, and that political authority of the community rested in age-group leadership.[44] This leadership was, and continues to be, appointed through the consensus of elders and of the age group itself. Leaders are identified in childhood for their exceptional qualities, which are nurtured throughout their lives and given special attention to their education. Age groups form through the education of Maasai men in warrior training which unites them in common knowledge and creates an identity that may exceed other identification by section or family; women join the age group of their husbands at marriage and adopt the status of that age. Esther Mwangi and Elinor Ostrom found in their research that it was (and is) this "social ecological system" of "nested governance" in Maasailand that accounts for the skill and success of Maasai diplomacy and ability to remain united in the face of British manipulations.[45] The age-group leadership in particular remained uncorrupted through the colonial era through its dense webbing of relationships. Naomi Kipury found that age groups across Maasailand were unified through the colonial period in spite of the distance between sections. She found that different *iloshon* maintained nearly identical stories of history across the breadth of Maasailand, and attributes that to the density of cultural unity among age mates.[46]

The British did consider a few Maasai men to be "friendly."[47] They worked with one genuine age-group leader of the *Iltuati*, Ole Gilisho. But according to Tignor and also to oral history, Ole Gilisho was known in the community to be "intensely suspicious of the British," who, when he cooperated with colonial authorities, "did so with the larger vision of preserving as much of Maasai tradition as possible."[48] That interpretation is consistent with Sandford's and other accounts. Nkapilil Ole Masikonte is another genuine age-group leader, of the *Iltalala*, who shows up in British records around the time of the 1910 evictions. But in general, government-appointed "chiefs" among the Maasai either used those positions to gain intelligence or were thought to have little social standing in the community. Maasai chiefs never built military organizations among their people to serve the British as Kamba and Kikuyu chiefs apparently had done.

Unable to find a genuine ally among the Maasai, the British invented one in the *oloiboni* Olonana. Olonana would have been the last person chosen by the British had they understood Maasai culture, as he was not an age-group leader and so had no culturally recognized leadership. Most importantly, Olonana came from a family of *Iloibonok*, spiritual leadership, and was thus a rare Maasai person prevented from involvement in governance of any kind. His role was to be available for spiritual guidance and to remain neutral about political issues. He was a young man likely occupied with his family's cattle before the British drew him into their orbit under the pretense that they had found a friendly *Purko* chief. *Iloibonok* are expected to welcome all seeking spiritual advice, even strangers, and the British likely found Olonana when they sought out his father Mbatiany at his home in Ngong, just west of Nairobi and a place of early encroachment by European settlers.[49] It is not clear whether Olonana exercised free will in his time in the British orbit. There is some recollection in oral history that he was imprisoned by the British "in a cage" at some point from which he escaped using the special powers of *oloiboni*. Significantly, Olonana died from a lingering illness in British custody, apparently without medical intervention, rather than the care of his family which would have been nonsensical in Maasai culture had he been free to choose where to convalesce. But unlike any other Maasai chief, Olonana was photographed sitting with British officers, in a picture widely used to create the impression of Maasai cooperation.

The British claimed that Olonana thumb-printed the "Agreement" they drafted in 1904 to provide cover for evictions from the Maasailand that would become the core of white settlement, in Naivasha and Nakuru, onto two Masai Reserves. He was said to have rejected the second eviction, of Maasai people from Laikipia, and would not support the second "agreement" drafted and signed by the British in 1911. But then British sources claimed that he reversed himself on his deathbed surrounded by British officers, as still a young man of about forty, and encouraged his people to accept the loss of Laikipia. To their superiors in Britain, local administrators often characterized Olonana as a man motivated by power hunger and petty jealousies.[50] Oral history does not provide a definitive answer to why Olonana was in the British orbit; elders suggest that being of the age group traumatized by the Kedong massacre, he may have sought to use British interest in him to establish diplomatic lines of communication and avoid the kind of violence of which he knew the British to be capable. What is clear is that the British kept him close just long enough to rationalize the last of the major evictions of the early colonial period, and the circumstances of his death suggest that he was not free to leave. Olonana's entire family left the area immediately after his death and settled in a new permanent home on the border of Tanzania where they continue to live. Maasai historian Donkol Ole Keiwa said, after visiting Olonana's family, that their move from the lush land at Ngong to dry hard land to the south suggests that his sons might have believed that the British killed their father and would now come for them. The family must have been traumatized. They moved to a place surrounded by hills that could be very well defended.[51]

There is also no evidence that either Olonana or his family benefited from his proximity to the British beyond a small chief's salary.[52]

The story of Olonana as a British ally was created after the massacre at Kedong. In spite of their own recorded evidence of escalating war with the Maasai, the British claimed to the Home Office in London that their skillful handling of the situation at Kedong had led them to win the support of a man they claimed to be the "supreme" Maasai chief, who they called "Lenana." In Sandford's account, Lenana,

> was so impressed with the impartial hearing given to the Masai witnesses, and with the justice of the decision [to not retaliate against the Maasai] that he vowed allegiance to the British Government, a vow which he faithfully kept. British justice on this occasion gained the friendship of the most powerful man in the Masai tribe, and rendered his influence warmly loyal to the administration from that day to the day of his death.[53]

This story apparently seemed plausible to those steeped in the racist hubris of the colonial imagination. As the progressive Norman Leys said, "Very typical is the immediate recognition by a savage people of a standard of justice higher than their own."[54] The myth of Lenana was used to reconstruct the broader story of British conquest of Maasailand as non-violent, and Maasai people as savages who were kept in check by a uniquely enlightened leader. In contradiction of its own earlier recounting of events, Sandford's *Administrative History* would later claim,

> No punitive expedition has ever been undertaken against the Masai, an omission which was very largely due to the authority and sagacity of Olonana, the chief medicine-man at the time when the European Government was first encountered, who survived long enough to keep his people in check until such a degree of administration had been effected as to render the dispatch of a punitive expedition a measure that would only be resorted to in the last extremity.[55]

When recognition of the British war in Maasailand was unavoidable, the British tried to recast it as a "civil war" among Maasai themselves, claiming that two armies led by Olonana and his brother Sendeu fought over supreme leadership of the Maasai people. Oral history recognizes rivalry between the brothers at the time of their father's death in 1890. But that matter was resolved by a Maasai court that deliberated and came to a solution by creating two territories and assigning one to each brother, to move forward with two chief *iloibonok*, instead of one. The claim of a civil war between *iloibonok* would never have been intended for a Maasai audience as it does not align with common sense. Physical conflict among *iloibonok* would have been a cultural breach of such magnitude that it would have destroyed permanently the entitlement of the family of Sendeu and Olonana and their position as spiritual leaders. However, today Maasai people still travel from across Maasailand to the family's home for spiritual guidance. The British account embeds other contradictory claims. Sandford suggests that while Olonana was a British ally, he also had to be constantly watched, and threatened with violence, to prevent him from aligning with Sendeu in a joint uprising of Maasai in the German and British territories. Commissioner Hardinge wrote in 1897:

> Of late there have been symptoms of unrest among the Masai, which have made it necessary to keep a careful watch on them. Sendeyo, Chief of the Loita division of the race, who wander sometimes in English and sometimes in German territory, has been endeavouring to persuade his brother Olonana, the Chief of the Masai of Naivasha, all of them on our side of the border, to join him in a general movement against the Germans in Kilimanjaro ....In anticipation of trouble in this quarter, I sent reinforcements to Taveta, and the simultaneous arrival of troops from Uganda at Naivasha and at Ngongo Bagas from Machakos seems to have induced Olonana to decline Sendeyo's proposals, which, though primarily directed against the Germans, really aimed at a general rising against all European control.[56]

Through the jumble of conflicting information, we can glimpse some coherent stories in Sandford's presentation of the escalating violence at the end of the nineteenth and early twentieth centuries. Occasional references to troop mobilization, such as the one cited above, support the oral history understanding of this period as one of large-scale war. The British appear to have been genuinely confused about who comprised Maasai leadership and the dynamics among them, suggesting that even Olonana was not an insider source on what would have been general knowledge in the community. Sandford's account suggests that the Maasai military used the British/German border strategically, raiding into German territory from the Kenyan colony, and vice versa, and then retreating back beyond the reach of either British or German troops who would not venture into each other's province.

Sandford's account also suggests that the British failed in their effort to recruit Maasai warriors to paid service as the military arm of the colonial administration. The British believed that Maasai might acquiesce in their weakened state following the Kedong massacre. Sandford said, "Masai raids may be said to have ceased after the year 1898, the last year in which they carried out a successful expedition against another tribe in the Protectorate."[57] At that point, beginning in 1899, Sandford claims that Maasai warriors in groups of a few hundred traveled alongside British forces and their punitive raids on other communities, which has been characterized in written history as an "alliance."[58] According to Sandford's own claim, the warriors were never paid wages, did not fight the communities under attack, agreed only to ride under their own leaders in separate columns, and were detailed specifically "to round up stock."[59] If true, the arrangement would not have favored British interests as it would have enabled Maasai to rebuild herds without engaging in war against other communities.

But there is no memory of an "alliance" between Maasai and British in oral history, where another interpretation is suggested. Maasai memory of this period is dominated by violence: the "total war" waged by the British that targeted the Maasai specifically, the advantage taken by other communities of sudden Maasai decline, and Maasai's own intensification of *injorin*, raiding other communities, to rebuild herds to regain strength. In oral history, Maasai were too weakened after the Kedong massacre to engage the British directly so they rebuilt their herds through raiding. It is from the British records that we learn that communities were subjected to the "punitive expeditions" of British troops, and the different agendas of the Maasai and British may have overlapped in ways that favored each at points. But there is no evidence in either British or Maasai history that Maasai shared the British agenda to conquer other East African communities, or to defeat them militarily, and no evidence that Maasai fought other communities directly alongside the British. Had there been an actual alliance, the British would have secured their own benefit in the arrangement as they would have enjoyed, by all accounts, the upper hand. What happened instead was that Maasai rebuilt their strength in this period after nearly perishing in the decade before, and their armed resistance continued into the twentieth century. The British lost significant ground in their war against the Maasai, complaining later that as it closed, Maasai had resumed their own "independent" raiding.[60]

The British understood Maasai raiding to be a tactic of war, and in the first decades of the twentieth century they moved swiftly to curtail it. They passed an extreme "stock theft ordinance" in 1913, through which they fined Maasai villages ten times the value of any cattle taken by warriors, a punishment which apparently had a "severe impact." British apparently hoped that this policy would drive a wedge between warriors and the elders who were ultimately held responsible to pay the fines for raiding undertaken by the young men.[61]

The story that Maasai collaborated with the British is not substantiated by the historical record yet it persists. Beyond the fictionalized account of Olonana, and the British claim that a brief alliance was formed as described above, no evidence has been offered of "collaboration," none found in archival or oral history, certainly none that can counter the volumes of evidence of warfare and resistance. There is no corroboration of British claims of collaboration in Maasai oral history. The historical record supports instead an opposite narrative: British colonization of Maasailand has been brutal and Maasai nearly did not survive the violence of British conquest. But they did survive through cultural unity, the strength of Maasai military, and by rebuilding and maintaining herds. Beyond the British claims about Olonana, Maasai leadership by all accounts was not corruptible, the community did not relinquish its own governance, and they emerged from the colonial era with some of their former lands under their cultural control, and with unbroken claims of the lands that had been occupied.

The British drafted two "agreements" to rationalize evictions of Maasai people undertaken in the course of the war between them. These were the only treaties[62] that the British apparently felt were necessary to justify removals of the peoples they conquered in all of East Africa. The "agreements" were each assembled in haste in an attempt to legitimate a prior seizure or promise of land for European settlement, and while the British claimed that known Maasai leaders thumb-printed written documents, there is no collective recognition in Maasai oral history, and all but a few of the signers are unknown as leadership or even as members of Maasai sections and families.[63]

Terms of the documents were hashed out among British administrators, and Maasai brought in once they were drafted to create an illusion of compliance. The 1904 Agreement followed a promise made by Commissioner Eliot to sell 500 square miles of Maasailand in the Rift Valley to the East African Syndicate, including 100,000 acres to Lord Delamere and 32,000 acres each to two British South Africans who immediately offered it for resale on the Johannesburg market.[64] Whistleblowers in the colonial administration got Eliot relieved of his post for this illegal action. But the sales were nonetheless honored, and a treaty drafted to legitimize the subsequent evictions of Maasai from the area. Eliot claimed he only did what was expected. He said,

> No doubt on platforms and in reports we declare we have no intention of depriving natives of their lands, but this has never prevented us from taking whatever land we want.[65]

The Agreement would evict Maasai from watered land to only the driest land in two separate reservations, one far north in Laikipia, and the other to a portion of Kajiado district today, initially excluding all of what is Narok County. Some British administrators sympathetic to the Maasai inserted language into that document in an attempt to safeguard their rights even to this land. The "Agreement" claimed that Maasai vacated the land "of our own free will" and "best interest."[66] But Maasai people expressed the opposite by refusing to leave where at all possible, and returning after forced removal, and "so neglected to carry out the terms of the agreement, as largely to destroy its meaning."[67] Colonial administrators admitted that "some pressure had to be put on the Masai of the Rift Valley to induce them to leave their grazing grounds"[68] and Norman Leys wrote that the Rift "was most unwillingly evacuated." An anonymous letter written to the Anti-Slavery Society claimed: "Masai very loth to leave. Villages burnt by Government."[69] The British also did not honor their own promises included in the Agreements, including that a road would be constructed to connect the northern and southern reserves, and that Maasai would have access to ceremonial grounds at *Kinapop*, Kinangop.

The second agreement of 1911 adopted the same strategy. A new EAP Commissioner, Percy Girouard, followed in Eliot's footsteps by illegally promising to sell to twenty-four settlers the same land at Laikipia promised for Maasai resettlement in 1904. Through Lotte Hughes' reconstruction in *Moving the Maasai*, we learn that Girouard lied to the Colonial Office in London about this and other things including the quality of the land in the Southern Reserve to which Laikipia Maasai were to be resettled.[70] The Colonial Office acknowledged the corruption later, one administrator asking rhetorically, "How far is it permissible to believe anything said to anybody in the East Africa Protectorate!"[71] But by then, by British count, 3,000 Maasai had been evicted from Laikipia, along with 15,000 cattle and 250,000 sheep and goats.[72] The British claimed that "no compulsion of any kind was used" in the move from Laikipia and only accompanied by "administrative and veterinary officers."[73] But other accounts claim that Maasai were removed at gunpoint from their villages in the north beginning long before the British drafted the Agreement. A person claiming to be an eyewitness reported that many Maasai people and cattle on the migration from Laikipia were dying of starvation, children and old people, who "begged to be allowed to return to the nearest available grazing" but were forced on "to the effect that they might stop and die, or go on and die." The informant said that what Maasai "feared most [was] death and outrage at the hands of the savage native soldiers at the orders presumably of those at the head of affairs."[74]

This account aligns with the community's oral history in which the evictions were unexpected and violent.

Maasai oral history continues to question whether any Maasai people participated in the "Agreements." According to Lotte Hughes in *Moving the Maasai*, Normal Leys "claimed to have proof that Maasai leaders had been ordered to sign a ready-made petition," and that Ole Gilisho had been "threatened with flogging and deportation" into signing. Ole Mootian "confirmed that such a petition had existed and was not signed willingly: 'There was nobody who agreed to be on the list. But if you have a gun pointed at you, will you agree or won't you?'"[75] Even if a handful of Maasai people had been forced to contribute their thumb-prints, they did not represent the recognized leadership of the whole community. Maasai oral history suggests that there were no Maasai people competent and trusted to both read and translate a document written in English, and that thumb-printing would have been an alien and meaningless ritual. As Maasai were known throughout East Africa for their fearless approach to defending Maasailand, Maasai people today argue that the claim that their grandparents would have agreed to vacate their homeland on the mere *threat* of British force lacks common sense.

In 1912, a group of Maasai men including Ole Gilisho, with the support of British reformers, filed a landmark legal action, the first indigenous litigation against the colonial state in East Africa. The suit sought to invalidate the 1911 treaty, which Ole Gilisho claimed that he had only thumb-printed under the threat of deportation, assumed in oral history to mean that he would have been covertly assassinated.[76] The case was heard by the East Africa Protectorate High Court but it was thrown out. One cause was that the treaties were considered to be "acts of state" and so colonial courts, defined as local courts, had no jurisdiction.[77]

The war with the British continued into the 1910s as the British colonial government turned its focus to destroying the culture of warriors and settling young Maasai men into "more productive occupations." But oral history and colonial records seem to agree that Maasai people completely and uniformly rejected British attempts to commercialize the economy of Maasailand and employ Maasai people. Maasai herds had become affected by inbreeding as raiding was curtailed and cows confined to the Masai Reserve. Nonetheless, Maasai refused British attempts to crossbreed their cows with European stock, which would have made them less able to survive drought, or to establish a cattle industry in Maasailand which would have transformed cattle into a commodity. Sandford complained that the "wealth of the Masai, therefore, is turned to no good purpose; their style of living does not change; they are still content to live in low buildings constructed of poles, grass and mud, in conditions of filth that defy description." Yet Maasai showed "no great desire to utilize their wealth in the purchase of imported articles and in the improvement of their diet."[78]

British records also acknowledge what is known in oral history that Maasai consistently refused to cooperate with colonial police through the years of formal colonization. Through the British colonial Collective Punishments Ordinance of 1909, colonized subjects who refused to assist police in finding "criminals" on tribal reservations would be punished as whole sections rather than individuals. Sandford reported that "the great majority of impositions of fines" under the ordinance were applied in the Masai reserve. He continued,

> Under any circumstances, the "Muran" [warriors] offer no assistance in the tracking down of the criminal and the elders, though professing detective zeal, are powerless to intervene. The attitude of the section involved in such cases is one of surprise and listlessness–they never know anything–and the collective fine which may ensue has not hitherto had the result of discouraging the adoption of such an attitude.[79]

The long-standing British agenda to force Maasai into paid police work was equally ineffective. Specifically, after 1902, the British sought to enlist Maasai warriors in the King's African Rifles (KAR), a colonial regiment that trained and employed Africans as the security forces in British colonies, under British officers and who fought abroad for the British during the First and Second World Wars. KAR service came with perks; it paid relatively well and rank-and-file *askaris*, police, enjoyed some limited power in exchange for their work protecting the British against the African people. But the British were discouraged in Maasailand. Even when Maasai were physically forced into service, they could not be made to work. They had "proved to be passive resisters, who had generally been discharged, after months of training, as unlikely to become efficient policemen."[80]

Maasai also refused government attempts to educate them in inferior and racist colonial schools.[81] Tignor found that a planned school in Narok was "part of a larger scheme being developed by the British officer in charge of the Masai Reserve" R.W. Hemsted, to destroy Maasai culture. In 1918 Hemsted imposed a tax on head of cattle to force Maasai to shrink their herds and transform the reserve into "a big ranch or estate." Maasai warriors were to be turned into wage workers, and it was in the context of this agenda that children would be forced into government "Native" school in Narok. While this strategy was employed by Europeans across the continent, few societies fought as hard against schooling as the Maasai. As Tignor found in his interviews with Maasai of this generation,

> It is difficult for an outsider to grasp the full measure of their opposition. [Maasai] likened school going to an unbearable loss comparable to the death or enslavement of a person. They felt that if children went to school they would be lost forever to Maasai society.[82]

British pressure on Maasai conscription mounted during the First World War and reached a tipping point in 1918. In that year, a failed campaign to conscript Maasai warriors into the KAR resulted in the *Ololulunga* massacre. According to British sources, On August 25 "a half company of King's African rifles, with machine guns" were sent to Narok where *Purko* warriors were refusing conscription. The warriors were "displaying a defiant attitude," and the KAR would "enable the Government to be in a position to deliver an ultimatum" and arrest the "ringleaders."[83] An even more aggressive policy was agreed upon at a meeting held in Nairobi with the Acting Governor, Assistant Commandant of the KAR, and the Officer in Charge of the Masai Reserve. All men in the Masai Reserve under age thirty-five would be conscripted into the KAR; a full company of KAR were stationed at Narok to carry out this order, and all warriors and elders who defied these orders would be imprisoned.[84] In response, Maasai elders and the "head moran," *olaig'uanani* Ole Pere of the *Iltareto* age group, were said by the British to have agreed to provide recruits, and the warriors were to receive training at Bukoba on Lake Victoria. But in spite of the claim of compliance, all of *Iltareto* warriors defied the KAR when it arrived to collect them. According to the interviews conducted by Robert Tignor, the warriors "had decided to live in the forest where they would rather die than be taken for the King's African Rifles."[85] Thus either there was no agreement between the elders and Ole Pere, or the elders and Ole Pere did not speak for the warriors.

In Sandford's account of the *Ololulunga* massacre, the KAR troops followed the warriors to a village where they were believed to have slept, and surrounded it, and then opened fire to destroy the village. But after their attack they found no warriors; instead, they had killed two women, an old man, and ten cows. In that account, the warriors retaliated on September 10 by attacking the same company before dawn at the Ololulunga trading center. Fourteen warriors were reported to have been killed and another fifty or sixty wounded, many dying later, including the leaders of the resistance. After this Sandford says, "Order collapsed throughout the district." He recorded that Maasai burned more than fifty shops in Narok and Mara, and cut telegraph lines between Narok and Elmenteita in Naivasha. British military stamped out the revolt, which led to the further militarization of Narok, but the *Purko* Maasai never did turn over conscripts. A system of continuous mounted patrols was thereafter established in the settler areas to the north of the reserve to prevent warriors from returning to the Mau Forest.[86]

As was the case regarding the Kedong Massacre, a very different story of the *Ololulunga* massacre exists in the oral history of the Maasai community. For Maasai people, *Ololulunga* represents a resolute stand of Western Maasai society against British colonization: a unified rejection of forced education, taxation, enforced military recruitment, and a deep-seated desire to return to *Kinopop* and *Entorror* and regain the lost territory from the 1911 evictions. The interviews conducted by Tignor support this understanding. They reveal that the Maasai community saw schooling for the danger it presented and the role it played in larger British designs to destroy the culture. It is not clear in oral history who struck first at *Ololulunga*; the conflict is grouped in Maasai memory with others happening at the same time, as part of more or less continuous violent conflict. While the warriors did not win the skirmish in the short term, Tignor affirms, "they were more successful than they realized."

> The school which they opposed opened under inauspicious circumstances. Probably its limited impact among the Purko owed much to the rebellion. Moreover, no other government schools were opened in Narok district for some time, and a government school was not started in Kajiado district until 1927. The independent warrior action had the effect of slowing educational work among the Maasai.[87]

Hemsted, who had been the "architect" of the plan, apparently learned from this experience that Maasai would not be controlled until the military arm of Maasai society had been destroyed, and that became the focus of administrative policy in Narok for the next two decades—to disarm warriors and take apart *manyattas*, warrior villages. A 1927 annual report from Kajiado describes this policy, which would turn Maasai into British-style stock managers through

> the gradual elimination of the old warrior companies of "sirits" [*isirito*, warrior companies] and the whole of the military tribal organization bound up with them: [and] the gradual spread of education among the boys now growing up.[88]

This period of war culminated in a more serious massacre in 1922 known as *Oloisuisho* in Maa and the Ilkitoip Rebellion in English. Maasai warriors of the *Iltareto* age group, *Ilmeiruturrut* age set, were hounded by the newly aggressive level of British warfare. Government troops were present throughout Narok district which included the European and Kikuyu settler colonial farms in Nakuru and Naivasha. Threatened with disarmament and with no *manyatta* safe from attack, warriors from as far away as Transmara moved to isolated areas in the Mau Forest to establish a compound that could be defended. Maasai accounts state that there had been talk among the warriors about leading their people from there back to Laikipia, to the north, *Entorror*. British administrators claimed that the warriors, led by "Laitetti and al-Kanyara,"[89] had leveled death threats against their own elders, including Ole Masikonte and Ole Gilisho. The British also claimed that the warriors threatened their own age-group spokesperson, Kuntai ole Sangalle, who had advocated "negotiation," rather than fighting.[90] Oral history contradicts the claim that the warriors threatened to assassinate their own leadership. The claim should be scrutinized in any case as it was used to justify an otherwise illegal first-strike British attack on the warrior's *manyatta* in the forest. In British accounts, the "massacre" would be described as a skirmish, a surprise attack on the *manyatta* to prevent a planned "guerrilla warfare" and the threatened assassinations.

Maasai sources remember something very different. The then-current warriors, the *Iltareto* age group, refused to be conscripted and they were determined to return to reclaim Laikipia. Hundreds of warriors gathered in a clearing buried deep in the Mau Forest, with ample pasture and water, and they built a *manyatta*. The clearing was shown to them by Ogiek neighbors and surrounded like a fortress by dense thicket, guarded by warriors stationed a mile outside along the only "road" providing passage. The *manyatta* is referred to by descendants of the survivors as a "training camp" where members of a whole generation were based with enough pasture, cattle, and water to survive for many years. According to these descendants, the British attack was undertaken to destroy the *Iltareto* in one motion. British troops were led around the back of the encampment by an Ogiek guide[91] and attacked at dawn, using machine guns for the first time in people's memory. The bullets from the guns continued to be lodged in surrounding trees hundreds of yards from where the *manyatta* stood, trees that were said to have become warriors themselves, protecting the *Iltareto* who ran from the British as they pursued the warriors deeper into the forest.[92] At least several wounded warriors escaped along the main path, and they ran another mile to caves where they nursed their wounds with soups made from herbs. Their attempts at recovery and eventual deaths are evidenced by stone bowls strewn around the site, and by their bones which still reside in the cave.[93]

British records say that they killed ten warriors and wounded fifteen and drove the rest out of the *manyatta* and then took 2,300 head of cattle. They say that an additional 210 warriors were arrested and 167 were jailed, and seven of these were executed.[94] Maasai say many hundreds died that day in the forest. But in oral history, the spirit of the *Iltareto* was not broken as the British intended. What is remembered is the brutal violence of guns and the fact laid bare that, in spite of their pretense of educating and "civilizing" the Maasai, the British agenda was to annihilate them.

The British issued a final report on the events of 1922 three years later. It claimed that the conflict at *Oloisuisho* had no "political" significance and was due to an excess of "animal spirits" of the warriors. The report claimed that Ole Masikonte blamed the conflict on the rebelling warriors, and quoted him saying that "if there were no more moran, there would be no further trouble." But the report also, in a contradictory fashion, supported the interpretation of the event in oral history. It acknowledged that the massacre arose in the context of "the endeavors of the administration to carry out a policy which intended the elimination of [the warrior] institution and the consequent abolition of the cattle manyattas."[95] *Oloisuisho* has great significance to many *Purko* elders, for whom the entire period is a time of heightened British warfare waged to finally destroy the Maasai warrior class, a period generally referred to by the name *Ololulunga* massacres. The massacres continue to resonate in the everyday life of Maasai people, who still ask, *Ishomo e suuji enaa Ilmeruturut?* translated as, "what is the offense that our people made to be attacked with such violence by the British?" People remind each other of the lesson learned by the *Ilmeruturut* age set, when they are about to undertake something risky, that you may face a punishment beyond your imagination. Even today the trauma of British war is evident every time Maasai children run into the bush in fear at the sight of a police uniform, and people assume that no one survives being arrested. The current generation was not alive at that time of British war, but they remember.

The *Oloisuisho* massacre culminated the early colonial period, a time in which the resistance of warriors was most disruptive to the primary British agenda: to secure land for settlement. That first era of mass evictions ended with *Oloisuisho* and a stalemate: the British had failed to force Maasai to fight for them. But as settlement grew so had the infrastructure of British police in the settlement areas, and so warrior resistance was curtailed. The following roughly forty years until Kenyan Independence are characterized by more typically stealthy resistance and, as some Maasai achieved literacy and English language, insipient organizing in response to new colonial policy. Less research has been done into the oral and written source history of this period, but a few events stand out.

One of these is the Rotian Riot in British history, the *Ilterito* uprising in Maasai, a revolt against forced labor of the *Ilterito* age group. In 1935, colonial authorities had built forced labor camps in parts of Maasailand to try again to dismantle the community's own cultural education in warrior training. By forcing wage work, the British were also trying to create the conditions in which they could tax Maasai people. They created a forced labor camp in Narok and incarcerated all Maasai warriors of *Ilterito* age group whom they could capture. The warriors were made to construct a trade road from Narok to Nakuru, running through Rotian and the farm of Powys Cobb at Mau Narok. Oral history suggests that they had been compromised by their age-group leader who had come to accept the British offer to collaborate with them, for which he received special treatment. But the *Ilterito* rejected his leadership, and they organized, and 100 of them came from far away Mellili and Mau Forest to liberate their agemates. They raided the police station and managed to leave with 120 warriors. The age-group leader who had collaborated with the colonial government was subject to *Aawuparie Orinka*, removal of his leadership club and in essence culturally dethroned, remembered as a rare occurrence in Maasai history.[96]

There is also insipient evidence of Maasai resistance that took the form of lobbying the colonial government in this period, creating a trail of written evidence still accessible in the Kenyan National Archives. The 1934 Kenya Land Commission (KLC) was convened to hear complaints about land allocation and management, and Maasai sought a hearing. Authors of a memorandum to the KLC described the Masai Reserve as

> waterless and without forest [and] it will be agreed that it is totally inadequate and utterly unsuitable for the requirements of a nomadic people with a pastoral occupation as we are invariably described.

The KLC dismissed the Maasai request for a hearing. But one member, a Provincial Commissioner S.F. Deck, filed a minority report that agreed that Maasai needed land, as 2 million acres of the Reserve were "either waterless of fly infested." This was supported that same year by a government scientific report on the Reserve, which suggested that almost one-third of the reserve, 3 million acres, was either arid or semi-arid, and that 800,000 acres were infested with tsetse fly and 300,000 with East Coast Fever. Maasai argued that the loss of the drought reserves and generally diminished land base led to overgrazing and soil erosion.[97] When the KLC ruled in favor of outside settlers encroaching on the Masai Reserve, Maasai people delivered a series of letters and petitions to the Commission, calling for an acknowledgment of their land rights.[98] In one letter Maasai in Kajiado reported the theft of 1,045 cattle by government officials and sixty-five arrests of Maasai herders for "trespassing" on their own land. When the government offered below-value compensation to resolve the growing complaints, the Maasai replied "No," in a petition with 134 signatures, "we prefer land to cash."[99]

There was less settlement of Maasailand across the border in Tanganika through most of the colonial era. There were attempts to introduce livestock economies to Maasailand in the 1930s, mass production of milk and meat, and sights set on converting wildlife-rich areas to National Park status, as was happening also north of the border in Kenya. Serengeti National Park was demarcated, but Maasai still had their traditional access to grazing there. But that changed with the British need to fund the Second World War, and more Maasailand was grabbed and converted to wheat, barley, and coffee farms. The critical shift happened in 1959 when all Maasai were evicted from Serengeti in anticipation of Tanganikan Independence in 1961. Maasai were promised that Ngorongoro and other lands would be theirs "for all time," and water sources were promised but not delivered. The economy of the state of Tanzania today continues to be reliant on trophy hunting in Maasailand, which has been fused there with "conservation" as it was originally in Kenya. Maasai in Tanzania were drawn into the very different nation-state governance than those in Kenya, attempting a more "socialist" model through Julius Nyere's Ujamaa "cultural revolution," which pushed collective farming and villagization on Maasai and other Tanzanian people. These policies explicitly sought to erase separate cultural identities: Maasailand was most impacted by "Operation Dressup," which extended regulatory power to the state over cultural expression through hair, clothes, and jewelry; and Operation Mparnet, or permanent settlement, which involved forced evictions through which families were often separated.

The Second World War brought new pressures to force Maasai into armed service, but these continued to be unsuccessful. Thus, the pressure shifted to confiscation of Maasai cattle for sale to white settlers, who had few of their own following war-time food shortages. In 1946, the then District Commissioner of Narok, Major Grant, undertook a massive cattle confiscation effort throughout the district. A conflict erupted, well known in oral history, when one Maasai man, Sendeu from *Olosho le Loita*, asked that a particular bull that he was attached to not be taken and substituted for another. For whatever reason, Major Grant refused and insisted on that particular bull. In the ensuing struggle, Sendeu speared Major Grant in the head, killing him instantly.[100] In oral history, a military contingent was sent to Loita and scores of people were killed, and many others arrested. Sendeu himself was hanged. But the British are also said to have not returned and they stopped that particular taxation effort.

Through this era leading up to Independence in 1963, Maasai communities retained the memory of the occupied land in specificity. We know this because of the work of the Maasai United Front (MUF). As described in Chapter 3, the MUF traveled through Maasailand to gather information from local places about specific illegal instances of occupation, and they produced a document that presented this research to the British government in London. While they were defeated in their immediate effort to be recognized in the formation of the Kenyan state, their work was clearly not in vain. The precious knowledge they gathered might well have been lost otherwise. The MUF also articulated a vision to reunite the broader community of *Olosho le Maa* under one political sovereignty that could coexist in some form with the states of Kenya and Tanzania. And they emerged from the colonial era with the Masai Reserve still in the hands of the community in spite of having lost 75 percent of their original homeland. As there is no evidence that any British or Kenyan representatives to the constitutional process advocated Maasai land rights, the community's retention of even this small part may be attributed to the MUF.

After Independence, the MUF continued their fight for the return of lost land, and they maintained that unless satisfied, they would take steps to form a semi-autonomous nation of Maa people.[101] It is known in oral history that the Kenyatta government responded to this threat by undertaking an aggressive campaign to destroy Maasai leadership, using a combination of bribery and coercion, and eventually the MUF was neutralized. It is also known that some members of the MUF accepted the government's offer of land and political positions, including John Keen, who ended up with a large parcel in the affluent Karen neighborhood outside of Nairobi. Ole Tipis served as a member of the Kenyan Parliament and when he moved to Nairobi, his role as a community leader was usurped by William Ole Ntimama, an age-group mate of Tipis who had not taken part in the MUF-era activism. Ntimama used his position as Chairman of Narok County Council to curry the favor of Kenya's second president Daniel Arap Moi by giving him 1,000 acres, bloated later to 3,000 acres, in the protected Mau Forest. Moi himself then engineered further invasion by his own Kalenjin community. Ntimama discredited Tipis and drove him from leadership by 1988.[102]

In spite of the collapse of elected Maasai leadership, a new generation of Maasai people began to take up the fight for land rights again in the early 1990s. The turn was marked in 1992 by a violent conflict over election rigging and an illegal expansion of Kikuyu settlers in Maasailand, in Enoosupukia water catchment area, and Naisoya in the Mau Forest. In 1998, Maasai began to organize a legal challenge in anticipation for the expiration of the temporary titles issued in

1904 to settlers for occupied land at Laikipia, and organizers began recruiting people through a popular education program on the history of Maasai land loss.[103] The year 2002 marked another turning point for Maasai land rights as the Moi regime ended, and the activists who left Kenya because of government repression were able to return. In 2004 a challenge to the continued occupation of Laikipia by the families of British settlers was filed in Kenyan court. In 2008 hundreds of Maasai moved back onto disputed land at Mau Narok where they remain today, while a suit for the land's return to the community was filed in 2010 and continues to make its way through Kenyan High Court. Later that year Kenyan people approved the first constitution drafted on Kenyan soil, and it created the Kenya Land Commission to manage all land issues to investigate historical land injustices, and Mau Narok was one of the first cases they took up. In 2016, Maasai organized a protest against a government attempt to remove people from Kedong Ranch for a dry port railroad system that had sold the land out from under the community without its consent. Recently, Mau Forest has seen the eviction of illegal settlement following a thirty-year effort by Maasai people with the support of the global community, and the forest is regenerating and refilling rivers, its regrowth credited with the rainfall that is transforming parts of Maasailand to the south. This event has injected a new hope in the more than a century-long Maasai land rights struggle.

One of many things that we learn about cultural survival by following new questions into Maasai history is the importance of Maasai leadership: when leadership has been true to the Maasai community, our integrity has remained in check, but when leadership is corrupted, the community itself has fallen into chaos. Leadership must remain steeped in a belief in the integrity of Maasai culture, and detach their interests from the manipulations and corruption of national politics. We ask, what would it mean for Maasai to defy the story so common in history, of a people being defeated by the confusion of their own privileged classes? What would it look like to instead be empowered by a leadership committed to Maasai cultural survival?

Conclusion: *Entaisere* (the Future)

We approached the gathering in early morning as the night fog that had settled on the land began to dissipate, touched by the first rays of sun. Looking out on the sea of people, the largest gathering of Maasai people in the twentieth or twenty-first century, we saw the movement. Fifteen thousand community members had arrived on this day in January 2011, to protest the killing, arrest, and harassment of our community by the state of Kenya in our legal claim for the return of Mau Narok. With no food for a crowd that size, we fasted for three days and renewed our strength for the fight ahead.

Just a few weeks before, a thousand Maasai community members converged on the High Court in Nairobi to demand a hearing on their case for Mau Narok. On that same day, as dusk began to settle, two Mau Narok activists were assassinated in Nakuru, the city closest to Mau Narok. Ole Mpoe and Ole Punyua were killed by men on motorcycles with machine guns as they slowed into a long line of traffic. Images of the bullet-ridden car had been immediately televised, but that exposure did not stem the violence. Two months after the January vigil, fifty-two people were arrested in a sweep of movement leadership as crowds of hundreds, sure that those detained would be killed, surrounded the jail and demanded their release. The leading presidential candidates, former and current presidents Uhuru Kenyatta and William Ruto, were prevented from proceeding through Narok town in Maasailand for seven hours, their cars blockaded by thousands of Maasai people demanding to know their position on Mau Narok. Back in Mau Narok, police retaliated by arbitrarily brutalizing Maasai people: women were raped; others forced at gunpoint to carry heavy bundles of wood on their backs while crawling on their knees. These tactics are not new to us: we are subject to unaccountable violence by the state because of our lack of political power. That lack is demonstrated again by the most recent evictions of Maasai people from Ngorongoro and Loliondo in northern Tanzania, along the common border with Kenya, in June of 2022. Police arrived unannounced, shooting into villages and lighting houses, schools, and churches on fire. Again, people were killed, women were raped, and many small children were lost permanently in the chaos as they sought shelter alone in the vast wildlife-dense wilderness. The degree of this brutality is exposed by the many people, including small children, who went missing in the chaos and remain unaccounted for.

Our future as a community is in no way guaranteed. Many other Indigenous communities in colonized places have been finished, their languages and memories and ways of knowing erased from the earth. As *Olosho le Maa*, we exist on this precipice every day. We are vulnerable because our lives are not valued by the states that claim us, and because we still hold precious things that the states want from us: land, natural resources, and our culture. To erase Maasai from history and to invalidate our identity are not benign acts: they facilitate our actual erasure. However, our own knowledge of history teaches us that we have survived many similar moments. Maasai culture teaches us that *ng'en enkong'u olapurroni kake melang enolopeny enkiteng'*: The eye of a thief may be clever, but no more so than the cow's owner. Our greatest strength is that we know ourselves, and we know that our survival depends on the sustaining resilience of our culture.

And as it happens, even as we face a new and extreme violence against the Maasai community, a cultural renaissance is also underway in Maasailand.

For the past several generations, the ceremonial life that has bound the Maasai people for centuries or millennia had been increasingly muted, held more and more in smaller gatherings, almost in hiding as if our ceremonies were a shameful secret. But, starting in the spring of 2021, Maasai of the *Ilmeshuki* age group began gathering across the whole of Maasailand for the *Olng'esherr* ceremony, the graduation of junior elders to elders. *Olng'esherr* is a powerful time for the transmission of oral history, where a deeper layer of cultural teachings can be shared between older and graduating generations. The emergence of this revival was decades in the making, the expression of age-group mentorship which is the skeletal structure of the Maasai education system. The *Ilmeshuki* had been mentored by the older age group of *Ilkitoip* from their time of initiation until elderhood. As the *Ilkitoip* completed their role of mentorship at *Olng'esherr*, the slightly younger *Ilkisaruni* were in the process of graduating the next generation, *Ilmerisho* warriors, into junior elderhood in a separate ceremony called *Eunoto*. Mentorship is a cultural responsibility and it infuses everything we do, and graduations are times of cultural renewal, where deep information is shared, and rituals passed on. Before colonization, thousands of people gathered for these ceremonies, for which preparation would take years. Ceremonial villages were constructed, fermented honey beer made and stocked, and people would live together for months. When the time arrived for this 2021 *Olng'esherr*, we anticipated that the ceremonies would draw more than usual recent numbers.

But no one was prepared for the depth of the return. Because, through our colonization, Maasai have come to know ourselves as a community divided, into traditional Maasai and those with Western education. Maasai in towns and cities live different lives from those who do not have literacy or English language, who care for the cattle and the land in rural areas. The more Western education a Maasai person has, the more vulnerable to being seduced, their imaginations altered to lose sight of the power of Maasai culture. Before *Olng'esherr* we thought we might be already destroyed by the artificial trappings that have come to divide us in our interests, those transient individual identities offered by different kinds of employments, styles of houses and dress. Yet here we were together at *Olng'esherr*, urban and rural Maasai, wearing Maasai clothes and beads, sleeping on skins, smearing ochre, creating songs and sharing the fire, living in our traditional homes, speaking Maa, using our real names, knowing each other through our clans and families. Maasai taxi drivers abandoned their cars, while Maasai bankers and teachers took leaves of absence from their jobs. For months we participated in the songs and rituals, the education and celebration, just as our community has done these many generations.

This renaissance begins the work of Maasai futures because it focuses our minds and clears our deeper sight. From the ceremonial grounds, we "see" through the fog of trauma, the confusion created by a long century of violence. We regain sight through the minds and hearts of our grandparents, and we remember in our bones the power of our collectivity. This ability to see again is awakened by the ceremonial rehearsal of who we are in history, the longevity of our resilience. Steeping in our culture creates a cognitive shift, a mental liberation, and the challenges that we face crystalize, as well as the solutions to those challenges.

From the ground of ceremony, we can see that in spite of efforts on every possible front to convince us otherwise, the culture of the West is not superior to our own Indigenous African culture. We see that the West today has been captured by colonial capitalism, an economic system, and a culture which takes what is alive and transforms it into dust—land, wildlife, cows, and even human beings. To us, this aspect of Western culture is madness that masks as the lifestyle of "the civilized." We find it everywhere, in the privatization and sale of land, the pollution of rivers and air, the separation of human beings into smaller and smaller units of accountability, individuals taught to compete rather than cooperate for the basic things we all need to live. Capitalism surrounds and invades us, forcing us to trade livestock, and our time and culture, for the money that makes us dependent on more money. It nips at our heels like packs of hyenas, circling our villages at night looking for a point of entry. Our culture feeds our resistance. We know that sharing food builds power. Relationships are a more tangible reality than money, which is printed on the same paper as false treaties, and faked land titles.

From the ceremonial ground, we hear the occupied lands, the rivers and trees, and other beings, crying out to be protected. We see our duty to recover as many of these lands as possible and to bring them back into the fold of the community. Privatization has been the most effective tactic of colonization, a means to break our cultural unity. It has been accomplished through the seemingly benign neoliberal policy of "willing buyer, willing seller." Thus, the future of this community lies in protecting land that is unsold, strengthening community land control boards with local appointments, and continuing to claim illegally occupied lands. We need to recover and protect the land that has survived allotment, our common lands including the Maasai Mara, Mau Forest, Loita Forest, Purko Development Trust, Kedong Ranch, Amboseli National Park, Morompi Lands, land returned to the community at Mau Narok, Ngorongoro, Loliondo, and many others.

We are also reminded at *Olng'esherr* of the integrity of Maasai cultural leadership. We live in a time of Western electoral politics that comes with access to corrupt political patronage through national parties. It is up to our community to rebuild political power through our culture. The Western political system is oriented to the past, to a future bound by the rigid structures imagined by past generations. But Maasai leadership express a different vision, especially those leaders who have pursued every aspect of our cultural learning, who are skilled at diplomacy, negotiation, and restorative justice. We can use the electoral process to strengthen our own cultural leadership if we find sufficient unity.

It is from the ceremonial ground that we see a future for *Olosho le Maa*. We see generations of Maa people born into a culturally grounded society with ecologically sustainable economies, our own blended education systems, political leadership accountable to the community, led again by our elders. This future builds on our current work: communal land rights, Maasai workers associations, community-driven tourism, and restored "conservation" through Maasai management. We see reclaimed forest, rivers, and grazing land reignited through a new pastoralism that applies cultural knowledge to current realities. We see our collective power expressed in physical space through community organizing and research centers built in rural areas. Ultimately, we see *Olosho le Maa* defining our own social, economic, and political space within the nation-states of Kenya and Tanzania. This is what we mean by self-determination and cultural sovereignty.

Our future and our history are one and the same, and our knowledge of the past is our path to survival.

Notes

Introduction

1   Their participation has been through two primary organizations: MERC (the Institute for Maasai Education, Research, and Conservation) is an organizing collective founded by Meitamei in the 1980s in Maasailand; Prescott College is a fierce liberal arts college in Arizona with a social justice mission. Together they established the Dopoi Center in Maasai Mara as an institute for decolonizing education and research. In addition, many dozens of Maasai people have shared their knowledge and insights through over a dozen large community presentations conducted in the course of researching this book.

2   "Mau Narok" is used to refer both to the broader forested area and to a particular 30,000 acres occupied by the Welsh settler Edward Powys Cobbs.

3   See Parselelo Kantai, "How African Politicians Gave Away $100bn of Land," *The Africa Report*, August 2012, https://www.theafricareport.com/6835/how-african-politicians-gave-away-100bn-of-land/; Antony Gitonga, "Kenya's Maasai Accuse Flower Growers of Undermining Their Access to Lake," *Associated Press Worldstream*, November 1, 2004.

4   Quoted in Parselelo Kantai, "In the Grip of the Vampire State: Maasai Land Struggles in Kenyan Politics," *Journal of Eastern African Studies*, 1:1, March, 2007, 107–22.

5   The full story is told in Chapter 3.

6   See Eve Tuck and K. Wayne Yang, "Decolonization Is Not a Metaphor," *Decolonization: Indigeneity, Education & Society*, 1:1, 2012, 1–40.

7   Meitamei Olol Dapash was the lead signer of this suit and also the leader of the land rights movement that emerged from it.

8   The Kenyans to be resettled at Mau Narok were Internally Displaced Persons, IDPs, who had been impacted by the post-election violence in 2007.

9   From the Report of the Working Group on Indigenous Populations, *Indigenous People in Africa: Contestations, Empowerment and Group Rights*, edited by Ridwan Laher and Korir Sing Oei (Pretoria, South Africa: Africa Institute of South Africa) 2014, 3.

10 Quoted in Dorothy Hodgson, *Being Maasai, Becoming Indigenous: Postcolonial Politics in a Neoliberal World* (Bloomington: Indiana University Press) 2011, 26.

11 This process is described in Chapter 2.

12 And for the botanical diversity of Maasailand. See, for example, Patrick Maundu et.al, "Ethnobotany of the Loita Maasai: Towards Community Management of the

Forest of the Lost Child," Loita Ethnobotony Project, People and Plants Working
Paper, December, No. 8 (Paris: UNESCO, 2001).

13 The Maa word *elokunoto* is the closest to the English word "freedom" but its exact
meaning refers to the freeing of a cow refusing to nurse a new baby and therefore
has been bound to a tree to allow access for the calf.

14 Maasai courts are described in Dorothy Hodgson, *Gender, Justice, and the
Problem of Culture: From Customary Law to Human Rights in Tanzania*
(Bloomington: Indiana University Press) 2017. A Maasai methodology for
deliberating on issues, *Enkiguena,* is presented in Mara Goldman, *Narrating Nature:
Wildlife Conservation and Maasai Ways of Knowing* (Tucson, AZ: University of
Arizona Press: Critical Green Engagements) 2020.

15 The most recent example is of the *Olng'esherr* graduation ceremony of a new
generation of elders, for which dozens of ceremonial villages were constructed and
thousands of people assembled for several weeks to months beginning in 2020.

16 See for example the description of water projects funded by Rotary International on
the website of the Maasai Education, Research and Conservation Institute (MERC),
www.maasaierc.org.

17 This is the consensus narrative of Maasai history as it is currently written, presented
in Thomas Spear and Richard Waller, eds., *Being Maasai: Ethnicity and Identity in
East Africa* (Athens, Ohio: Ohio University Press) 1993.

18 See Lotte Hughes, *Moving the Maasai: A Colonial Misadventure* (London: Palgrave
Macmillan, 2006). This book is an excellent source of British accounts of British-
Maasai treaties of 1904 and 1911, drawn from a dissertation which also includes
very useful research into Maasai resistance. Beyond the book, Hughes' work
has engaged with internal Maasai community politics and of Maasai "memory
making." Lotte Hughes, "Rough Times in Paradise: Claims, Blames and Memory
Making Around Some Protected Areas in Kenya," *Conservation and Society*, 5:3,
2007, 307–30; Lotte Hughes, "The Use and Abuse of Maasai Treaties: Fact and
Fantasy in a Land Claims Process," The Open University, Milton Keynes, UK,
"Land Alienation and Contestation in Kenyan Maasailand." The Open University,
Milton Keynes, UK, "Malice in Maasailand: The Historical Roots of Current
Political Struggles," *African Affairs*, 104:215, 2005, 207–24. While the book affords
her expertise on British colonial history in Maasailand, she has come to represent
expertise in Maasai history itself, which led to authorship of the first edition of The
No-Nonsense Guide to Indigenous Peoples (Verso), 2003.

19 Hughes writes,

> There is little mention in the published literature of two of the most
> momentous events in the last hundred years of Maasai history: the forced
> moves which robbed the "Kenyan" Maasai of the greater part of their
> territory, and resistance to the second move from Laikipia to the Southern
> Reserve which culminated in a 1913 court case brought by the Maasai,
> with the assistance of Leys and other Europeans in and outside the colonial

service. The few historians who have covered these events fail to analyse fully their significance and effects, or to include a Maasai perspective and direct, attributable quotes. The resistance is typically dismissed as insignificant, largely assumed to end at the court case, and not placed within the context of other African resistance movements.

(Hughes, *Moving the Maasai*, 5)

Hughes herself expresses support for Maasai land rights in the preface to her book when she writes, "[I]ndigenous communities have fought to assert their rights, separate identity and cultural heritage in the face of attempts by governments and mainstream society to assimilate, marginalise or even exterminate them. Rights to land and natural resources are central to this struggle" (xv).

20   The story that Maasai agreed to cede their land to the British is repeated on the popular encyclopedic source, Wikipedia, at: wikipedia.org/wiki/Anglo-Maasai_Treaty_(1904).

21   Michel-Rolph Trouillot, *Silencing the Past: Power and the Production of History* (Boston, MA: Beacon Press) 1995, 2015, xxiii.

22   R.W. Hemsted, "Masai Reserve, Annual Report," 1921, KNA, PC/SP 1/2/1, quoted in Robert Tignor, *The Colonial Transformation of Kenya: The Kamba, Kikuyu, and Maasai from 1900–1939* (Princeton, NJ: Princeton University Press) 1976, 17. The spelling of "Maasai" is correct though unusual in this era.

23   Anibal Quijano describes the continued functioning of a "coloniality of power" under statehood. Toyin Falola discusses the use of "neocolonialism" by African intellectuals. Mahmood Mamdani and Hamid Dabashi offer necessary critiques of the function of nation-statehood and especially, in the words of the former, the "two-state solution to the problem of the native." Roxanne Dunbar-Ortiz is one of many scholars exploring the terrain of power under settler colonialism. See Anibal Quijano, "Coloniality of Power, Eurocentrism, and Latin America," *Nepantla*, 1:3 (Durham: Duke University Press) 2000, 533–80; Toyin Falola, *Nationalism and African Intellectuals* (Rochester: University of Rochester Press) 2001; Mahmood Mamdani, *Neither Settler Nor Native: The Making and Unmaking of Permanent Minorities* (Cambridge: Belknap Press) 2020, 39; Hamid Dabashi, *The Emperor Is Naked: On the Inevitable Demise of the Nation-State* (London: Zed Books) 2020; Roxanne Dunbar-Ortiz, *An Indigenous Peoples' History of the United States* (Boston: Beacon Press) 2014.

24   The subtext of many current books published in and about Kenya today is that ethnic identity is dangerous to peace. For example, in *Remembering Kenya: Identity Culture and Freedom*, Mbugua and Gona emphasize the injustice done to Kenya's Internally Displaced Persons, refugees from post-election violence in 2007–8, while occluding the broader context of "historical injustice" claimed by Indigenous and other cultural community to the land from which IDPs were ostensibly removed during the violence. Mbugua wa-Mungai and George Gona, eds., *(Re)membering Kenya Vol 1: Identity, Culture and Freedom* (Nairobi: Twaweza Communications, African Books Collective) 2010.

25 The International Criminal Court (ICC) conducted an extensive investigation into the 2007 Kenyan post-election violence which focused on the political leadership of the dominant ethnic communities and their party apparatuses; while that process ultimately collapsed as a result of tampering, enough information was disseminated to indicate the clear production of that violence as a function of party politics. Almost no violence occurred on Indigenous lands.

26 Rudolph Ryser, *Indigenous Nations and Modern States: The Political Emergence of Nations Challenging State Power* (Abingdon: Routledge) 2012.

27 Bogumil Jewsiewicki and David Newbury, eds., *African Historiographies: What Histories for Which Africas?* (Beverly Hills: Sage) 1986, 114. Quote taken from: Trevor-Roper, "The Rise of Christian Europe," *The Listener*, November 1963, 871.

28 Stewart Hall, "The West and the Rest: Discourse and Power," in Stuart Hall and Bram Gieben, eds., *Formations of Modernity* (Cambridge: Polity Press in Association with Blackwell and the Open University) 1992, 186.

29 Linda Tuhiwai Smith, *Decolonizing Methodologies: Research and Indigenous Peoples* (London: Zed Books) 2006.

30 Trouillot, *Silencing the Past*, 48.

31 Ibid, 52.

32 Ibid, 7–8.

33 The source of the now widely reproduced claim that Maasai ate wildlife as "second cattle" is an anecdote in David Western's 1997 memoir, *In the Dust of Kilimanjaro* (Washington, D.C.: Island Press) in which he says that a Maasai man Ole Purdul Parashino tells him that "Before the white man said wild animals belonged to them … [my community] ate wildlife to survive the big droughts. Wild animals were our second cattle, you know" (145–56). The community he refers to is *Iloodokilani*, who live in the area of Magadi Lake, and border hunting communities including the Sonjo, and the practice described is unknown throughout Maasailand. Citing this single source, the claim has been reproduced widely in scholarship. See, for example, Álvaro Fernández-Llamazares et al., "Historical Shifts in Local Attitudes towards Wildlife by Maasai Pastoralists of the Amboseli Ecosystem" (Kenya), *Journal for Nature Conservation*, 53, 2020, 1–11.

34 William Mullen, "David Western," *The Chicago Tribune*, October 19, 1997. Western says that he gave up hunting himself at 16, but that "I support hunting as a conservation tool." Raymond Bonner, *At the Hand of Man: Peril and Hope for Africa's Wildlife* (New York: Knopf) 1993, 240.

35 Hughes, *Moving the Maasai*, 181–2.

36 This myth of the lost Eden has been read more broadly onto the continent of Africa, and used to sell both the safari tourism and conservation industries there to Western subjects. See Jonathan S. Adams and Thomas O. McShane, *The Myth of Wild Africa: Conservation without Illusion* (Oakland, CA: University of California Press) 1997.

37 Lotte Hughes, "Rough Time in Paradise: Claims, Blames and Memory Making around Some Protected Areas in Kenya," *Conservation and Society*, 5:3, 2007, 307–30, 308.

38 See Kantai, "In the Grip of the Vampire State," 107–22.

39 Robert Young says, "If so-called 'poststructualism' is the product of a single historical moment, then that moment is probably not May 1968 but rather the Algerian War of Independence," noting that "Sartre, Althusser, Derrida and Lyotard among others, were all either born in Algeria or personally involved with the events of the war." Robert Young, *White Mythologies: Writing History and the West* (London: Psychology Press) 2004.

40 Sartre argued that the very concept of the ethical civilization the West claimed to be could not exist in thought except in opposition to the production of the colonized as savage. Sartre described humanism as "an ideology of lies," that now the white settler must face as it is being "savagely rooted out." Barthes says humanism makes invisible the possibility for the colonized to exist as difference. Though diversity may be celebrated on the surface as exotic, it is in fact erased as the sameness of all of humanity is thought to exist just below the skin. 1978; Young, *White Mythologies*, 121–2.

41 Aileen Moreton-Robinson says that the construction of identity as "fluid" is a strategy of Indigenous silencing. Settler identity is fluid because the fluidity creates, literally, the means to elude, escape being pinned down in a settler position. The identity of Indigenous peoples is a contest over power, as they can be "modernized," and separated from land, by attributing to them a "fluid" identity with the same effect. See Aileen Moreton-Robinson, *The White Possessive: Property, Power & Indigenous Sovereignty* (Minneapolis, MN: University of Minnesota Press) 2015, 13.

42 "Gender" is a "category of analysis" invented by Western feminist scholars to analyze the different rights and identities afforded people in Western societies, originally solely on the basis of their reproductive anatomy. In Westernized cultures, gender is understood to be a totalizing form of identity, lasting from birth to death, which marks Western subjects as members of social classes with differential rights, as a means to exploit the labor of "women." "Women" have been devalued as a class in Western societies through their association with a "private sphere," also an invention of Western capitalism, an otherwise illogical exclusion of the economic activities of "the home" from the larger economy. Gender accompanied industrialization in the West, and the ideal (white) woman was trained to develop opposite qualities from men, to be meek and pious, while (white) men were unleashed to be aggressive and acquisitive, suited for business and full citizenship. The Western economic and social order rests on the literal marriage of the two genders in a privatized family economy dedicated to its own personal economic security. Gender, in its current usage, is thus like "race," an invention of Western colonial racial capitalism; the entire model embeds white supremacy. These many years after that origin in industrialization, "gender"

continues to comprise a core of Western understanding of personal and collective identity, and is a means of power through various forms of compliance—or resistance, through rejection of privatization and gender nonconformity. This scholarship is too vast to reproduce here, but further reading would include some essential texts: Jean Boydston, *Home & Work: Housework, Wages, and the Ideology of Labor in the Early Republic* (New York: Oxford University Press) 1990; the works of Alice Kessler-Harris, including *Gendering Labor History* (Champaign, IL: University of Illinois Press) 2006; Kimberle Crenshaw, "Mapping the Margins: Intersectionality, Identity Politics, and Violence Against Women of Color," *Stanford Law Review*, 43:1291, 1993, 1241–99; Michel Foucault, *The History of Sexuality* (New York: Pantheon Books) 1978; Jonathan Katz, "The Invention of Heterosexuality," *Socialist Review*, 20:1, 1990, 7–34; Sandra Bartky, "Foucault, Femininity, and the Modernization of Patriarchal Power," in *Feminism and Foucault: Reflections on Resistance* (Boston: Northeastern Press) 1998; Dean Spade, "Resisting Medicine/Remodeling Gender," 18 *Berkeley Women's Law Journal*, 15 (2003) 15–37. Scholarship offering an anticolonial perspective includes, Chandra Mohanty, "Under Western Eyes: Feminist Scholarship and Colonial Discourses," *Feminist Review*, 30:1, 1998, 61–88; Chandra Mohanty, *Feminism Without Borders: Decolonizing Theory, Practicing Solidarity* (Durham, NC: Duke University Press) 2003. The second piece especially suggests a ground of solidarity based in women's exploitation under global capitalism to replace a "sisterhood" based in biology.

43 While Western scholarship has detailed the history of the Western production of the biological fiction of "race," Yoruban scholar Oyèrónké̩ Oyěwùmí notes that "gender," as a totalizing identity, is typically treated as universal. Oyěwùmí says that in Yorubaland, the idea that anatomy forms *permanent, ranked social identities* of all kinds, including race and "gender," was foreign before "sustained contact with the West." In that way, gender is inseparable, she says, from "biological determinism." Before colonization, there were no "women" in Yorubaland using a Western definition of the term. Oyèrónké̩ Oyěwùmí, *The Invention of Women: Making an African Sense of Western Gender Discourse* (Minneapolis: University of Minnesota Press) 1997, ix, 122, 124.

44 Oyěwùmí, *The Invention of Women*, 124.

45 For example, allotment policies that broke up communal Maasailand into Group Ranches in the 1970s and 1980s distributed it only to "male heads of households." When the Kenyan government began extending Western education to Maasai people at the same time—on the US Indian school model, it excluded women. Women were barred from political office in Maasailand for the first more than fifty years of Kenyan statehood. However, the new Kenyan constitution of 2010 has provided for a sudden expansion of education to girls and women throughout Kenya, and set aside political offices for women only, creating a promising structural change that has been put to use rapidly throughout Maasailand.

46   Victorian-era European women were ironically enabled to leave their own
     entrapment in a "domestic sphere" through missionary work in colonized
     places. See Louise Michele Newman, *White Women's Rights: The Racial
     Origins of Feminism in the United States* (Oxford: Oxford University Press)
     1999. Western women imagined themselves to be less oppressed than those
     of colonized places, and understanding that was expanded during the years
     of the second wave of feminism in the United States and Europe, in the
     1960s–80s. At that time, feminist scholarship promoted the idea that all women
     throughout the world, and throughout history, share an oppression mirroring
     that experienced by mid-twentieth century Western women. See Robin
     Morgan, *Sisterhood Is Global: The International Women's Movement Anthology*,
     1984 (New York: The Feminist Press at City University of New York) 1986.
     Women's rights have in some cases been harmed by the uncritical imposition
     of Western feminisms in in colonized places. See Nima Naghibi, *Rethinking
     Global Sisterhood: Western Feminism and Iran* (Minneapolis, MN: University of
     Minnesota Press) 2007.

47   Hodgson, *Gender, Justice, and the Problem of Culture*, 123.

48   Spivak says of the Third World Woman, "She is a signifier, whose distinction is that
     she is shifted from one position to another without being allowed any content."
     Gayatri Chakravorty Spivak, *A Critique of Postcolonial Reason: Toward a History
     of the Vanishing Present* (Cambridge, MA: Harvard University Press) 1999, 14.
     Rosalind Morris, ed., *Can the Subaltern Speak? Reflections on the History of an Idea*
     (New York: Columbia UP) 2010, 3.

49   See especially Chapters 3, "Criminalizing Culture: Human Rights, NGOs, and the
     Politics of Anti-FGM Campaigns," and Chapter 4, "Demanding Justice: Collective
     Action, Moral Authority, and Female Forms of Power," in Dorothy Hodgson,
     Gender, Justice, and the Problem of Culture.

50   "Arjun Appadurai argues convincingly that rules about what he calls 'the
     debatability of the past' operate in all societies" all of which are aimed at
     guaranteeing credibility: "authority, continuity, depth, and interdependence. No
     where is history infinitely susceptible to invention." Trouillot, *Silencing the Past*, 8.

51   The reference is to a quote from Audre Lourde, *The Master's Tools Will Never
     Dismantle the Master's House* (London: Penguin Books) 2018.

Chapter 1

1   Thomas Spear, "Part One: Introduction," in Thomas Spear and Richard Waller, eds.,
     Being Maasai: Ethnicity and Identity in East Africa (Athens, Ohio: Ohio University
     Press) 1993, 1.

2   An exception to this rule will be discussed further below.

3   The details of the appropriation of Maasailand at Kenyan statehood are described in the next chapter.

4   See for example file titled "Interchange of Professional and Technical Staff between U.K. and Kenya," Files of the Ministry of Agriculture, Fisheries and Food, [1966] British National Archives, MAF 184/172m.

5   See Lotte Hughes, "Mining the Maasai: The Story of Magadi," *The Journal of East African Studies*, 2:1, 2008, 134–164; Amos Kareithi, "A Tale of Bogus Maasai Agreements and Lost Mineral Rights," *The Standard*, January 28, 2012.

6   Michel Cahen, "Anticolonialism and Nationalism: Deconstructing Synonymy, Investigating Historical Processes: Notes on the Heterogeneity of Former African Portuguese Colonial Areas," in Eric Morier-Genoud, ed., *Sure Road? Nations and Nationalisms in Guinea, Angola and Mozambique* (Leiden: Brill Academic Publishers, African Social Studies Series, 28) 2012, 10.

7   See Conor Gaffey, "Kenya Just Opened a $4 Billion Chinese-Built Railway, Its Largest Infrastructure Project in 50 Years," *Newsweek*, May 31, 2017; Cobus van Staden, "How China Is Changing Africa's Future: Moving Away from Western Influence, Africa Is Already Getting a Glimpse of a Different Future," "The World Post," *Huffington Post*, April 8, 2018.

8   Anibal Quijano, "Coloniality of Power: Eurocentrism and Latin America," *Nepantla: Views from the South*, 1:3, Duke University Press, 2000, 533–580.

9   Stuart Hall defines "The West" as those societies that have evolved hegemonic power by consolidating resources, those that are "developed, industrialized, urbanized, capitalist, secular and modern." "The West" was originally established through Western European colonization of much of the rest of the world, and the Atlantic slave trade that preceded and coexisted with colonization. Since the end of the Second World War its epicenter has resided in the United States, though the West now exists throughout the world, having been distributed beyond geography through the advance of global capitalism. When we use the term "The West," in this book we are referring to that consolidated power with origins in the cultures of Europe but that now include elite classes in the Global South. Stuart Hall, "The West and The Rest: Discourse and Power," in Stuart Hall and Bram Gieben, eds., *Formations of Modernity* (Cambridge: Polity Press, in Association with Blackwell and the Open University) 1992, 186.

10 Reference to the Berlin Conference of 1884–5 where European states divided Africa into spheres of influence in preparation for formal colonization.

11 Jay Walljasper and Nikil Aziz, "The Neo-Colonial Land Grab in Africa: Outside Nations Are Once Again Dividing Up Africa—This Time for Biofuel and Mineral Rights," *On the Commons*, April 15, 2011, http://www.onthecommons.org/neo-colonial-land-grab-africa.

12 "Land Grabbing in Africa: The New Colonialism," Bwesigye Bwa Mwesigire, *This Is Africa*, May 28, 2014, https://thisisafrica.me/land-grabbing-africa-new-colonialism/.

13 Data from the US-based, Global Financial Integrity (GFI), and the Centre for Applied Research at the Norwegian School of Economics, Presented in Jason Hickel, "Aid in Reverse: How Poor Countries Develop Rich Countries," *The Guardian*, January 19, 2017. Dambiso Moyo has also critiqued development agendas for undermining the relationship of African people to African states, as the global aid industry becomes the providers of basic services, a function denied to African states through the mechanisms of Western control of African economies, leaving African people beholden directly to the West for the needs like food, education and health care. See Dambisa Moyo, *Dead Aid: Why Aid Is Not Working and How There Is a Better Way for Africa* (New York: Farrar, Straus and Giroux) 2009.

14 See Ellen Meiksins Wood, *Empire of Capital* (London: Verso) 2005; David Harvey, *The New Imperialism* (Oxford: Oxford University Press) 2003. The scholar Toyin Falola says: "Africa has no control of prices and no say in determining the quantities demanded. It is subject to price and demand fluctuations with devastating consequences for its people and economies. The gains from selling its products are channeled back to the West from which Africa processes manufactured products and virtually all the major items it requires for industrialization and manufacturing. Even things that could be produced domestically are imported." Toyin Falola, *Nationalism and African Intellectuals* (Rochester, NY: University of Rochester Press) 2001, 132.

15 Mainstream Development discourse has used an uncritical interpretation of history to justify the destructive outcomes of development strategies in the Global South, of rapid urbanization and impoverishment driven by landlessness for example. Jeffrey Sachs, former Director of The Earth Institute at Colombia University, explains that the misery produced by rapid industrialization is a necessary step toward modernization in the postcolonial world today as it was in Western imperial societies. Jeffrey Sachs, *The End of Poverty: Economic Possibilities for Our Time* (New York: Penguin) 2005.

16 Quijano, "Coloniality of Power," 541. See also Walter Mignolo, *The Darker Side of Renaissance: Literacy, Territoriality, and Colonization* (Ann Arbor: U Michigan Press) 2003; James Morris Blaut, *The Colonizer's Model of the World: Geographical Diffusion and Eurocentric History* (New York: Guilford Press) 1993.

17 Quijano, "Coloniality of Power," 556.

18 The splitting of human societies into either "primitive" or "civilized" is a powerful tool of ideology that cannot make logical sense outside of its own frame. Europeans imagined all things European to be "civilized," simply by virtue of the fact that they occurred, were made or thought of, in Europe. The streets of

industrial London that were caked with human and animal waste, air blackened
with coal dust, people sick with disease and hunger—these conditions were read
as stages in the progress of civilization, as was European penchant for violence and
warfare, its bizarre by some standard religiosity, and crude political system relying
on all manner of capital punishments. Only its art and architecture informed its
identity in its own imagination. In contrast, in the same seventeenth century of
linear time, Europeans believed the nations of the eastern region of North America
to be "primitive," even though their sophisticated networks of diplomacy and
governance would otherwise have been recognized as elements of the greatest
achievements of "civilization." The complex interwoven political structures of the
Maasai and their systems of justice, the city-states of West Africa with their iron
works and powerful militaries, even the kingdoms of Ethiopia that were revered
in Medieval Europe, would come to be diminished in the mind of colonization.
European food was civilized but not the food of the colonized peoples, whose
technologies were considered primitive, along with their religions, ways of
dressing, languages, medicines, and sciences. Western scholars have produced an
extensive literature critiquing this core ideology of Western imperialism beginning
with Edward Said, *Orientalism* (New York: Vintage Press) 1978. Much of this
work has emphasized the use of ideas of the primitive in art and culture. See
Marianna Torgovnick, *Gone Primitive: Savage Intellects, Modern Lives* (Chicago, IL:
University of Chicago Press) 1990; Jan Nederveen Pieterse, *White on Black: Images
of Africa and Blacks in Western Popular Culture* (New Haven: Yale UP) 1992. While
the West has critiqued itself, the most important work on the creation of Africa in
the Western imagination, widely cited by African scholars, is that of V.Y. Mudimbe.
See V.Y. Mudimbe, *The Invention of Africa: Gnosis, Philosophy, and the Order of
Knowledge* (London: James Currey) 1988.

19 Gustavo Esteva, "Development," in Wolfgang Sachs, ed., *The Development
Dictionary: A Guide to Knowledge as Power*, 1992, 2nd Ed. (London: Zed Books)
2010, 2.

20 See for example Sachs, *The Development Dictionary*.

21 Kwame Nkrumah, *Neo-Colonialism, The Last Stage of Imperialism* (London:
Thomas Nelson & Sons Ltd.) 1965, 1.

22 See Carol Ann Cosgrove, "The Common Market and Its Colonial Heritage," *Journal
of Contemporary History*, 4:1, Colonialism and Decolonization, January, 1969,
73–87.

23 Interview with Kwame Nkrumah, Basil Davidson, *AFRICA: A Voyage of Discovery*,
"Episode 8: The Legacy" (28:50).

24 Interview with Julius Nyerere, Basil Davidson, *AFRICA: A Voyage of Discovery*,
"Episode 8: The Legacy" (30:00).

25 These include Amical Cabral of the West African liberation movement from
Portuguese, Felix Moumie of Cameroon, Sylvanus Olympio of Togo, Mehdi Ben

Barka of Morocco, and Eduardo Mondlane of Mozambique's Frelimo. See "Africa: A Continent Drenched in the Blood of Revolutionary Heroes," *The Guardian*, January 17, 2011, https://www.theguardian.com/global-development/poverty-matters/2011/jan/17/lumumba-50th-anniversary-african-leaders-assassinations.

26 Quoted in M.H. Khalil Timami, "African Leaders and Corruption," *Review of African Political Economy*, 32:104–5, 383–93, 2005.

27 B.A. Ogot, "Chapter Three: The Decisive Years: 1956-1963," in B.A. Ogot and W.R. Ochieng, eds., *Decolonization and Independence in Kenya, 1940–1993* (Nairobi: East African Educational Publishers) 1995, 64.

28 See Robert M. Maxon and & Peter Ndege, "Chapter 6: The Economics of Structural Adjustment," in B.A. Ogot and W.R. Ochieng, *Decolonization & Independence in Kenya, 1940–1993* (Nairobi, Kenya: East African Educational Publishers) 1995, 151–186.

29 Nkrumah, *Neo-Colonialism*, 2.

30 See Charlotte Lydia Riley, "'The Winds of Change are Blowing Economically': The Labour Party and British Overseas Development, 1940s–1960s," in Andrew W.M. Smith and Chris Jeppesen, eds., *Britain, France, and the Decolonization of Africa: Future Imperfect?* (London, UK: UCL Press) 2017; Ebere Nbwauni, "Getting behind a Myth: The British Labour Party and Decolonisation in Africa, 1945–1951," *Australian Journal of Politics and History*, 39:2, 1993, 197–216.

31 Ramon Grosfoguel, "The Epistemic Decolonial Turn: Beyond Political Economy Paradigms," *Cultural Studies*, 21:2–3, 2007, 219.

32 Samin Amin, *Eurocentrism: Second Edition* (New York: Monthly Review Press) 2009.We might add control of political capital, especially in African contexts, as leadership and political ideology is imposed on African people by the West.

33 Sabelo J. Ndlovu-Gatsheni, *Coloniality of Power in Neocolonial Africa: Myths of Decolonization* (Dakar: Council for the Development of Social Science Research in Africa) 2013, 12.

34 Falola, *Nationalism and African Intellectuals*, 127.

35 Ibid, 113.

36 No. 14 in the World Conference against Racism, Racial Discrimination, Xenophobia and Related Intolerance, Declaration. Accessed July 26, 2012, http://www.un.org/WCAR/durban.pdf. Quoted in Ichiro Maekawa, "Neo-Colonialism Reconsidered: A Case Study of East Africa in the 1960s and 1970s," *The Journal of Imperial and Commonwealth History*, 43:2, 2015, 317–241.

37 Mahmood Mamdani, *Neither Settler Nor Native: The Making and Unmaking of Permanent Minorities* (Belknap: Harvard University Press) 2020, 39.

38 Hamid Dabashi, *The Emperor Is Naked: On the Inevitable Demise of the Nation-State* (London: Zed Books) 2020.

39 Ogot and Ochieng, eds., *Decolonization and Independence in Kenya, 1940–1993*.

40 Basil Davidson said "British colonial policy claimed that its task in Africa was 'nation-building,' it being supposed in London that the task had been beyond the capacity of Africans themselves." Basil Davidson, *The Black Man's Burden: Africa and the Curse of the Nation-State* (New York: Random House) 1992, 11–12.

41 Falola, *Nationalism and African Intellectuals*, 85.

42 Ibid, 38.

43 Ibid, 111, 134, 136, 140, 142.

44 Maasai were among those who articulated a vision of a different model of statehood that might coexist with African nations as will be described in Chapter 3.

45 "The Kikuyuisation of Kenya: Although the state continued to talk of Kenya as one nation, and to de-emphasise ethnicity in its public statements and policies on land, service delivery and jobs, the unifying rhetoric of nationhood concealed a less palatable truth. The 1970s saw the entrenchment of Kikuyu power via a web of both formal and informal networks. As with the security forces, the senior civil service was increasingly Kikuyu dominated." Charles Hornsby, *Kenya: A History Since Independence* (London: I.B. Tauris) 2013, 85. It is the children of the Kikuyu elite, the Koinanges, Kenyattas, Thukus, Kinyanjuias, Waiyakis, Ngonjos, Waruhius, Magugus, Wawerus, who trace their descent from colonial Chiefs, who still comprise the core of political and economic power. Marshall Clough, *Fighting Two Sides: Kenyan Chiefs and Politicians, 1918–1940* (Niwot: The University Press of Colorado) 1990.

46 Title deeds to the land have been found to be missing from the Kenyan National Lands Office and few published sources exist to back up what is known among the Maasai communities who have lived through this distribution and occupation of land at Mau Narok. An exception is found in the autobiography of one of the land's recipients, Simeon Nyachae, a Provincial Commissioner under President Kenyatta whose family occupies over 10,000 acres; David K. Leonard, *African Successes: Four Public Managers of Kenyan Rural Development* (Berkeley, CA: University of California Press) 1991. According to *Forbes*, Kenya's former President Uhuru Kenyatta, son of Jomo, owns 500,000 acres of the best land throughout Kenya. Raymond Ackerman, "Africa's #26: Uhuru Kenyatta," in Kerry Dolan, "Tallying Africa's Wealthiest People: Forbes Inaugural List of Africa's 40 Richest People in Africa," *Forbes*, November 16, 2011, https://www.forbes.com/lists/2011/89/africa-billionaires-11_Uhuru-Kenyatta_FO2Q.html. A secret CIA report issued in the year of Jomo Kenyatta's death in 1978 hints at both the extent of the wealth, in land and also a near monopoly on trade in elephant tusks, but also concern with the depth of resentment of the people over this theft of the country's assets and potential for revolution and land redistribution Alphonse Shiundu, "The Untold Story of the Kenyatta's Wealth," *The Standard*, January 29, 2017, https://www.standardmedia.co.ke/article/2001227584/the-untold-story-of-the-kenyattas-wealth.

47 A glance at land values in Nairobi suggest that ethnicity operates similarly to
    the way "whiteness" is afforded market value in settler colonial contexts such as
    the United States. For that context, see Cheryl Harris, "Whiteness as Property,"
    Harvard Law Review, 106:8, June, 1993, 1707–91, and specific studies of urban
    contexts in the United States, including Thomas Segrue, *The Origin of the Urban
    Critis: Race and Inequality in Postwar Detroit* (Princeton, NJ: Princeton University
    Press) 1996; Beryl Satter, *Family Properties: Race, Real Estate, and the Exploitation
    of Black Urban America* (New York: Metropolitan Books) 2009.

48 See John Akama, "The Creation of the Maasai Image and Tourism Development
    in Kenya," in John Akama and Patricia Sterry, eds., *Cultural Tourism in
    Africa: Strategies for the New Millennium: The Proceedings of the ATLAS Africa
    International Conference, Mombasa 2000* (Arnhem, Netherlands: Association for
    Tourism and Leisure Education) 2002, 43–54. Also see Edward Bruner, "Maasai on
    the Lawn: Tourist Realism in East Africa," *Cultural Anthropology*, October, 2009.

49 Ngugi Wa Thiongo is the best-known Kenyan writer of African nationalism and
    often cited as a representative of Indigenous Africans internationally, though his
    work can also be seen to universalize the Kikuyu experience, language, and culture
    and in that way to erase the existence of Maasai and other Indigenous communities.
    His work emphasizes the betrayal of Independence and suffering of the non-elite
    of Kenyan people and so speaks to a general experience. But his stories also present
    "tribalism" as the great evil that has divided Kenyans since Independence, erasing
    the self-presentation of the communities like Maasai. Maasai are incorporated
    into his work through characters like "Ole Masai" in *Petals of Blood*, who is never
    identified as Maasai, in spite of his name, but stands instead for "every Kenyan." See
    Ngugi Wa Thiongo, *Petals of Blood* (London: William Heinemann) 1977.

50 Patrick Wolfe, "Settler Colonialism and the Elimination of the Native," *Journal of
    Genocide Research*, 8:4, December, 2006, 389.

51 For further insight about the mechanisms of such "belonging," see also Eileen
    Moreton-Robinson, *The White Possessive: Property, Power, and Indigenous
    Sovereignty* (Minneapolis, MN: University of Minnesota Press) 2015, 5.

52 Fear of ethnic identity is the subtext of many recent books published in Kenya,
    such as *Remembering Kenya: Identity Culture and Freedom*, by Mbugua and Gona.
    The victims of their story are IDPs, Kenya's Internally Displaced Persons, mostly
    Kikuyu refugees from a campaign of interethnic violence that followed election
    rigging in 2007 and was initiated by political leaders of rival parties: Kenya's former
    president and deputy president were indicted by the International Criminal Court.
    As ICC witnesses disappeared and the court's case collapsed, an extensive process
    of "Truth and Reconciliation" was undertaken in Kenya to hear from the Kenyan
    people, and what they said that such violence would only be prevented with an
    honest engagement with the "historical injustices" that put Kenyan land into the

ownership of its wealthy political elite. The IDPs are gone home now, having been paid by the government to buy land. But their stories of dislocation were used for years to fan the flames of political tensions. There is irony in the role of IDPs in the national narrative. Much of the land that they were driven from in the Rift Valley is the same contested land from which Maasai were driven out by the British only decades before. The suffering of the IDPs, their "forced trek in the rain dying of pneumonia" is dislodged from the history of the earlier forced removal of Maasai from much of that same land under similar conditions. IDP emerged to absorb the position of those victimized by historical injustices, and to keep the eye of the public on the threat of "dangerous" ethnic identity. Mbugua Wa-mungai and George Gona, eds., *(Re)membering Kenya Vol 1: Identity, Culture and Freedom* (Nairobi: Twaweza Communications, African Books Collective) 2010.

53 Daniel Branch, *Kenya: Between Hope and Despair, 1963–2012* (New Haven: Yale UP) 2011, 292.

54 John Parker and Richard Reid, "But Whose Dream Was It Anyway?," in *From the Oxford Handbook of Modern African History* (Oxford: Oxford University Press) 2013, 12.

55 The Biafra conflict with Nigeria illustrates the use of state power by an ethnic community, the Igbo, to impose statehood on Indigenous communities in resistance. Rudolph Ryser, *Indigenous Peoples and Modern States: The Political Emergence of Nations Challenging State Power* (New York: Routledge) 2012, 22, 25. Other examples include the Somali people bifurcated by the Kenya/Somali border, the Dan in West Africa, Makonde in Tanzania and Mozambique, all sought reunification with their people on the other sides of borders in conflicts described as Civil Wars. Falola, *Nationalism and African Intellectuals*, 118.

56 Ryser, *Indigenous Peoples and Modern States,* 25.

57 Ryser said in 2012 that there are there are 200 states in the world, over 6,000 nations, 6,170 languages spoken. No organization exists to mediate relationships between states and nations. Ryser, *Indigenous Peoples and Modern States,* 12; 39–40.

58 This history is described by Ryser, *Indigenous Peoples and Modern States*; Dorothy Hodgson, "Comparative Perspectives on Indigenous Rights Movement in Africa and the Americas," *American Anthropologist*, January, 2008; Dorothy Hodgson, *Being Maasai, Becoming Indigenous: Postcolonial Politics in a Neoliberal World* (Bloomington: Indiana University Press) 2011, 32, 33.

59 Ryser, *Indigenous Peoples and Modern States,* 15.

60 One that has not been settled. There is no agreement on a definition of "Indigenous," and many communities to which the term might refer reject it. The main reason is that the term "Indigenous" can be used in a backhanded way to incorporate Indigenous nations within the polity of states. The ILO definition of Indigenous peoples adopted in 1989 defined Indigenous as those with "aspirations ... to

exercise control over their own institutions, ways of life and economic development and to maintain and develop their identities, languages, and religions *within the frameworks of the States in which they live.*" [emphasis added.] ILO preamble, 1989, quoted in Hodgson, *Being Maasai, Becoming Indigenous,* 39. The structure of the UN study houses Indigenous peoples as a "Disadvantaged Populations" reifying state hegemony. Ryser, *Indigenous Peoples and Modern States,* 15. The Working Group on Indigenous Populations was located under the Sub-Commission on the Promotion and Protection of Human Rights, "formerly the Sub-Commission on Prevention of Discrimination and Protection of Minorities." Hodgson, *Being Maasai, Becoming Indigenous,* 32, 34. A second issue is that "Indigenous" inevitably collapses an impossible diversity of societies, economies and cultures—the array of currently lived alternatives–into a single false binary opposition to the "modern" capitalist nation-state. A third issue is that Indigenous identity may or may not be strategic in the context of specific state power. After years of conflict through the process of crafting UNDRIP, Indigenous activists successfully argued a compromise. The power to define "Indigenous" lies with each community who adopts that identity, and thus the UNDRIP uses but does not define the term. Hodgson, *Being Maasai, Becoming Indigenous,* 40. UNDRIP does however offer a context for that self-definition. Indigenous peoples are those who have experienced "historical injustice" through their dispossession from land and other resources through colonization into the present moment.

61   The administration of Kenya's second president, Daniel Arap Moi, had banned political gatherings and used torture and incarceration to snuff out political resistance, and many Kenyan activists left during those years. Also at this time, Western donors began to shift their agendas from funding states to supporting local community "grassroots" work and organizations, which created opportunity for Indigenous peoples. Hodgson, *Being Maasai, Becoming Indigenous,* 27.

62   Hodgson, *Being Maasai, Becoming Indigenous,* 25.

63   But that involvement waned in the next few years. The UN Working Group was not a policymaking body and had no teeth, no authority to investigate complaints, and the purpose it had served to enable the cross fertilization of activists, researchers, and donors could be taken to other forums See Hodgson, *Being Maasai, Becoming Indigenous,* 32–5; Boaventura de Sousa Santos, *Rise of the Global Left: The World Social Forum and Beyond* (London: Zed Books) 2006.

64   Ryser, *Indigenous Peoples and Modern States,* 45.

65   The quote is from G.W.F. Hegel, *The Philosophy of History* (New York: Wiley Books) 1944, 99. The book collects a series of lectures given by Hegel in the years shortly before his death in 1831.

66   See for example: G.R. Sandford, *An Administrative and Political History of the Masai Reserve* (Nairobi, 1918; Governor's House, Mombasa, 1919); H.A. Fosbrooke, *An*

Administrative Survey of the Maasai Social System (Nairobi, Kenya: Boyd & Co. Ltd.) 1948; Lord Claud Hamilton, "The E-Unoto Ceremony of the Masai," Bodleian University of Oxford (cir 1900) GB 161 MSS.Afr.s.1810; Dr. Edward Margetts, "On the Masai E-Unoto," *Man*, 63, December, 1963, 190; Alfred Claud Hollis, "A Note on the Masai System of Relationship," *Journal of Anthropological Institute of Great Britain and Ireland*, 40, 1910, 493; "Masai Penal Code," Founded in Memory of Mary Kinglsey, Contents of Vol. XXVIII, 1928–1929, London: Macmillan and Co. Ltd, 12. Similar study was made of African communities throughout colonized Africa. Falola, *Nationalism and African Intellectuals,* citations on p. 296, endnote 24.

67   The British did produce some Maasai history in their administrative manuals, but these were not professionally undertaken, but rather repeated the suppositions of travel writers and administrators. Sandford's *Administrative and Political History of the Masai Reserve* is an example. Because African history was constructed under colonialism as a story of Europeans in Africa, "no common African history could emerge, but only fractured histories, reflecting the various contacts with the Portuguese, British, French, Italians, and Germans. The assumption was that the period before the fifteenth century belonged to the domain of archeology, linguistics, and related disciplines. Controlled by British faculty, the orientation imitated the University of London, with courses on political ideas and outline courses on European and English history." Falola, *Nationalism and African Intellectuals*, 230.

68   Bogumil Jewsiewicki and David Newbury, eds., *African Historiographies: What Histories for Which Africas?* (Beverly Hills: Sage) 1986, 114. Quote taken from: Trevor-Roper, "The Rise of Christian Europe," *The Listener*, November, 1963, 871.

69   Falola says that "The writers were many, but among the most famous are Sir Apollo Kagwa of Uganda, Carl Reindorf of Ghana, Samuel Johnson, Jacob Egharevba, and Akiga Sai of Nigeria, Hampate Ba of Mali, and Boubou Hama of Niger." They did this to preserve knowledge for future generations and to "provide an alternative way of looking at a variety of institutions and events in contrast to the way in which European sources had presented them." Falola, *Nationalism and African Intellectuals*, 66–7, 72.

70   Transcribing oral history was a tool of cultural survival, in Falola's words, "the tool of identity." As Akiga wrote on the Tiv, "You, then, my Tiv brothers of the new generation that can read, read [my book] and tell others, who cannot, of the things of our ancestors; so that, whether we have learnt to read or not, we all may still know something of our fathers who have gone before us. And do you, however great your knowledge may be, remember that you are a Tiv, remain a Tiv, and know the things of Tiv; for therein lies your pride. Let us take heart. The old mushroom rots, another springs up, but the mushroom tribe lives on." Falola, *Nationalism and African Intellectuals*, 68, 195.

71 Frederick Cooper, *African in the World: Capitalism, Empire, Nation-State* (Cambridge, MA: Harvard University Press) 2014, 1.

72 Cooper, *African in the World*, 6, 38.

73 The United States asserted control over the form of nation-statehood in African places within its sphere of influence, like Kenya, long before Independence. See Korwa G. Adar, "Kenya-U.S. Relations: A Recapitulation of Paradigmatic Conceptualizations, 1960s–1990s," in Macharia Munene, J.D. Olewe Nyunya, and Korwa Adar, eds., *The United States and Africa: From Independence to the End of the Cold War* (Nairobi: East African Educational Publishers, Ltd.) 1995.

74 The full quote is: "World peace could not occur without democratic social relations, and this in turn required economic prosperity for all societies. Poverty drove desperate peoples to support irrational beliefs of the sort that had led to World War II. It was only Western scientific rationality and technical expertise that could boost economic prosperity for poor societies, thereby attracting people to rational forms of political participation. Consequently, it was the duty of Western societies to increase their scientific and technical research and to disseminate the results to poor societies." Sandra Harding, "Beyond Postcolonial Theory: Two Undertheorized Perspectives on Science and Technology," in *The Postcolonial Science and Technology Reader* (Durham, NC: Duke University Press) 2011, 2.

75 Falola says that the universities were founded to disseminate and "implant" in "the minds of young intellectuals" in Africa, "certain models of development" and "appreciation" of Western culture. Falola, *Nationalism and African Intellectuals*, 206.

76 Christopher Fyfe, ed., *African Studies Since 1945: A Tribute to Basil Davidson: Proceedings of a Seminar in Honour of Basil Davidson's Sixtieth Birthday at the Centre of African Studies, University of Edinburgh Under the Chairmanship of George Shepperson* (London: Longman) 1976, 1. See also, Jewsiewicki and Newbury, eds., *African Historiographies*, 151.

77 "The US-based Ford Foundation, the Rockefeller Foundation, and the International Council for Educational Development, Carnegie Trust of America, and the Colonial Development and Welfare Fund, USAID, the United Nations, UNESCO, the World Bank, the IMF, the International Association of Universities, and specific US university systems all were involved in the planning and funding of African universities." (Falola, *Nationalism and African Intellectuals*, 207, 233–4).

78 Michael Adas, "Social History and the Revolution in African and Asian Historiography," *Journal of Social History*, 19:2 (Winter 1985) 2001, 335–48.

79 Philip D. Curtin, "Precolonial African History," in *Issue 501 of American Historical Association Pamphlets* (Washington, D.C.: American Historical Association) 1974, 14. Newbury, *African Historiographies*, 153.

80 Basil Davidson, *Let Freedom Come: Africa in Modern History* (Boston: Little, Brown and Company) 1978, 17.

81 Ernest Renan, "Qu'est-ce qu'une nation?," translation: "What Is a Nation?" Lecture at the Sorbonne, Paris, March 11, 1882.

82 The origin story of the United States has become exposed as mythology weaponized to maintain an illusion that issues of native conquest were settled in a long-ago past. Roxanne Dunbar-Ortiz says, "Origin narratives form the vital core of a people's unifying identity and of the values that guide them. In the United States, the founding and development of the Anglo-American settler-state involves a narrative about Puritan settlers who had a covenant with God to take the land." That part of the origin story is supported and reinforced by the Columbus myth and the "Doctrine of Discovery." As Patrick Wolfe says, "The question of genocide is never far from discussions of settler colonialism. Land is life—or, at least, land is necessary for life." Quoted in Roxanne Dunbar-Ortiz, *An Indigenous Peoples' History of the United States* (Boston: Beacon Press) 2014, 2–3.

83 Most Indian land has been lost since Independence, and even more since the 1930s, as British treaties with Indigenous nations were nullified by the United States. Those treaties had prevented British settlers from expanding west of the Appalachian Mountains under the proclamation of 1763, which was a primary factor in the settler revolt known as the American Revolution. Roxanne Dunbar-Ortiz says, "After the war for independence but preceding the writing of the US Constitution, the Continental Congress produced the Northwest Ordinance. This was the first law of the incipient republic, revealing the motive for those desiring independence. It was the blueprint for gobbling up the British-protected Indian Territory ('Ohio Country') on the other side of the Appalachians and Alleghenies." Dunbar-Ortiz, *An Indigenous Peoples' History of the United States*, 3. Anibal Quijano argues that even though the era of British settlements in North America is referred to as the Colonial Era, that colonization was not initiated until after the establishment of the United States as Native people were removed but not occupied under the British and the colonial model only realized after "Independence." Quijano, "Coloniality of Power."

84 In *Decolonizing Methodologies: Research and Indigenous Peoples*, Linda Tuhiwai Smith summarizes Indigenous and other critics of Western history (London: Zed Books) 2006, 30.

85 W.E.B. Du Bois, *The Negro*, 1915 (Project Gutenberg, 2011) (New York: Henry Holt and Co.); W.E.B. Du Bois, *Black Reconstruction in America: An Essay Toward a History of the Part Which Black Folk Played in the Attempt to Reconstruct Democracy in America, 1860–1880*, 1935 (New York: Oxford University Press) 2007. David Levering Lewis, *W.E.B. Du Bois: A Biography 1868–1963* (New York: Henry Holt and Co.) 2009. C.L.R. James, *The Black Jacobins: Toussaint L'ouverture and the San Domingo Revolution* (London: Secker & Warburg Ltd.) 1938.

86 See for example of this work Mehrsa Baradaran, *The Color of Money: Black Banks and the Racial Wealth Gap* (Cambridge, MA: Harvard University Press) 2017. These

counter-narratives were studied in universities in the 1960s where history was a
tool of consciousness raising and organizing; the second wave feminist movement,
Black Panther Party, and anti-imperial Students for a Democratic Society trace
their origins in part to university study groups. See Donna Murch, *Living for the
City: Migration, Education, and the Rise of the Black Panther Party in Oakland,
California* (Chapel Hill: U North Carolina Press) 2010.

87 The Colonial Development and Welfare Act finally allowed higher education in the
British colonies in 1940.

88 Bethwell A. Ogot, "Rereading the History and Historiography of Epistemic
Domination and Resistance in Africa," *African Studies Review*, 52:1, April, 2009, 18.

89 Professor Ogot has contributed extensively to Kenyan historiography and also has
made himself personally accessible through his autobiography, which provides rich
ground for understanding the moment into which Kenyan history was first written.
Bethwell Allan Ogot, *My Footprints on the Sands of Time* (Bloomington: Trafford
Pub.) 2006.

90 In his autobiography, Ogot reports that the previous chair referred to "nineteenth
century Central Africans as 'these impulsive children of nature.'" Ogot, *My
Footprints*, 133–5.

91 Ogot, *My Footprints*, 140–3; 150. Ogot said later, "By the end of the 1960s African
history and historiography had been successfully introduced in numerous
academic institutions in Africa, Europe, and the United States. Africa-based
historians and social scientists founded academic journals, formed historical
associations, and held academic and professional conferences in Africa. The
most remarkable legacy of these activities was the writing of UNESCO'S General
History of Africa, published in eight volumes and translated into more than fifteen
international languages. This was the response of African intellectuals to the
colonialist history of Africa and the colonial library. These activities constituted our
intellectual resistance to the Western epistemic domination." Ogot, "Rereading the
History and Historiography of Epistemic Domination and Resistance in Africa," 18.

92 Ogot and others have emphasized the lost potential for a broader coalition
Kenyan government that briefly existed as the Kenyan African Union, KAU,
which was formed in 1944 but banned during the Mau Mau revolt in 1953. B.A.
Ogot, Review Article, "Britain's Gulag. Review of David Anderson, *Histories of the
Hanged: Britain's Dirty War in Kenya and the End of Empire* (London: Weidenfeld
& Nicolson) 2005, and Caroline Elkins, *Britain's Gulag: The Brutal End of Empire
in Kenya* (London: Jonathan Cape) 2005," *Journal of American History*, 46, 2005,
493–505. See also John Lonsdale, "KAU's Cultures: Imaginations of Community
and Constructions of Leadership in Kenya after the Second World War," *Journal of
African Cultural Studies*, 13:1, 2000, 108.

93 Kenyan statehood was initially brokered by a coalition of Luo and Kikuyu political
leadership who together formed the KANU political party and worked closely

with representatives of the Crown in London to draft Kenya's constitution. They also drafted together the plan for Kenya's capitalist economy under the direction of Mboya, a young Luo leader with international appeal and popular support to succeed Kenyatta as Kenya's second president. Mboya was assassinated in 1969, Ogot says by "the Kikuyu mafia." Ogot, *My Footprints,* 228. At the time of Mboya's assassination, Ogot says of Kenyan historians, "All of us were Luos" and that Ogot was himself put under surveillance for a time. Ogot, *My Footprints,* 183.

94 Ogot developed this method, in fact through his PhD dissertation, before the value of Oral History was recognized in the Western Academy through the work of Jan Vansina, the man credited with its invention in Western historiography. Vansina recognized the challenges faced by Western historians conducting Oral History in Africa. He said, "Traditions should be recorded in the language in which they were transmitted. This is usually done for most kinds of oral transmission, with the exception of narratives, commentaries, and epics. Indeed, it has been suggested that historians rely on instantaneous translations for immediate understanding of narratives, but those who have recorded 'live' traditions in the original would not agree with this suggestion. In a translation the linguistic 'markers,' the exact shadings or nuances, the multiple meanings of the original narration, the whole literary climate of the performance is lost. With that loss, the impact of the language on the content of the tradition will remain largely undetected." Jan Vansina, "Once Upon a Time: Oral Traditions as History in Africa," *Daedalus*: 100: 2, "The Historian and the World of the Twentieth Century," Spring, 1971, 452.

95 Ogot, *My Footprints,* 144. He said later that the "pioneers" of African history "discovered purposive change in an African past which dealt not with 'tribes' but with human communities whose institutions and ideas deserved respect in their own terms." Ogot, "Rereading the History and Historiography of Epistemic Domination and Resistance in Africa," 18.

96 Ogot, *My Footprints,* 138. African Oral history is methodical, in the words of George Dei, "not just talk. Cultures relying on oral transmission of history and religion need specially selected individuals to carry and pass on that knowledge. These are caretakers of knowledge who perform a similar task, keeping watch over a particular history. In many cultures, only these custodians of knowledge are permitted to pass it on. Many Indigenous groups in Africa and North America used this system to protect their culture and histories from invading Europeans who sought to exterminate their culture and histories." Dei is among those who have continued this "transgressive" African-centered approach to research and all academic work and teaching in his call for collaboration and rejection of the "prism" of individualism, and the segregation of "the sources of raw data" and "the place of academic theorizing." George J. Sefa Dei, *Teaching Africa: Towards a Transgressive Pedagogy* (University of Toronto: Ontario Institute for Studies in Education) 2010, xxii, 2.

97 Ogot, *My Footprints,* 157.

98 Ibid, 150, 152.

99 Ogot said later that "The aspect of western science most offensive and destructive was that Africans as a race are only capable of 'concrete' thought, as opposed to Europeans for whom abstract thought is second nature." Bethwell A. Ogot "Rereading the History and Historiography of Epistemic Domination and Resistance in Africa," *African Studies Review*, 52:1 (April, 2009), 1–22. Kenya in the end settled on a nationalist curriculum reminiscent of what is taught across the continent of Africa. See Solomon Monyenye, "Education and Development of Nationhood in Kenya," *Reinvigorating the University Mandate in a Globalizing Environment: Challenges, Obstacles, and Way Forward* (Conference Proceedings May 26–27, 2005, Kenyatta University).

100 Two key members of this group, Thomas Hodgkin and Christopher Fyfe, were known as radical historians, friends of the British historian Eric Hobsbaum, both outsiders to the field in their politics and also exemplary in their entitlement to academic resources, both born to families with prominence in academics. Neither finished school and both received honorary degrees. Fyfe became involved in history in 1950 at age thirty when his brother-in-law invited him to colonial headquarters in Sierra Leone to salvage moldy archives, and was appointed national archivist and ten years later, he published an 852-page book on Sierra Leone history modeled on Joyce's Ulysses. Thomas Hodgkin was self-taught, travelled through Africa, joined the Communist Party as a young man, and wrote *Nationalism in Colonial Africa* in 1956. *The Scotsman: Scotland's National Newspaper,* September 16, 2008; "Christopher Fyfe," John Hargreaves, *The Guardian,* October 27, 2008.

101 "Basil Davidson," *The Telegraph,* July 19, 2010; Caroline Neale, *Writing "Independent" History: African Historiography, 1960–1980* (Westport: Greenwood Press, 1985). The second quote is by Edward Said. Victoria Brittain, "Basil Davidson Obituary" *Guardian,* July 9, 2010; "Basil Davidson," *The Telegraph,* July 19, 2010.

102 Brittain, "Basil Davidson Obituary" *Guardian,* July 9, 2010; "Basil Davidson," *The Telegraph,* July 19, 2010.

103 Davidson said, "There isn't a single literate East African aged 35 to 50 who wasn't educated on my textbooks." He was also reported to have said, "What good did it do? Very little." "Basil Davidson," *The Telegraph,* July 19, 2010. Christopher Fyfe educated a generation of historians in Sierra Leonne, condensed versions of his book taught in schools throughout the country and was "cherished in many Freetown homes," according to his obituary in the *Guardian.* "Christopher Fyfe," John Hargreaves, *The Guardian,* October 27, 2008.

104 Thomas Hodgkin said, "the real conflict [among historians] was between those who, from whatever philosophical standpoint, sought the end of empire—who

were opposed to the colonial relationship as such—and those who wished to modify, reform and 'humanise' it. The test of seriousness was willingness to attack, or seek to overthrow, one's own imperialism. This meant that one must, naturally and necessarily, support the demands of national movements for total independence, even if this seemed likely to lead immediately to what we thought of then as the dictatorship of the national bourgeoisie—what Fanon later called 'false decolonisation'—though we were hopeful, over-hopeful no doubt, of the possibility of other kinds of outcome." Thomas Hodgkin, "Where the Path Begins," in Christopher Fyfe, ed., *African Studies Since 1945: A Tribute to Basil Davidson, Proceedings of a Seminar in Honour of Basil Davidson's Sixtieth Birthday at the Centre of African Studies, University of Edinburgh, Under the Chairmanship of George Shepperson* (London: Longman Group Ltd.) 1976, 12.

105 Terence Ranger claimed, in John Lonsdale's words, that "Post-colonial critics failed to realize that Africa's historians did not depend for their data on colonial accounts alone. We could read or hear African narratives too. The critics' other mistake was theoretical. They did not appreciate that all human enterprise necessarily rests on a narrative sense of its actors' place in a fruitfully linear, or redemptively recursive, sense of time. Historians were as warily conscious of this need in colonialists as in their subjects. In response to the first criticism, Ranger stated his own belief that the disciplined, scholarly, representation of locally constructed, autonomous, liberating, narrative was technically the equivalent to any other historical practice." John Lonsdale, "Agency in Tight Corners: Narrative and Initiative in African History," *Journal of African Cultural Studies*, 13:1, 2000, 5–16, 8.

106 Carolyn Neale, "The Idea of Progress in the Revision of African History, 1960–1970," in Jewsiewicki and Newbury, *African Historiographies*, 112.

107 Davidson, *Let Freedom Come*, 44. Davidson reversed his position later, arguing that the nation-state model must be dismantled and greater continental unity built through greater local power. Davidson, *Black Man's Burden*; "Basil Davidson," Arna Biney, *Pambazuka News: Voices for Freedom and Justice,* July 28, 2010.

108 Neale, *Writing "Independent" History*; Jewsiewicki and Newbury, eds., *African Historiographies*. The critiques of this cohort were influenced by those of African historians. See Arnold Temu and Bonaventure Swai, *Historians and Africanist History: A Critique: Post-Colonial Historiography Examined* (London: Zed Books) 1981. Neale, "The Idea of Progress," 116.

109 Ibid, 116.

110 Ibid, 119.

111 Ibid, 116. Africanist Philip Curtin defined the "stateless societies" as "historical blank spots on the map of Africa" that may *continue* to exist "into the twentieth century." Curtin, "Precolonial African History," 11.

112 See Andrew Zimmerman, "Africa in Imperial and Transnational History: Multi-Sited Historiography and the Necessity of Theory," *The Journal of African History*, 54:3, 2013, 331–40.

113 Neale, Jewsiewicki and Newbury, *African Historiographies*, 115. For example, she cites: "Kinship and Statelessness among the Nilotes," Ogot, B., in J. Vansina et al., *The Historian in Tropical Africa* (Oxford: Clarendon) 1964. Herders and cities continue to coexist today despite their assignment into different historical moments. Maasai communities live today in villages made of cow dung within view of the skyscrapers on the outskirts of Nairobi; both the skyscrapers and the villages are here and now. Lions sometimes wander across highways from the fenceless national park that sits in the center of Nairobi to prey on Maasai herds, a drama that in this place is a fully urban issue. "Lions on the Loose in Nairobi Again," *Daily Nation*, Mary 21, 2016. The article describes the Maasai village at City Cabanas, Nairobi, which lost over 100 sheep in an attack from a lion wandering from the adjacent Nairobi National Park.

114 Neale, *Writing "Independent" History*, 37.

115 Toyin Falola says that in the 1970s, "disciplines such as history, religious studies, and philosophy were challenged to justify themselves. The state began to regard some disciplines as producing 'useless knowledge,' useless because their contribution to development was hard to see." He says, "Medicine, law, pharmacy, and engineering became the kings among offerings, the social sciences the civil servants, and the humanities the slaves." Falola, *Nationalism and African Intellectuals*, 211–12, 268. David Newbury claims that as funding was cut for African Studies in the 1970s, "enrollment in graduation programs fell dramatically" though "undergraduate enrollment in Third World courses often remained high" Bogumil Jewsiewicki and David Newbury, "Historians and Africanist History," in Jewsiewicki and Newbury, *African Historiographies: What History for Which Africa?* (Thousand Oaks, CA: SAGE Publications) 1985, 154.

116 The Rockefeller and Ford Foundations had provided the main support for Kenyan history and also acted as gatekeepers to World Bank loans, and their funding had never been secure: for example, faculty positions had typically been created on a temporary basis and every program and project created by African history departments, every scholarship, appointment, library, research agenda, was vetted by the funding agencies themselves. Ogot's description of the founding of the History Department at the University College of Nairobi demonstrates one example of the involvement of funding agencies in prioritizing projects, faculty, and activities. Bethwell A. Ogot, *My Footprints on the Sands of Time: An Autobiography* (Kisumu: Anyange Press Ltd.) 2003, 102, 130–3, 166. Elsewhere Ogot said, "Carnegie Corporation sought to redefine the mission of African universities and the contributions which they might make to national

development" in 1960. Ogot, "National Identity and Nationalism Concepts and Ideologies," Keynote Address, *Commonwealth Association of Museums,* September, 1995, South Africa and Botswana, 1. Tovin Falola and E.S. Atieno Odhiambo, *The Challenges of History and Leadership in Africa: The Essays of Bethwell Allan Ogot* (Trenton, NJ: Africa World Press) 2002, 646, 651.

117 Abiola Irele, "The African Scholar: Is Black Africa Entering the Dark Ages of Scholarship?," *Transition,* 51, 1991, 58. Toyin Falola says, "African scholars who want to publish in the West risk disaster: their inability to obtain current materials diminishes the quality of their contributions, and they face the difficulty of situating themselves in agendas and concerns that are decidedly external to their interests. Rejection of African authors has become so commonplace that Western publishers and journals have been accused of turning publication into a major opportunity to exercise cultural and intellectual power over Africa." Falola, *Nationalism and African Intellectuals,* 268.

118 Jewsiewiki, "One Historiography or Several?," in Jewsiewiki and Newbury, *African Historiographies,* 9.

119 Falola, *Nationalism and African Intellectuals,* 270, 276.

120 Thandika Mkandawire, "Three Generations of African Academics: A Note," *CODESRIA Bulletin,* 28:3, 1995, 9.

121 Ogot, *My Footprints,* 157–8.

122 John Lonsdale, *Mau Mau and Nationhood: Arms, Authority, and Narration* (Athens, OH: Ohio University Press) 2003, 2.

123 Mau Mau historiography will be discussed in Chapter 2.

124 E.S. Atieno-Odhiambo, "Introduction: The Invention of Kenya," in B.A. Ogot and W.R. Ochieng' eds., *Decolonization and Independence in Kenya: 1940–93* (Nairobi: E.A.E.P) 1995, 2.

125 Ogot, *My Footprints,* 157–8.

126 Annie E. Coombes, Lotte Hughes, and Karega Munene, *Managing Heritage, Making Peace: History, Identity and Memory in Contemporary Kenya* (London: I.B. Tauris) 2014, 186; Atieno-Odhiambo, "Introduction," 1.

127 A Kenyan identity will be built, in Ogot's words, as a "multicultural nation continuously and ceaselessly engaged in a crusade" for greater freedom, democracy, and equality of Kenyan citizens. Lonsdale agrees. "The people of Kenya," he said, "have to broaden their historical experiences to embrace the multi-cultural and multi-ethnic nature of the Kenyan state." Lonsdale, *Mau Mau and Nationhood,* 5.

128 Ndeywel E. Nziem, "African History and Africanist Historians" in Jewsiewiki and Newbury, *African Historiographies,* 25.

129 Nziem, "African Historians and Africanist History," 20. The school at Dar also critiqued the culture of the field of Western History, which Temu said is a

"man's profession" noting that there was only one woman of thirty historians at Cambridge in 1975. Temu and Swai, *Historians and Africanist History,* ix, xiv, xvi.

130 Temu and Swai, *Historians and Africanist History*, x.

131 Arnold Temu said that *How Europe Underdeveloped Africa* reveals the specific ways that Western thought gets read onto African places and helps historians and their students to challenge the "Development Ideology" of imperial history and in that way has practical application. Temu and Swai, *Historians and Africanist History*, 9. Walter Rodney, *How Europe Underdeveloped Africa,* 1972 (Abuja, Nigeria: Panaf Publishing) 2009. See also Falola, *Nationalism and African Intellectuals,* 129.

132 Falola, *Nationalism and African Intellectuals*, 256, 259.

133 Nziem, "African Historians and Africanist History," 20.

134 For the role of universities in the formation of radical movements, see Murch, *Living for the City*; Todd Gitlin, *Years of Hope, Days of Rage* (New York: Bantam Books) 1989.

135 Michael Adas, "Social History and Revolution in African and Asian Historiography," *Journal of Social History*, 19:2, December, 1985, 336.

136 This repudiation of the first generation of African history and call for greater professionally reflects a broad consensus. See: Lonsdale, "KAU's Cultures: Imaginations of Community and Constructions of Leadership in Kenya after the Second World War," 107; Newbury, *African Historiographies*, 119–20. Joseph C. Miller, History and Africa/Africa and History, *The American Historical Review*, Volume 104, Issue 1, February 1999, 1–32; Parker and Reid, *Oxford Handbook of Modern African History,* 12.

137 David Newbury, "Africanist Historical Studies in the United States: Metamorphosis or Metastasis?" in Jewsiewicki and Newbury, *African Historiographies,* 154.

138 Newbury, "Africanist Social Studies," in Jewsiewicki and Newbury, *African Historiographies,*152.

139 Scholars of the western academy derided those Africanists who critiqued post-colonial nation-statehood as "Pessimists," and some saw this "Pessimism" to be the greatest threat to African statehood. Terence Ranger claimed that he and other "optimists" promoted African agency while the Pessimists' thinking was Eurocentric. He saw himself as, "The historian who persists in treating national movements as something of genuine importance and formidable energy; who sees the African peoples winning their independence in the face of colonial reluctance and repression; who believes that mass participation was at various points crucial; has to argue his case against a wide belief that national independence was an episode in a comedy in which the colonial powers handed over to their selected and groomed bourgeois successors and in which nothing fundamental was changed … The Africanist historian … who emphasizes African activity, African

adaptation, African choice, African initiative, will increasingly find his main adversaries not in the discredited colonial school but in the radical pessimists." Terence Ranger 1968, quoted in Lonsdale, "Agency in Tight Corners," 7. The historiography has adopted this perspective: "Since the late 1950s,we have seen the demise of Eurocentric colonial historiography, the rise and decline of African historiography encapsulated in the modernization paradigm, the emergence of a school of African agency and its rejection by "radical pessimists" who embrace underdevelopment theory, and a short lived flirtation with modes of production analysis. The absence of a dominant paradigm today is a sign of the field's growing maturity." Allen Isaacman, "Jewsiewiki and Newbury, Review: *African Historiographies: What History for Which Africa?*," 1986, *Contemporary Sociology,*17:2, 1968, 162. A great source on the past and future of "Pessimism," is Abubakar Momoh, "Does Pan-Africanism Have a Future in Africa? In Search of the Ideational Basis of Afro-Pessimism," *African Journal of Political Science,* 8:1, 2003. On a revival of African Nationalism as anti-imperialism, Issa G. Shivji, "The Rise, the Fall, and the Insurrection of Nationalism in Africa," Paper from Keynote Address to the CODESRIA East African Regional Conference held in Addis Ababa, Ethiopia, October 29–31, 2003. See also Alan Isaacman, "Reviewed Work: African Historiographies: What History for Which Africa?", Edited by Bagumil Jewsiewicki and David Newbury (Beverly Hills: Sage) 1986, in *Contemporary Sociology*, Vol. 17, No. 2, (March, 1988), 162.

140 Adas, "Social History," 337.

141 Newbury, "Africanist Social Studies," 153.

142 Africanist historians in the West had to fight to extend the "People without History" approach to Africa. Michael Adas says, "Most African and Asian historians who came of age in the 1960s and early1970s can … recall moments of confrontation that made them all too aware that their avid interest in peasants, untouchables, or other varieties of non-elite groups was not history for those in positions of academic power." Adas, "Social History and the Revolution in African and Asian Historiography," 336. That included apparently Marxist historians whose work had produced the approach of the new history in the West. Eric Hobsbawm was a leading British Marxist historian whose reconstruction of British History from the perspective of its working classes was instrumental in the larger project. Yet Hobsbawm continued the argument that Africa had no useful history into the 1990s. John Lonsdale said, "In his history of 'the short twentieth century,' *Age of Extremes*, Hobsbawm had dismissed Africa, along with the rest of the Third World. It had no relevance to what mattered, 'the dynamics of global transformation.'" For the Africanists who undertook the search for "People without History" in Africa, the project stood in defiance of Hobsbawm, but also of the Dar School, as an alternative to the more radical theory generated there and especially the critique of neocolonialism. Terence Ranger introduced the focus on

a "people-oriented historiography" at the Dar School in 1960, to shift from a focus he said on the Cultural Nationalism based in anti-imperial theory, which he said students did not want, and he called instead for a new history, one that will study poverty and underdevelopment. Falola, *Nationalism and African Intellectuals,* 252. Eric Hobsbawm, *The Age of Extremes: The Short Twentieth Century, 1914–1991* (London: Michael Joseph) 1994, 200. See also Eric Hobsbawm, *The Age of Revolution in Europe: 1789–1848* (London: Abacus) 1962. Quoted in Lonsdale, "Agency in Tight Corners," 9.

143 Temu and Swai, *Historians and Africanist History,* 5.

144 Miller said that "tribe" was used as a litmus test to differentiate the insider Africanist from the older out-of-touch historians, the "nonspecialists." Miller, "History and Africa," 15–16.

145 Miller, "History and Africa," 20.

146 Adas, "Social History," 340. See also Lonsdale, "Agency in Tight Corners," 7.

147 The full quote: "Our present perceptions of Africa and our understanding of its past are conditioned by the epistemological categories well established by 1900, and in large part derived from the observations of administrators, missionaries, and various travelers. Their perceptions were translated directly, uncritically, into their conclusions, and, once published, these have often been accepted as fact, as if they were similar to incontrovertible experimental observations of the structures of crystals." Vanisina says that his own field was based on the writings of "Early colonialists [who] produced false African societies that were then 'discovered' by Anthropologists in the 1950s." Vansina, Jewsiewicki and Newbury, *African History and Africanist Historians,* 29, 35.

148 Miller, "History and Africa," 12.

149 Tignor compares the impacts of early colonization on the three most affected communities, and King describes colonialera resistance of Maasai. Robert Tignor, *Colonial Transformation of Kenya: Kamba, Kikuyu and Maasai, 1900–1939* (Princeton, NJ: Princeton University Press, 1976); Kenneth King, "The Kenya Maasai and the Protest Phenomenon, 1900–1960," *The Journal of African History,* 12:1, 1971, 117–37.

150 Richard Waller's *first* intervention was to reframe the Maasai community's known armed resistance to their colonization as cultural "conservatism," a general refusal to change and hostility "to attempts to penetrate their society from without or to change it from within." *Second,* he used a brief period of Maasai cooperation with the British, during a time of starvation at the turn of the twentieth century, to argue that Maasai more broadly were allies of the British, a claim that has characterized Maasai in Kenyan history since. He argued that Maasai would have embraced colonization and British culture had they not been "relegated to the periphery, politically as well as geographically" onto reservations after 1904, which forms the basis of the argument that Maasai identity is a product of British

agency. *Third*, he argued that Maasai were heading toward cultural annihilation before the arrival of the British, the implication being that Maasai culture survived due to colonization. *Fourth*, Waller said that Maasai were undermined by their own corrupt leadership who he says hired Maasai out as "military clients of local chiefs" to "harness Maasai raiding impulses for their own advantage." These leaders, he said, betrayed Maasai, especially the oloiboni Olonana who "lent his authority to recruitment [of Maasai warriors] in return for a share of the spoils." All of these claims will be addressed in Chapter 5. Richard Waller, "The Maasai and the British 1895–1905: The Origins of an Alliance," *Journal of African History*, XVII:4, 1976, 529–53.

151 Swahili language sources have not been explored in English scholarship to the knowledge of the authors. John Berntsen questioned "how much the Swahili really knew and understood about the life, customs, and past of the Maa-speaking peoples, and about how well they communicated any such knowledge to the Europeans. A number of Swahili had accompanied several caravans to Maasailand and spoke the Maa language, which was a lingua franca or [*sic*] the northern Rift Valley region. No doubt they understood the general characteristics of Maasai life, but it is not clear that they appreciated the more subtle distinctions which a Maa-speaker might have found important." John Berntsen, "The Enemy Is Us: Eponymy in the Historiography of the Maasai," *History in Africa*, 7, 1980, 1–21; see also "The Maasai and Their Neighbors: Variables of Interaction," *African Economic History*, 2, Autumn, 1976, 7.

152 Berntsen, "The Maasai and Their Neighbors," 1.

153 Thomas Spear and Richard Waller, eds., *Being Maasai: Ethnicity and Identity in East Africa* (Athens, OH: Ohio University Press) 1993.

154 Thomas Spear, "Introduction," in Spear and Waller, Being Maasai, 2.

155 This argument is made through the other chapters: "[The Maasai] developed a formal ethnic identity not because they were in search of a community but because, as boundaries hardened under colonial definition, the loosely articulated community that they had could not deal effectively with outsiders without one." "In this sense, aliens took the place of 'Dorobo' as 'the mirror in the forest', defining the community by positing its opposite." Richard Waller, "Acceptees and Aliens: Kikuyu Settlement in Maasailand," in *Being Maasai*, 242–3.

156 Waller, "Acceptees and Aliens," *Being Maasai*, 238.

157 Ibid, 237.

158 Ibid.

159 Spear, "Introduction," 1.

160 Bill Bravman, "Ethnicity and Identity—*Being Maasai: Ethnicity and Identity in East Africa*," Review, *Journal of African History*, 35:1, March, 1994, 134–5.

161 Paul Spencer, "Becoming Maasai, Being in Time," Spear and Waller, *Being Maasai*, 161.

162 See, for example, Dorothy Hodgson, *Once Intrepid Warriors: Gender, Ethnicity,*
    and the Cultural Politics of Maasai Development (Bloomington: Indiana University
    Press) 2001; Hodgson, *Being Maasai, Becoming Indigenous*. Agency over Maasai
    identity is routinely attributed to British colonizers, and assumed to be used
    strategically by Maasai people today. Dorothy Hodgson summarizes, for example,
    "These pastoralist Maa speakers were eventually called 'Maasai' by Europeans to
    distinguish them from Maa speakers who continued to farm, gather and hunt, and
    sometimes herd. By the late colonial period, people themselves came to fiercely
    identify themselves as 'Maasai,' an assertion of ethnic identity that continues today,
    despite (or because of) continued attacks on their land, livelihoods, appearances
    and practices." Dorothy Hodgson, *Gender, Justice, and the Problem of Culture:*
    From Customary Law to Human Rights in Tanzania (Bloomington: University of
    Indiana Press) 2017, Chapter 1.

163 See for example a recent article in *The New Yorker*, which (mis)uses at length
    a complex exploration by Dorothy Hodgson of contemporary Maasai identity
    to claim that it is "Time" (for *New Yorker* readers) to "Rethink" the self-
    definition of Indigenous peoples, especially the Maasai. No living Maasai people
    were apparently consulted in the drafting of the article, and *The New Yorker*
    declined to print a letter in response from at least one Indigenous Maasai
    person, Meitamei Olol Dapash. Manvir Singh, "It's Time to Rethink the Idea
    of 'Indigenous': Many Groups Who Identify as Indigenous Don't Claim to Be
    First Peoples; Many Who Did Come First Don't Claim to Be Indigenous. Can
    the Concept Escape Its Colonial Past?" Analysis of Inquiry, *The New Yorker*,
    February 27, 2023 Issue.

164 An extensive international body of scholarship has emerged which seeks to
    include "Land" as a human right of Indigenous peoples. See Jeremie Gilbert, "Land
    Rights as Human Rights: The Case for Specific Rights to Land," *Sur International*
    Journal on Human Rights, 10:18, 2013, https://sur.conectas.org/en/land-rights-
    human-rights/; Brian Asa Omwoyo, "A Critical Evaluation for the Regime of
    Protection for Protection of Indigenous Peoples' Rights Under International
    Human Rights Law," 2014; Ademola Oluborode Jegede and Thohoyandou, "The
    Protection of Indigenous Peoples' Lands by Domestic Legislation on Climate
    Change Response Measures: Exploring Potentials in the Regional Human Rights
    System of Africa," *International Journal on Minority and Group Rights*, 24:1, 2017,
    24–56; Jérémie Gilbert and Valérie Couillard, "International Law and Land Rights
    in Africa: The shift from States' Territorial Possessions to Indigenous Peoples'
    Ownership Rights," in Robert Home, ed., *Essays in African Land Law* (Pretoria,
    South Africa: Pretoria University Press) 2011, 47–68; Stefaan Smis, Dorothée
    Cambou, and Genny Ngende, "The Question of Land Grab in Africa and the

Indigenous Peoples' Right to Traditional Lands, Territories and Resources," *Loyola Los Angeles International and Comparative Law Review*, 35:3 (Summer 2013), 493; George Mukundi Wachira, *Vindicating Indigenous Peoples' Land Rights in Kenya* (Faculty of Law: University of Pretoria) 2008.

165 Sankaran Krishna, *Globalization and Post Colonialism: Hegemony and Resistance in the 21st century* (Lanham, MD: Rowman & Littlefield) 2009, 122. Aileen Morten-Robinson describes the construction of identity as "fluid" as a strategy of silencing Indigenous peoples, as it enables settler societies to elude themselves, to escape being pinned down in their settler position. Indigenous people on the other hand are constructed as fixed in time and space, and one strategy of assimilation is to bring them into fluid identities, which means assimilating, adopting the mark of the "civilized." She says that Indigenous identity is not in fact fixed, and it does not conform to this framing. It exists in different communities differently, and is communal not individual, and is essentially a factor of a relationship to a place forged outside of colonization. Moreton-Robinson, *The White Possessive*, 13.

166 David M. Anderson, "Cow Power: Livestock and the Pastoralist in Africa," *African Affairs*, 92:366, January, 1993, 123.

167 "From the mid-twentieth century, when governments throughout Africa first began to implement far-reaching policies for rural development, the pasturelands and the kraals have witnessed a battle between two sets of protagonists; one advocating the protection of pastoralist societies, through sometimes within a paradigm of gradual change; the other advocating rapid transformation through social and economic 'modernization.'" Anderson, "Cow Power," 122.

168 Terence O. Ranger, "The Invention of Tradition in Colonial Africa," in Eric Hobsbawn and Terence Ranger, eds., *The Invention of Tradition* (Cambridge: Canto Press) 1993/1992, 248. Joseph Miller said, "African politicians and intellectuals created ethnicity itself by manipulating supple, collective identities to meet historical circumstances." His source for this claim is nineteenth-century European observers. Miller, "African History," 17.

169 Ranger, "The Invention of Tradition," 249.

170 Meitamei Olol Dapash was designated the lead representative of the Maasai community in the BBI process.

171 Lotte Hughes, "Why Maasai's BBI Demands Are Unworkable, Especially on Land," February 27, 2020, *Saturday Nation*, Kenya.

172 Lotte Hughes, "Building Bridges or Sowing Division? Maasai, BBI, and a Century of Misinterpretation," August 6, 2021, *The Elephant*, theelephant.info/analysis/2021/08/06/building-bridges-or-sowing-division-maasai-bbi-and-a-century-of-misinterpretation/.

Chapter 2

1   See Robert Tignor, *Colonial Transformation of Kenya: Kamba, Kikuyu and Maasai, 1900–1939* (Princeton: Princeton University Press) 1976.

2   Letter from Provincial Commissioner to the Chief Secretary of the Colony at Nairobi titled *Masai Kikuyu Boundary*, April 8, 1913, 82–5, Kenya National Archive, DC/MKS10A/5/1.

3   Joseph Thomson, *Through Masai Land: A Journey of Exploration among the Snowclad Volcanic Mountains and Strange Tribes of Eastern Equatorial Africa* (London: Sampson, Lowe, Marston, & Rivington) 1885.

4   Fischer was turned back by Maasai and Thomson met a similar reception of what he called "hostile" Maasai near Mt. Kilimanjaro. He did reach Naivasha but said that Maasai there were "troublesome" and at Laikipia he was forced to flee in the night. In 1887, Count Teleki reported to the Germans, traveling from Zanzibar to Mt. Kilimanjaro, through the land of the Kaputiei Maasai, to Ngong, to Laikipia, and all the way to Lake Turkana without conflict. In 1889, when Dr. Carl Peters reached *Entorror* and undertook a massive raiding of Maasai livestock for which three of his party were killed. George R. Sandford, *Administrative and Political History of the Masai Reserve*, 1918 (London: Waterlow & Sons) 1919, 10–11.

5   Sandford, *An Administrative and Political History of the Masai Reserve.*

6   H.W.O. Okoth-Ogendo, *Tenants of the Crown: Evolution of Agrarian Law and Institutions in Kenya* (Nairobi: African Center for Technology Studies Press) 1991, 12–13.

7   Okoth-Ogendo, *Tenants of the Crown,* 12–13.

8   Ibid, 13.

9   Ibid, 12–13.

10 Ibid, 30.

11 Dr. Likimani, "Kenyan Constitutional Conference, 1962: Record of the First Meeting of the Masai Delegates and a Group of Representatives of the Conference, Held in the Music Room, Lancaster House, on March 21, 1962, 5:00 pm." Kenya National Archive, CO822/2000/115261.

12 Norman Leys, *Kenya* (London: Hogarth Press) 1924, 113.

13 Ibid.

14 Bruce Berman and John Lonsdale, "Coping with the Contradictions: The Development of the Colonial State 1895–1914," in *Unhappy Valley: Conflict in Kenya and Africa: Book I: State and Class* (London, UK: James Currey) 1992, 89.

15 Caroline Elkins, *Imperial Reckoning: The Untold Story of Britain's Gulag in Kenya* (New York: Henry Holt) 2005, 8–9.

16 Leys, *Kenya,* 108.

17 David Anderson, *Histories of the Hanged: The Dirty War in Kenya and the End of Empire* (New York: W.W. Norton) 2005, 5.

18 Anderson, *Histories of the Hanged*, 11.

19 Capitalism created a field of opportunity for "workers" of the agricultural communities.

> Colonial rule entrenched power; it also enlarged markets. The African poor could exploit the new demands for their produce and their labour because there was also new competition for the prestige of their protection. They even found a market in land, despite its alienation to Europeans. As workers they were oppressed but as dependents they benefited from the rivalry for their service among a wider range of patrons. Their chiefs were fastened more securely over them with administrative sanctions but, as before, they were not the only masters. The power of the state had made room for others.

John Lonsdale, "The Conquest State of Kenya 1895–1905," *Unhappy Valley: Conflict in Kenya and Africa: Book I: State and Class* (London: James Currey) 1992, 15.

20 Berman and Lonsdale, "Coping with the Contradictions," 90.

21 The later figures came from a Danish source, Ole Wivel, "Karen Blixen," August 29, 2013, *Dansk Biografisk Leksikon (in Danish). Copenhagen, Denmark: Gyldendal.* David Anderson cites a different number, of 1,000 acres for Kikuyu workers. Anderson, *Histories of the Hanged*, 23–4.

22 The museum tells us that Blixen, an avid hunter, hosted thousands of "guests" to her mostly forested land, which was known to the Maasai as a deep rhino homeland. The Maasai name for the Ngong hills especially suggests the eye of a stream where rhinos gather.

23 Anderson, *Histories of the Hanged*, 24.

24 Ibid.

25 Ibid.

26 Berman and Lonsdale, *Unhappy Valley*, 363.

27 The chroniclers of white settlement in Kenya describe these as the halcyon days of "the pioneers," who carved their farms out of the African wilderness. "Pioneering itself may be a sort of art," wrote Elspeth Huxley, "in its own way as creative as the painting of a picture." Anderson, *Histories of the Hanged*, 24.

28 E.S. Atieno-Odhiambo, "The Formative Years: 1945–55," in B.A. Ogot and W.R. Ochieng, eds., *Decolonization & Independence in Kenya: 1940–1993* (London: James Currey) 1995, 35–7.

29 Lonsdale, *Unhappy Valley*, 418.

30 Berman and Lonsdale, "Coping with the Contradictions," 90.

31 Lonsdale, "The Conquest State of Kenya, 1895–1905," 36.

32 Anderson, *Histories of the Hanged*, 24.

33 Londsdale, *Unhappy Valley*, 430.

34 See Patrick Wolfe, "Settler Colonialism and the Elimination of the Native," *Journal of Genocide Research*, 8:4, December, 2006, 388.

35 Wolfe, "Settler Colonialism," 389.

36 Aileen Moreton-Robinson traces the invention of British settler belonging in the colony of Australia. For the first generation of migrants in the 1880s, "their sense of belonging was to Britain." They were "pioneers" developing "resource for the empire." Franz Fanon says,

> The settler makes history and is conscious of making it. And because he constantly refers to the history of his mother country, he clearly indicates that he himself is the extension of that mother country. Thus, the history which he writes is not the history of the country which he plunders but the history of his own nation in regard to all that she skims off, all that she violates and starves.

Aileen Moreton-Robinson, *The White Possessive: Property, Power, and Indigenous Sovereignty* (Minneapolis, MN: University of Minnesota Press) 2015, 5; Franz Fanon, *Wretched of the Earth* (Harmondsworth: Penguin) 1961, 40.

37 Moreton-Robinson, *The White Possessive*, xxi.

38 Aloysha Goldstein, "Where the Nation Takes Place: Proprietary Regimes, Antistatism, and U.S. Settler Colonialism," *South Atlantic Quarterly*, 107:4, Fall, 2008, 835–6.

39 Koigi Wa Wamwere, *I Refuse to Die: My Journey for Freedom* (New York: Seven Stories Press) 2003, 24.

40 Moreton-Robinson, *White Possessive*, 5.

41 Anderson, *Histories of the Hanged*, 10.

42 Ibid, 10, 12–13.

43 Daniel Branch, *Kenya: Between Hope and Despair, 1963–2011* (New Haven, CT: Yale University Press) 2011, 7.

44 Lonsdale, *Unhappy Valley*, 418.

45 Anderson, *Histories of the Hanged*, 27–8.

46 Lonsdale, *Unhappy Valley*, 383.

47 Anderson, *Histories of the Hanged*, 16.

48 Wunyabari O. Maloba, *Mau Mau and Kenya: An Analysis of a Peasant Revolt* (Bloomington, IN: Indiana University Press) 1998, 61.

49 Ogot and Ochieng, *Decolonization and Independence*, 35–7.

50 Elkins, *Imperial Reckoning*, 42–3.

51 Many books on Mau Mau repeat a trope that the British in Kenya only used brutal force near the end of their rule, in the 1950s. But that only applies to Central Kenya, as Maasai, Nandi, and other peoples experienced brutality throughout the colonial period. B.A. Ogot says, in his review of books on Mau Mau by Caroline Elkins and David Anderson, "The problem is that many writers on Kenyan history, especially the history of decolonization, view everything from Central Kenya. Otherwise, they would know that colonial rule in Kenya had always been brutal and dirty methods

were always used to crush any rebellion." B.A. Ogot, "Review Article: Britain's Gulag," *Journal of African History*, 46, 2005, 495.

52 It is estimated that there were 25,600 Homeguard and 20,000 Mau Mau insurgents, and 80,000 Kikuyu civilians held in detention camps and 800 emergency villages were enclosed and guarded—a total of 1.5 million Kikuyu, nearly the whole of the population, were detained. Ogot, "Review Article," 493–505, 499–500. In uncovering Mau Mau, historians found not a unified story as much as a "patchwork of local narratives." Bethwell A. Ogot, "Revolt of the Elders: An Anatomy of the Loyalist Crowd in the Mau Mau Uprising 1952–1956," in Bethwell A. Ogot, Toyin Falola, Atieno Odhiambo, eds., *The Challenges of History and Leadership in Africa: The Essays of Bethwell Allan Ogot* (Trenton, NJ: Africa World Press) 2002. Daniel Branch argues that at different stages of the war, most Kikuyu were both supporters of the Mau Mau and allies of the government, sometimes even simultaneously. "The great mass of the Kikuyu population was initially therefore neither loyalist nor Mau Mau. They dealt in the currency of survival rather than ideology." Branch, *Kenya: Between Hope & Despair,* 10, 14.

53 Michela Wrong, *It's Our Turn to Eat: The Story of a Kenyan Whistle-Blower* (New York: Harper Perennial) 2010, 105; Wa Wamwere, *I Refuse to Die,* 24.

54 "In the eyes of the squatters, the White Highlands were now part of the Kikuyu frontier, and they treated their loss of land with the same seriousness and anger as that evinced by the landless and dispossessed ahoi in the Kikuyu reserve." Maloba, *Mau Mau and Kenya,* 60.

55 Lonsdale, *Unhappy Valley,* 418.

56 Few such tightly defined periods of time in the history of such a small area of the world can have been subjected to such intensive scrutiny as Kenya's Central Highlands for the years between the end of World War II and independence in 1963. Historians, anthropologists, and political scientists have explored the roots of the Mau Mau insurgency within the colonial political economy of Kenya, detailed the movement's members, described the events of the 1950s, and considered the tortured position of members of the rebellion within the politics of the post-colonial state.

> E.S. Atieno Odhiambo and John Lonsdale, eds., *Mau Mau and Nationhood: Arms, Authority, and Narration* (Athens, OH: Ohio University Press) 2003, 45.

Oxford Bibliographies agrees: "[M]ore scholarly and popular work has been written about Mau Mau than almost any other topic in the history of sub-Saharan Africa." Myles Osborne, "Mau Mau," *Oxford Bibliographies,* July 26, 2017, http://www. oxfordbibliographies.com/view/document/obo-9780199846733/obo-9780199846733-0188.xml#. In addition to the synthetic histories cited in this chapter, books published on Mau Mau include narratives of Mau Mau detainees, including Jomo Kenyatta,

Suffering without Bitterness: The Founding of the Kenya Nation (Nairobi: East African Publishing House) 1968; J. M. Kariuki, *Mau Mau Detainee: The Account by a Kenya African of His Experiences in Detention Camps, 1953–1960* (Oxford: Oxford University Press) 1963; Bildad Kaggia, *Roots of Freedom, 1921–1963: The Autobiography of Bildad Kaggia* (Nairobi, Kenya: East African Publishing House) 1988.

57   Odhiambo and Lonsdale, eds., *Mau Mau and Nationhood*, 3.

58   See Gerald Horne, *Mau Mau in Harlem?: The U.S. and the Liberation of Kenya* (New York: Palgrave Macmillan) 2009.

59   B.A. Ogot mentions that 350 Maasai in Narok District were found in 1954 to have joined Mau Mau, though these may have been representative more of the borders of the Maasai community than its heart, as the names of those Maasai typically reflect mixed Kikuyu lineage. Maasai appear from these records to have more broadly sheltered Mau Mau on the run from British military within the Masai Reserve. See Ogot, "Review Article," 500; "Secret" File describing Mau Mau activity among the Maasai, "Administration," Secretariat of the Colony and Protectorate of Kenya, *British National Archives*, FCO 141/7196. Lonsdale reports that 800 Maasais and an unrecorded number of Kambas joined the Mau Mau.

60   Odhiambo in Mau Mau and Nationhood, with the "7 thesis" of Kenyan nationalism. Odhiambo and Lonsdale, *Mau Mau and Nationhood*, 47.

61   Branch, *Kenya: Between Hope & Despair*, xiii.

62   Odhiambo and Lonsdale, *Mau Mau and Nationhood*, 48, 227.

63   B.A. Ogot says, "[U]ntil the contributions of all Kenyan communities to the struggle for independence are acknowledged, and until Mau Mau is integrated in a genuinely harmonious way into the common historical consciousness of Kenyans, we are likely to view the British gulag as a kind of ethnic cleansing of the Kikuyu," which he says Elkins and Anderson both do. B.A. Ogot, "Review: Britain's Gulag," *Journal of African History*, 46, 2005, 498.

64   Odhiambo and Lonsdale, *Mau Mau and Nationhood*, 45.

65   E.S. Atieno-Odhiambo, "The Formative Years, 1945–55," in B.A. Ogot and W.R. Ochieng, eds., *Decolonization & Independence in Kenya: 1940–1993* (Nairobi: EAEP) 1995.

66   Small Farm Settlement Income Target Report from Ministry of Agriculture, 1962, Kenya National Archive, BN/11/17; Land Development and Settlement in Kenya Memorandum by the Ministers for Agriculture, Animal Husbandry and Water Resources [drafted by Hennings and Swynnerton, presented by Bruce McKenzie] March 9, 1960 7, 20, Kenya National Archive, BN/88/17; Notes from a Meeting held in the Chief Commissioner's Office on Friday, May 13, 1960, Kenya National Archive, BN/11/17.

67   G.B. Wasserman, "The Adaptation of a Colonial Elite to Decolonization: Kenya Europeans and the Land Issue 1960–1965," PhD Dissertation at Columbia University, 1972, 268.

68 Quoted in, Caroline Elkins, *Imperial Reckoning: The Untold Story of Britain's Gulag in Kenya* (New York: Henry Holt & Co.) 2005, 127.

69 Donkol ole Keiwa identifies three men from Kiambu who together orchestrated the settlement of Maasailand by Central Kenyans; they represent two factions of Kikuyu who do not always agree, from Kiambu and Nyeri, but they collaborated on distributing Maasailand together. The three were Njenga Karume, who helped Kenyatta settle Kikuyu in Rift Valley; J.M. Kariuki, a Member of Parliament whose original home was Nyeri, and Kihika Kimani from Nakuru. J.M. was thought to be bitter that Kenyatta was not doing enough for the Nyeri Kikuyus. Kenya's third President Mwai Kibaki was from Nyeri but loyal throughout to Kenyatta, which is why he was able to attain the presidency. But Kibaki retained his loyalty to Nyeri which was the home of the more radical, peasant-based part of the Mau Mau movement, and during his administration, Mau Mau was recovered and honored, and a monument was erected to Mau Mau leader Dedan Kimathi in Nairoib. Though Kimathi was a guerrilla fighter who was killed by British forces, his family was given Maasai land next to where J.M. Kariuki was from, in Laikipia, Nandarua County.

70 Odhiambo and Lonsdale, *Mau Mau and Nationhood*, 33.

71 Elkins, *Imperial Reckoning*, 362.

72 See Karuti Kanyinga, "The Legacy of the White Highlands: Land Rights, Ethnicity, and the Post-2007 Election Violence in Kenya," *Journal of Contemporary African Studies*, 27:3, 2009, 325–44.

73 Charles Hornsby is the source of this detailed research, published in, *Kenya: A History Since Independence* (London: I.B. Tauris) 2013, 75, 76, 303.

74 Ibid.

75 Wrong, *It's Our Turn to Eat*, 112.

76 Ogot, *Mau Mau and Nationhood*, (Columbus, OH: Ohio State University Press) 2003, 11.

77 Hornsby, *Kenya*, 97–8.

78 Kevin Bruyneel, *The Third Space of Sovereignty: The Postcolonial Politics of U.S.-Indigenous Relations* (Minneapolis, MN: University of Minnesota Press) 2007, 94. See also Esther Mwangi, "Subdividing the Commons: The Politics of Property Rights Transformation in Kenya's Maasailand" (Washington, D.C.: International Food Policy Research Institute) 2006.

79 Even the County Governments of Narok and Kajiado do not have rights to these mines.

80 Ogot and Ochieng, *Decolonization and Independence*, 87.

81 On the history of group ranches in Maasailand, see Esther Mwangi, "Subdividing the Commons: The Politics of Property Rights Transformation in Kenya's Maasailand," CAPRI Working Paper #46 (Washington, D.C.: International Food

Policy Research Institute) 2006; John Galaty, "Ha(l)ving Land in Common: The Subdivision of Maasai Group Ranches in Kenya," *Nomadic Peoples*, 34/35, 1994; Marcel Rutten, *Selling Wealth to Buy Poverty: The Process of the Individualization of Land Ownership among the Maasai Pastoralists of Kajiado District, Kenya* (Saarbrucken, Germany: Verlag Breitenbach Publishers) 1992; Elliot Fratkin, "Pastoral Land Tenure in Kenya: Maasai, Samburu, Boran, and Rendille Experiences, 1950–1990," *Nomadic Peoples*, 34/35, 1994; Hornsby, *Kenya: A History Since Independence*, 96–7, 251.

82 Esther Mwangi, "Fragmenting the Commons: The Transformation of Property Rights in Kenya's Masai Land" (Bloomington, IN: Indiana State University) 2001, 7. https://www.academia.edu/82493115/Fragmenting_the_Commons_The_Transformation_of_Property_Rights_in_Kenyas_Masai_Land?uc-sb-sw=59099620

83 Mary Poole and Meitamei Olol Dapash interview with Donkol ole Keiwa, Dopoi Center, Maasai Mara, June 23, 2018.

84 This issue is explored in Chapter 4 on the introduction of the Western science of grazing in Amboseli.

85 John Galaty, "This Land Is Yours: Social and Economic Factors in the Privatization, Sub-Division and Sale of Maasai Ranches," *Nomadic Peoples*, 30, 1992, 28. This number grew to thirty-one ranches by 2000.

86 Hornsby, *Kenya*, 96, 251.

Chapter 3

1 Report of Agricultural Feasibility Study Team, Narok District, Kenya presented to the Department of Agriculture by T.G. Willis, Department of Agriculture, Ottawa Canada, et al. p. 24, para. 5.1.3.1968, Kenya National Archive, BN/8/131.

2 Norman Leys, *Kenya* (London: Hogarth Press) 1924, 102.

3 Ibid, 101.

4 Leys concluded that "such statements were unlikely to induce the Secretary of State to consent to the removal of the tribe from Laikipia." Leys, *Kenya*, 108.

5 Copy of the 1911 Agreement located in the Ukamba Province Report on the Boundary of the Masai and Kikuyu Reserves from 1912–1915, 61, Kenya National Archive, DC/MKS10A/5/1.

6 George Ritchie Sandford, *An Administrative and Political History of the Masai Reserve* (London: Waterlow & Sons Ltd.) 1919.

7 Sandford, *An Administrative History*, 42.

8 Narok District Annual Report, 1916–1917, Kenya National Archive, DC/NRK/1/1/1; Letter from the Office of the Senior Commissioner Masai Province to the Chief Native Commissioner, Nairobi April 22, 1926 titled *Re: Masai Boundary Dispute*, Kenya National Archive, DC/NRK/1/8/1.

9   Narok District Annual Report, 1916–1917, 4, Kenya National
    Archive, DC/NRK/1/1/1.

10 Letter from District Commissioner H.E. Bader to F. Hopley Esqr., Advocate in
    Nairobi. July 31, 1926, para. 11(g), Kenya National Archive, DC/NRK/1/8/1.

11 The agreement confuses the Eunoto ceremony with the Enkipaata ceremony.
    The guarantees regarding Kinopop were carried forward from the Agreement of
    1904. Copy of the 1904 Agreement located in the Ukamba Province Report on the
    Boundary of the Masai and Kikuyu Reserves from 1912–1915, 3, Kenya National
    Archive, DC/MKS10A/5/1.

12 Copy of the 1911 Agreement located in the Ukamba Province Report on the
    Boundary of the Masai and Kikuyu Reserves from 1912–1915, 62, Kenya National
    Archive, DC/MKS10A/5/1.

13 Narok District Annual Report, 1916–1917, 1, Kenya National Archive,
    DC/NRK/1/1/1.

14 Letter from Office of the Senior Commissioner, Masai Province to Chief Native
    Commissioner, Nairobi. April 22, 1926, Kenya National Archive, DC/NRK/1/8/1.

15 Ibid.

16 The names of the six Maasai include: Sentoni Ole Langoe, Godidis Ole Lamungem
    Sadelon Ole Suru, Terat Ole Serat, Kibigorwar Ole Teganya, and Kinye Ole Todoki.
    Appellate Registrar Memo, His Majesty's Supreme Court of Kenya at Nairobi.
    Criminal Appeals Nos. 58–63 August 23, 1926. Kenya National Archive, DC/
    NRK/1/8/1.

17 Ibid, para. 11(f) Letter from District Commissioner H.E. Bader to F. Hopley
    Esqr., Advocate in Nairobi. July 31, 1926, para. 11(c), Kenya National Archive,
    DC/NRK/1/8/1.

18 Memorandums of Appeal, His Majesty's Supreme Court of the Colony of Kenya at
    Nairobi, August 5, 1926. Case No. 423 of the II Class Magistrate's Court at Nakuru,
    Kenya National Archive, DC/NRK/1/8/1.

19 1931 Map located in Narok District Handing Over Reports 1946–1959, Kenya
    National Archive, DC/NRK.2/1/1.

20 Memo from District Commissioner of Narok Wilkinson, February 1950, Kenya
    National Archive PC/NKU/2/16/3.

21 Letter from Agricultural Provincial Commissioner Rift Valley H. E. Welby to the
    Hon Colonial Secretary, Nairobi May 16, 1934, Kenya National Archive, LND
    3/1/83.

22 Letter from Powys-Cobb to the Provincial Commissioner of Rift Valley, December
    16, 1934, Kenya National Archive, BN/12/24.

23 Letter from the District Commissioner to the Officer in Charge, Masai October 12,
    1950, Kenya National Archive, PC/NKU/2/16/3.

24 Letter from Director of Surveys to the Provincial Commissioner October 6, 1953,
    Kenya National Archive, PC/NKU/2/16/3.

25   Letter from District Commissioner Hosking to the Director of Surveys, Nairobi
     and Provincial Commissioner of Southern Province, Ngong. November 23, 1953,
     Kenya National Archive, PC/NKU/2/16/3.

26   Notes from a "Masai Trespass" Meeting held at Mau Narok on Friday July 20, 1934.
     Present: Agricultural Provincial Commissioner Rift Valley, Officer-in-charge Masai,
     District Commissioner Nakuru, District Commissioner Narok, E. Powys Cobb,
     Asst. Supdt. of Police, Nakuru, Kenya National Archive, LND 3/1/83.

27   In November of 1949 the District Commissioner of Narok clarified that trespass as
     a punishable offense " … only applies to trespass by stock, not by casual travelers."
     In this meeting the Maasai agreed not to trespass under two conditions, " … that
     the boundary should be marked … " and that the administration, "allow Masai
     to cross with donkeys the narrow part of [Cobb's] farm to collect wood from the
     forest in Masai." Six months later, still without any sign of plans for a fence, the
     same Commissioner was baffled at the interpretation by the Maasai regarding the
     definition of trespass, that the "[Maasai] define trespass as entry by beast only and
     persons walking on the Mr. Cobb's land were not considered trespassers." In the
     eight-month time-span between when trespass was originally defined, there were
     only two cases of animal trespass.
     Letter from District Commissioner of Narok, Wilkinson to E. Powys Cobb.
     November 12, 1949, Kenya National Archive, PC/NKU/2/16/3; Extract from D.O's
     Safari Report May 22–26, 1950, Kenya National Archive, PC/NKU/2/16/3.

28   Letter from H.P. Warmington Spdt. of Police, Ngong to Commissioner of Police,
     Nairobi. November 10, 1958, Kenya National Archive, PC/NKU/2/15/23.

29   Ibid.

30   Colonial administrators acknowledged that the "Masai could easily refuse to pay
     compensation. They [the Maasai] could counter by citing many cases of poaching
     game in the Reserve by Mau Narok farmers, timber stolen from their forests,
     members of their tribe being shot and cases of trespass." The Southern Provincial
     Commissioner, K.M. Cowley, encouraged this kind of violence against Maasai,
     saying "We are trying to … [dispel] the current impression in the Rift that we
     are indifferent to the misdemeanours of our 'painted savages.' As you know I am
     anything but indifferent and should welcome a few more incidents like the one
     where Rift police caught up with a band of Masai and shot three dead when they
     resisted." Letter from D.H. Ruthven to the European Agricultural Settlement Board
     to the Executive Officer in Nairobi, quoting the District Commissioner of Narok on
     January 8, 1957, Kenya National Archive, PC/NKU/2/15/23; Letter from Southern
     Provincial Commissioner K.M. Cowley to the Minister of African Affairs, C.M.
     Johnston. September 24, 1958, Kenya National Archive, PC/NKU/2/15/23.

31   Letter from District Commissioner of Narok Galton-Fenzi titled *Theft of
     Sheep by Masai-Mau Narok District* January 26, 1957, Kenya National Archive,
     PC/NKU/2/15/23.

32 Memo from the Provincial Commissioner, Southern Province December 1, 1959, Kenya National Archive, PC/NKU/2/15/23.

33 Letter from the District Commissioner, Narok to the Officer in Charge, Masai District April 11, 1950, Kenya National Archive, PC/NKU/2/16/3.

34 Letter from the District Commissioner, Narok Wilkinson to E. Powys Cobb. March 31, 1950, Kenya National Archive, PC/NKU/2/16/3.

35 Narok District Annual Report 1934, Kenya National Archive, DC/NRK1/1/2.

36 Meeting notes from J.A. Miller District Commissioner Narok 10/9/1958, Kenya National Archives. PC/NKU/2/15/23.

37 David Goldsworthy, *Tom Mboya: The Man Kenya Wanted to Forget*, 1982 (New York: Africana Publishing Co.) 2008, 255.

38 Caroline Elkin, *Imperial Reckoning: The Untold Story of Britain's Gulag in Kenya* (New York: Henry Holt & Co.) 2005, 22.

39 Proposal for Settlement Scheme by the European Agricultural Settlement Board, sent to the Chairman of the European Settlement Board, Nairobi by J.F. Lipscomb, G.J.L. Burton, J.G. Evans. January 25, 1950, Kenya National Archive, BV/23/65.

40 C.K.C. Macharia, "Land Tenure Reform and Africanisation of the 'White Highlands' 1956–1970," PhD Dissertation at the University of Nairobi, May 1981, 36.

41 Elkin, *Imperial Reckoning*, 362.

42 Letter from E. Powys Cobb to his daughter February 21, 1927, Kenya National Archive, MSS/31/1.

43 Note on Discussion Held in the Minister for Agriculture and Natural Resources' Office on March 4, 1952, Kenya National Archive, LND/3/1/83.

44 [Biography of Ethel Powys Cobb,] Letter from Dr. A.C. Thurston, Oxford Colonial Archives Project, to Dr. Anne C. Thurston, August 10, 1987, "Papers of Edward Powys Cobb," Kenya National Archive, MSS/31/1.

45 B.A. Ogot and W.R. Ochieng, eds., *Decolonization and Independence in Kenya 1940–1993* (Nairobi: EAEP) 1995, 43, 87.

46 Macharia, "Land Tenure Reform and Africanisation of the 'White Highlands' 1956–1970," 36.

47 D. Leonard, *African Successes: Four Public Managers of Kenyan Rural Development* (Berkeley: University of California Press) 1991, 91.

48 Ogot and Ochieng, eds., *Decolonization and Independence*, 43.

49 Quoted in, Elkins, *Imperial Reckoning*, 127.

50 Land Development and Settlement in Kenya Memorandum by the Ministers for Agriculture, Animal Husbandry and Water Resources (drafted by Hennings and Swynnerton, presented by Bruce McKenzie) March 9, 1960, 24, para. 46, Kenya National Archive, BN/88/17.

51 Ibid, 24–7.

52 Land Development and Settlement in Kenya Memorandum by the Ministers
    for Agriculture, Animal Husbandry and Water Resources (drafted by Hennings
    and Swynnerton, presented by Bruce McKenzie) March 9, 1960, 2, para 2, Kenya
    National Archive, BN/88/17.
53 Small Farm Settlement Income Target Report from Ministry of Agriculture, 1962,
    Kenya National Archive, BN/11/17.
54 Notes from a Meeting held in the Chief Commissioner's Office on Friday, May 13,
    1960, Kenya National Archive, BN/11/17.
55 Land Development and Settlement in Kenya Memorandum by the Ministers for
    Agriculture, Animal Husbandry and Water Resources [drafted by Hennings and
    Swynnerton, presented by Bruce McKenzie] March 9, 1960, 7, 20, Kenya National
    Archive, BN/88/17.
56 G.B. Wasserman, "The Adaptation of a Colonial Elite to Decolonization: Kenya
    Europeans and the Land Issue 1960–1965," PhD Dissertation at Columbia
    University, 1972, 268.
57 The Meeting was held at Government House, Nairobi, on November 27, 1960.
    Present at this meeting were: Secretary of State Rt. Hon. R. Maudling; Sir Patrick
    Renison, Acting Governor of Kenya; K.M. Cowley, Provincial Commissioner for
    Southern Province, and other colonial administrators. The Maasai delegation
    from Narok included: Mr. J.K. Ole Tipis; Mr. Kaashu Ole Sumbulo; Mr. Moses
    Ole Lemein; Mr. Ole Nkumam; Mr. M.P. Nampaso; Mr. Paul Rurumban; Mr.
    James Naeku; Mr. Punyua; Mr. Sampuerap; Mr. Ole Nkuyayu; Mr. Ole Masikonte;
    Mr. Sironik; and Mr. Ole Masiar; and from Kaijiado: Mr. S.S. Oloitipitip; Mr. J.T.
    Mpaayei; Mr. M.M. Ole Ncharo; Mr. G.K. Ole Kipury; Mr. J.C. Lekimani; and Mr.
    S.S. Ole Paita. The eighteen Maasai delegates to that meeting included leadership
    from both the Narok and Kajiado areas of Maasailand, and appear to have included
    both politically elected and traditional leadership. Following Ole Tipis, all Maasai
    people spoke in turn. They advocated a regional constitution and all agreed that
    paramount was the survival of Maasai people as a "Tribe."
58 Ole Tipis said that these included Mokokodo, Sampur, Tamus, Sebei and Wuasi
    Nkishu.
59 "Appendix A: A Memorandum on the Masai Treaties and the Masai Lands,
    Presented to Her Majesty's Secretary of State for the Colonies, at Government
    House, Nairobi, on Monday the 27th of November, 1961," and "Memorandum on
    Maasai Lands in Kenya," [submitted by Maasai Delegates] Kenya National Archive,
    CO/822/2000, 115261.
60 Ibid.
61 Maudling was advised to (1) express sympathy for recent droughts and flooding
    that had plagued the Eastern area of the Masai Reserve and remind the delegates
    that Britain had provided aid, (2) encourage the delegates to bring their land
    claims to the constitutional conference in London, and (3) inform the delegates that

no decision has been reached about formal Maasai participation at the conference. "Record of a Meeting Between the Secretary of State for the Colonies and a Delegation Representing the Masai at Governor's House, Nairobi, on November 27, 1961," and "Secretary of State's Visit to Kenya, 1961: The Masai Problem," Kenya National Archive, Kenya National Archive, CO/822/2000, 115261.

62 "The Maasai: Their Special Position," attachment to "Secretary of State's Visit to Kenya, November, 1961: The Maasai Problem," Kenya National Archive, CO/822/2000, 115261.

63 Ibid.

64 "Secretary of State's Visit to Kenya, November, 1961: The Masai Problem," Kenya National Archive, CO/822/2000, 115261.

65 "Introduction" and "Memorandum: Maasai Claims under the 1904 and 1911 Treaties," attachments to "Brief No. 11, The Maasai: Official Eyes Only," Kenyan Constitutional Conference 1962, Kenya National Archive, CO/822/2000, 115261.

66 Kenyatta handed out the bulk of the 30,000 acres of Mau Narok to personal friends and family, including Koinange, whose family still occupies at least 5,000 acres.

67 Goldsworthy, *Tom Mboya*.

68 "Brief No. 11, The Masai: Official Eyes Only," Kenya Constitutional Conference 1962, 5, Kenya National Archive, CO/822/2000, 115261.

69 Ibid, 7.

70 The Maasai delegates were led by Ole Tipis, and also included Mr. J.l.H. Ole Konchellah, Mr. Ole Sein, Mr. P. Ole Lemein, Dr. Likiman, Mr. Partasio Ole Nambaso, Mr. John Ole Tameno, Mr. John Keen (Ole Kedampi), (Observer), and R.L. McEwen (Legal Advisor). One member of the Maasai delegation, Mr. P. Rurumban was refused admittance to the meeting on the grounds that he was a member of the Samburu tribe, but then allowed to attend as an observer. The meeting was chaired by Hon. Hugh Fraser, MP for the first half and Rt. Hon Reginald Maudling, MP, for the second, and was attended by three other representatives of the Crown, the Kenyan Colonial Governor, two other British Kenyan officials, and six representatives of the KADU political party, including Mr. Ngala and Mr. Towett of the Commission of Lands, and KANU representatives including Jomo Kenyatta and Bruce McKenzie, the colonial and soon-to-be independent governments' Minister for Agriculture. Ogot and Ochieng, eds., *Decolonization and Independence in Kenya 1940–1993*, 70. "Record of the First Meeting between the Masai Delegation and a Group of Representatives of the Conference held in the Music Room, Lancaster House, SW1, On Wednesday, March 21, 1962, at 5:00 p.m.," Kenya National Archive, CO/822/2000, 115261.

71 "Record of the First Meeting Between the Masai Delegation and a Group of Representatives of the Conference held in the Music Room, Lancaster House, SW1, On Wednesday, March 21, 1962, at 5:00 p.m.," Kenya National Archive, CO/822/2000, 115261.

72 Ibid.

73 Ibid.

74 Ibid.

75 Lacking trust in banks, and fearing government seizure, Maasai had hidden the money they raised for the voyage in bushes and under beds. (Lemein, Personal Communication, 2015).

76 "To Colonial Secretary, London, from United Front, Nairobi, March 30, 1962," Kenya National Archive, CO/822/2000, 115261.

77 "Secret" Memo, P.J. Kitgatt to Mr. H. Steel, February 19, 1962, Kenya National Archive, CO/822/2000, 115261.

78 Ibid.

79 Record of the Third Meeting between the Masai Delegation and a Group of Representatives of the Conference held in the Music Room, Lancaster House, SW1, on Tuesday, April 3, 1962, at 4:15 p.m., Kenya National Archive, CO/822/2000, 115261.

80 Ibid.

81 Ibid.

82 "The Masai: Their Special Position," Kenya National Archive, CO/822/2000, 115261.

83 Ibid.

84 Wasserman, "The Adaptation of a Colonial Elite to Decolonization," 268.

85 Letter from Justus Ole Tipis, V.P. of the Rift Valley Regional Assembly, to Bruce McKenzie, Minister for Agriculture and Animal Husbandry, October 12, 1964. Kenya National Archive, BV/104/49.

86 Letter from Justus Ole Tipis, V.P. of the Rift Valley Regional Assembly, to Bruce McKenzie, Minister for Agriculture and Animal Husbandry, October 12, 1964. Letter from Ethel Powys Cobb to Bruce McKenzie, Minister of Agriculture and Animal Husbandry, September 9, 1964. Kenya National Archive, BV/104/.

87 Letter from Bruce McKenzie, Minister of Agriculture and Animal Husbandry to Justus Ole Tipis, Vice President of the Rift Valley Regional Assembly, October 19, 1964. Kenya National Archive, BV/104/49.

88 Copy of Lease and Registration of Titles Ordinance, Chapter 160, Grant; Number I.R. 14607, in the personal collection of Moses Mpoe.

89 Report of Agricultural Feasibility Study Team, Narok District, Kenya presented to the Department of Agriculture by T.G. Willis, Department of Agriculture, Ottawa Canada, et al. 1968, 21, Kenya National Archive, BN/8/131.

90 Wasserman, "The Adaptation of a Colonial Elite to Decolonization."

91 Ministry of Agriculture and Animal Husbandry, "Background Paper on Masai Wheat" [1968] Kenya National Archive, BN/8/131.

92 Ibid, 131.

93   Report of Agricultural Feasibility Study Team, Narok District, Kenya presented to the Department of Agriculture by T.G. Willis, Department of Agriculture, Ottawa Canada, et al. 1968, 11–12, 34, Kenya National Archive, BN/8/131.

94   Ibid.

95   "Minutes of the Meeting of Narok District Agricultural Committee Held in the District Commissioner's Office on Tuesday May 21, 1968 at 10.30 A.M.," Kenya National Archive, AN 13/45.

96   "Minutes of the First Meeting (1968) of the Provincial Agricultural Board Rift Valley Province Held in the Conference Room of the Provincial Headquarters Nakuru on Friday March 8, 1968 at 10.30 A.M.," PAB and DAC Minutes for ADA, Rift Valley Province, Agriculture Department, 1968, Kenya National Archive, AN 13/45.

97   "Minutes of the Meeting of Narok District Agricultural Committee Held in the District Commissioner's Office on Tuesday May 21, 1968 at 10.30 A.M.," Kenya National Archive, AN 13/45.

98   "Minutes of the Meeting of Narok District Agricultural Committee Held in the District Commissioner's Office on Wednesday and Thursday, 10th and July 11, 1968 at 10 A.M.," Kenya National Archive, AN 13/45.

99   Leonard, *African Successes*, 107–8, 214.

100 Ibid, 214.

101 "Minutes of the Third Meeting (1968) of the Province Agricultural Board, Rift Valley Province Held in the Provincial Conference Room Nakuru on July 16, 1968 at 10.00 A.M.," Kenya National Archive, AN 13/45.

102 "Setting Apart of Land for Wheat Growing in Maasailand," S. Nyachae, Provincial Commissioner, Rift Valley Province, to The Permanent Secretary, Ministry of Agriculture and Animal Husbandry, June 7, 1968, Kenya National Archive, BN/8/131.

103 Ibid.

104 Letter to F.E. Charnley, Department of Lands, from Andrew M. Mercer, General Manager, MADO, July 9, 1968, Kenya National Archive, BN/8/131.

105 Letter from Andrew M. Mercer to F.E. Charnley, Ag. Commissioner of Lands, July 15, 1968, Kenya National Archive, BN/8/131.

106 Ministry of Agriculture and Animal Husbandry, "Background Paper on Masai Wheat" [1968] Kenya National Archive, BN/8/131.

107 The Maa word "Enkutoto" means "area," and the plural "Nkutot" would have been more accurate.

108 Mercer said that Nyachae "has at various committee meetings indicated his view that individual Masai have specific land rights and he could see no reason for this organization not entering into specific agreements with individuals." Letter to F.E. Charnley, Department of Lands, from Andrew M. Mercer, General Manager, MADO, July 9, 1968, Kenya National Archive, BN/8/131.

109 "Confidential" Letter from F.E. Charnley, Ag. Commissioner of Lands, to Andrew Mercer, July 12, 1968, Kenya National Archive, BN/8/131.

110 "Setting Apart of Land for Wheat Growing in Maasailand," S. Nyachae, Provincial Commissioner, Rift Valley Province, to The Permanent Secretary, Ministry of Agriculture and Animal Husbandry, June 7, 1968, Kenya National Archive, BN/8/131.

111 "Setting Apart of Land for Wheat Growing in Masailand," Letter from D.C. Mlamba, Permanent Secretary, Ministry of Agriculture, to Permanent Secretary, Office of the President, Nairobi, July 30, 1968, Kenya National Archive, BN/8/131.

112 Letter from S. Nyachae to Permanent Secretary Mlambo, August 8, 1968, Kenya National Archive, BN/8/131.

113 Letter from Andrew M. Mercer to F.E. Charnley, Ag. Commissioner of Lands, July 15, 1968, Kenya National Archive, BN/8/131.

114 "Setting Apart of Land for Wheat Growing in Masailand," letter from D.C. Mlamba, Permanent Secretary, Ministry of Agriculture, to the Permanent Secretary, Office of the President, and Permanent Secretary, Ministry of Economic Planning and Development, July 30, 1968, Kenya National Archive, BN/8/131.

115 Ministry of Agriculture, "Draft Paper for the Working Party: Policy for the Masai Wheat Area, 1969," September 30, 1968, Kenya National Archive, BN/8/131.

116 "Land Adjudication in Narok: Minutes of Meeting Held on Thursday, November 28, 1968 at 2 P.M. in the Conference Room, Ministry of Lands and Settlement," Kenya National Archive, BN/8/131.

117 Leonard, *African Successes,* 1991.

118 Ibid, 95.

119 Ibid, 100.

Chapter 4

1 The specific intention was to reverse Amboseli's status as a National Park to that of a Game Reserve, thereby devolving management from Kenyan Wildlife Services (KWS) to the Maasai-run Olkajaido County Council (OCC).

2 The African Conservation Centre describes its mission "to conserve biodiversity in East Africa and beyond through the collaborative application of scientific and indigenous knowledge, improved livelihoods and good governance through development of local institutions." https://www.accafrica.org/who-we-are/vision-mission/The founder of the African Conservation Center, David Western, is the author of *Natural Connections: Perspectives in Community-Based Conservation* (Washington, D.C.: Island Press, 1994).

3   See Erika Barthelmess, "Kenyan Government Degazettes Amboseli National Park," "Hot Topics," *African Conservation Telegraph*, 2:1, October/November, 2005, 5.

4   See Mark Dowie, *Conservation Refugees: The Hundred-Year Conflict between Global Conservation and Native Peoples* (Cambridge, MA: MIT Press) 2011.

5   Ian Parker, "Chapter 2: Jackson & Percival," in Ian Parker and Stan Bleazard, eds., *An Impossible Dream: Some of Kenya's Last Colonial Wardens Recall the Game Department in the Closing Years of the British Empire* (UK: Librario) 2001, 18–19.

6   John Muir founded the Sierra Club in 1892 through a philosophy that, while critiqued for its dismissal of Indigenous rights, recognized the intrinsic value of nature.

7   See "The White Man's Game," in Raymond Bonner, *At the Hand of Man: Peril and Hope for Africa's Wildlife* (New York: Knopf) 1993. Bonner describes the origin of the British conservation movement in policy designed to "keep elephants alive until they grow older and their tusks were worth more," for example, (49) the funding of the Kenyan game department through ivory trade beginning in the 1920s, (50) and the "patrician" class of private clubs of wealthy white men that created and ran the largest conservation organizations in the West who remained committed to hunting of African wildlife and to ivory through the 1980s and 1990s, even as they raised money from their donors to save elephants from the same (54).

8   Bonner, *At the Hand of Man*, 41.

9   Jonathan Adams and Thomas McShane, *The Myth of Wild Africa: Conservation without Illusion* (Berkeley: University of California Press) 1996, 29.

10 The preamble to the 1900 Convention on International Trade in Endangered Species, quoted in Bonner, *At the Hand of Man*, 40.

11 In the past, warrior training included a single collective hunt of one male lion, but this practice has long been discontinued.

12 Parker, "Chapter 2: Jackson & Percival," 18.

13 One of the draws to ownership of large parcels of land was the ability to hunt there without regulation, and game laws were typically fought by white settlers. Parker, "Chapter 2: Jackson & Percival," 17, 19, 24, 25.

14 "Somewhere after 1909, the laws that specifically permitted Africans who traditionally lived off game to go on doing so, vanished from the statues. After the First World War, the early official attitude that the game laws were primarily to control the activities of the white settlers disappeared altogether," Parker, "Chapter 2: Jackson & Percival," 27; Bonner, *At the Hand of Man*, 40.

15 Bonner, *At the Hand of Man*, 42.

16 The Society for the Preservation of the Wild Fauna of the Empire.

17 As late as the 1950s, American Russell E. Train founded the African Wildlife Leadership Foundation (now African Wildlife Foundation) and also became a

member of the "Hundred Pounder Club" for shooting an elephant with tusks weighing a collective 207 pounds. Bonner, *At the Hand of Man*, 55.

18 Peter Jenkins, "Chapter 4: Wildlife Use in World War II," in Parker and Bleazard, *An Impossible Dream*, 39–41.

19 Noel Simon, "Chapter 10: New Directions in the 1950s," in Parker and Bleazard, *An Impossible Dream*, 83.

20 Parker, "Chapter 2: Jackson & Percival."

21 The dedication of the book written by colonial era game wardens in Kenya, published in 2001, continues to refer to African land this way: "We dedicate this book to a Pleistocene Africa, which we so enjoyed and sought to preserve, but which is gone. It was an impossible dream." Parker and Bleazard, *An Impossible Dream*.

22 Of the Society for the Preservation of the Fauna of the Empire.

23 "Notes of a Conference Held at Government House, Nairobi, at 10 A.M. on the July 31, 1930, for the Purpose of Discussing Policy with Regard to the Preservation of Game," Kenya National Archive, GM 7/32.

24 Ibid.

25 "Memorandum II: Game Reserves, and the Possibility of Establishing Permanent Sanctuaries (National Parks)" Report presented to the Game Policy Commission explaining current policy, 1954, Kenya National Archive, "Game Control and Preservation, 1955–57," 8, PC/NGO/1/16/2.

26 Yellowstone National Park had been established in 1872 as a new status, and that became the model for parks in Africa. Albert National Park was established in 1925 in Belgian Congo, and Krueger in South Africa in 1926. Described in Bonner, *At the Hand of Man*, 167, 170.

27 "Notes of a Conference Held at Government House, Nairobi, at 10 A.M. on the July 31, 1930, for the Purpose of Discussing Policy with Regard to the Preservation of Game," Kenya National Archive, GM 7/32.

28 Ibid.

29 Bonner, *At the Hand of Man*, 169.

30 David Lovatt Smith, *Amboseli: Nothing Short of a Miracle* (Nairobi: East African Publishing House Ltd.) 1986, 26, 44.

31 "Extra from Masai District- Intelligence Report, February, 1948," in "Leases in Native Land Units," Kenya National Archive, PC-NKO-2-16-6.

32 Smith, *Amboseli*, 44.

33 "Amboseli National Reserve," Confidential Memorandum from the Provincial Commissioner, Southern Province, to The District Commissioner, Kajiado, November 1, 1955, and related correspondence through November 12, 1955, from the East Africa Tourist Travel Association, E.A. Paring, Governor of Kenya, Kenya National Archive, GA/22.

34 "Kenya National Parks: Amboseli," to the editor from Donald Ker, Nairobi, October 28, 1955; "National Parks-Amboseli," to the editor from S.H. Edwards Oakland California, October 18, 1955; "Game Preservation," to the editor from (Mrs.) Harold Ebinger, Aurora, Illinois October 18, 1955, *East African Standard*, Nairobi, Kenya.

35 "Amboseli National Reserve," Confidential Memorandum from the Provincial Commissioner, Southern Province, to The District Commissioner, Kajiado, November 1, 1955, and related correspondence through November 12, 1955, from the East Africa Tourist Travel Association, E.A. Paring, Governor of Kenya, Kenya National Archive, GA/22.

36 Confidential Letter from M.H. Cowie, Director Royal National Parks of Kenya, to the Director of Forest Development, Game and Fisheries, May 16, 1955, Kenya National Archive, GA/22.

37 "1956 Game Policy Committee, First Interim Report" 1956, Game Control and Preservation, 1956–58, Kenya National Archive, PC/NGO/1/16/2.

38 "Amboseli National Reserve: The Other Side of the Story," to the Editor, *East African Standard* [October, 1955] Kenya National Archive, GA/22.

39 "1956 Game Policy Committee, First Interim Report" 1956, Game Control and Preservation, 1956–58, Kenya National Archive, PC/NGO/1/16/2, 4.

40 "Memorandum II: Game Reserves, and the Possibility of Establishing Permanent Sanctuaries (National Parks)" Report presented to the Game Policy Commission explaining current policy, 1954, Kenya National Archive, "Game Control and Preservation, 1955–57," 8, PC/NGO/1/16/2.

41 Ibid, 9.

42 "Amboseli National Reserve," Confidential Letter from Provincial Commissioner, Southern Province, to the District Commissioner, Kajiado, November 1, 1955, Kenya National Archive, "Game Control and Preservation," 1955–57, PC/NGO/1/16/2.

43 Confidential Letter from M.H. Cowie, Director Royal National Parks of Kenya, to the Director of Forest Development, Game and Fisheries, May 16, 1955, Kenya National Archive, "Game Control and Preservation," 1955–57, PC/NGO/1/16/2.

44 "1956 Game Policy Committee, First Interim Report" 1956, Game Control and Preservation, 1956–58, Kenya National Archive, PC/NGO/1/16/2, 5.

45 Ibid, 7.

46 "Game Policy Committee; Ol Tukai Area" Confidential Letter from the Kajiado District Commissioner to the Provincial Commissioner, Southern Province, June 7, 1956, Game Control and Preservation, 1955–57, Kenya National Archives, PC/NGO/1/16/2.

47 Confidential Memo: "Game v. Masai," A.B. Simpson, District Commissioner, Kajiado, to The Provincial Commissioner, Southern Province, July 7, 1956,

Game. Control and Preservation Policy, 1955–57. Kenya National Archives, PC/NGO/1/16/2.

48 "Game Policy," draft reply from the District Commissioner Kajiado to E.A. Sweatman, Provincial Commissioner Southern Province [*c.* September 1954.] Kenya National Archive.

49 [Game Ranger Zaphiro] "Game Report-Kajiado District, 1954, Confidential report submitted to the Game Warden, Nairobi, January 7, 1955." Kenya National Archive, Game Control and Preservation, 1955–57, PC/NGO/1/16/2.

50 Sessional Papers No. 7 of 1957/58, *Report of the 1956 Game Policy Committee*, 7–8, Kenya National Archive, KW/23/28.

51 David Lovatt Smith, "Amboseli-The First Years," Draft Manuscript, Kenya National Archive, PC/NGO, 9.

52 Address to Governor. Statement by Chief Kisimir, Baraza Meeting at Ol Tukai August 8, 1958, "Amboseli National Reserve" Kenya National Archives, 1958–60 GA 3/13PC/NGO.1.16.8.

53 Smith, "Amboseli-The First Years."

54 Roughly $210 at the time.

55 Personal Communication, Wuala Ole Parsanka, Olgulului Group Ranch Campground, Amboseli, June 30, 2006.

56 These "protest killings" revived in the first decade of the twenty-first century. See "Conservation Refugees," San Francisco Chronicle, late May, 2006.

57 Personal Communication, Logela Melita, Olgulului Group Ranch Campground, Amboseli, August 1, 2006.

58 The quote is from Noel Simon, *Between the Sunlight and the Thunder: The Wild Life of Kenya*, Houghton Mifflin, January 1, 1963, quoted in Bonner, *At the Hand of Man*, 44.

59 Raymond Bonner describes the small donations that initially poured into the WWF's first big campaign to save elephants and rhinos in 1967, the "dirty ten-shilling notes" that arrived with notes of concern such as "I was saving up to buy a pair of shoes, but I think the elephants need it more," much of it he says from working-class people. But Bonner continues, the real money that WWF needed only came through a campaign called "1001 Club" for $10,000 donors with an anonymous member list that included corrupt African leaders like Mobutu Sese Seko, billionaires who destroyed wildlife habitat, embezzlers, and a large number of white South Africans, which was responsible according to Bonner for the WWF's reluctance to support a ban on ivory. Bonner, *At the Hand of Man*, 67–9.

60 Bonner, *At the Hand of Man*, 60, 82.

61 Mary Poole, Kaitlin Noss, Ann Radeloff, Walt Anderson, George Lupempe, Interview with Alex Legis, July 3, 2006, Loitokitok, Kenya.

62 Memo to the District Officer, Ngong Division, from J.K. Kuantai, Clerk to the Council, "Re:KSH 75,000/- Compensation for 2,500 Acres of Olosho Olbob,"

February 12, 1970. Kenya National Archive, Olkajiado County Council, "Full Council Minutes," JG/2/20, 35/6.

63 "Minutes of the District Joint Roads and Works Committee Held on May 17, 1971 at 10:30 a.m. In County Clerk's Office," "Full Council Minutes," Olkajuado County Council, Kenya National Archives, JG/2/20, 35/6. Letter from J.K. Huantai, Clerk to the Council, to The District Officer, Ngong Division, February 12, 1970, in "Full Council Minutes," Olkajuado County Council, Kenya National Archives, JG/2/20, 35/6, and "Minutes of the Full Council meeting Held on April 11, 1974 at 10.50 A.M. in the county chambers," Kenya National Archives, JC/12/19, "Full Council Minutes," Olkajuado County Council, 1974-9.

64 Personal Communication, Philip Ngatia, Maasai Mara, 7/8/06.

65 In 1969, the Reserve was reported to have taken in 2 million ksh ($285,000) in revenue and spending 50,000 ksh ($7,100) on Reserve management. Western, "Ecosystem Conservation."

66 Mary Poole, Kaitlin Noss, Ann Radeloff, Walt Anderson, George Lupempe, Interview with Alex Legis, July 3, 2006, Loitokitok, Kenya.

67 Outline of a Wildlife Utilisation Programme for Kajiado District, 1966, 1, Kenya National Archive, "Proposed New Parks," 5/8/483, KW 13/28, 2. This 1966 "secret" report on the OCC plan recommended that, "these 200 square miles [of the Amboseli Reserve] will be gazetted under that section of the National Parks Act dealing with National Reserves, and will in fact become (legally) a National Reserve though bearing the title 'Masai Amboseli Game Sanctuary.'" The details of the legal change would leave the land title with the Olkajiado Council, but made the National Parks Department of the central government "competent to exercise statutory powers and assume full management of the area." Outline of a Wildlife Utilisation Programme for Kajiado District, 1966, 1, Kenya National Archive, "Proposed New Parks," 5/8/483, KW 13/28, 2.

68 Outline of a Wildlife Utilisation Programme For Kajiado District, 1966, 1, Kenya National Archive, "Proposed New Parks," 5/8/483, KW 13/28.

69 Ibid, 2.

70 David Western, "Proposals for an Amboseli Game Park," Institute for Development Studies, University College, Nairobi, Staff Paper No. 53, September 1969, 4.

71 David Western and Philip Thresher, "Development Plans for Amboseli: Mainly the Wildlife Viewing Activity in the Ecosystem," September, 1973, 18, Kenya National Archive, GP 639.9.WES KW/9/15.

72 The Proposal said, "The traditional dependence of Maasai on livestock still largely prevails, and strongly influences their development objectives. This acts as a major constraint in the potential returns from wildlife utilization." 18, 68.

73 Western has written that he worked with Elders Ole Purdul, Ole Musa, and Stanley Oloitiptip, MP for Kajiado South, between 1968 and 1974 to try to get the OCC

and Elders to accept drafts of a park plan in 1968 and 1969. Western's eight-page 1969 report, he says, was written to be "simple and rudimentary" to leave room for Maasai opinion. He remembers that the plan was accepted by Maasai Elders, but then six weeks later was rejected; he attributes that denunciation to rising fears of a government take-over of the park stemming from the recent elections. After that negative response Western says "the die was cast for government intervention" and subsequently that the OCC abandoned the park to be taken by presidential decree in 1971. Western, "Ecosystem Conservation," 25, 30.

74 Western said that Oloitiptip "insisted on a local solution rather than one imposed from outside" and that he "squared solidly with the Maasai" against the government's "little-disguised takeover efforts." Western, *Natural Connection,* 26.

75 Interview with Logela Olol Melita, August 1, 2006, Amboseli Community Campsite, Mary Poole.

76 "Minutes of the Full Council Meeting" Held on April 11, 1974 at 10:50 A.M. in the County Chambers, "Full Council Minutes" Olkajuado County Council, 1974–1979 Kenya National Archive, JC/12/19.

77 Ibid.

78 Ibid.

79 "Special Full Council Meeting Agenda" Held on December 11, 1974 in the County Chambers. "Full Council Minutes" Olkejuado County Council, 1974–1979 and "Minutes of the Special Full Council Meeting" Held on December 27, 1974 at 10:30 A.M. in the County Chambers, Kenya National Archive, JC/12/19.

80 The group was composed of Chairman Legis, Secretaries for the Ministry of Tourism and Wildlife, the Director of Kenya National Parks, the Chief Game Warden, and the other members of the OCC.

81 "Minutes of Meeting on Amboseli National Park," Held January 21, 1975. At the Ministry of Tourism and Wildlife Conference Room in Nairobi. Kenya National Archives, 9/7 DCAW.

82 "Minutes of the Full Council Meeting" Held on January 30, 1976 at 12:15 P.M. in the County Chambers, "Full Council Minutes" Kenya National Archive, JC/2/19.

83 Interview with Daniel Laturesh, Ogulului/Olalarashi Group Ranch Chairman, and Joseph Saiyalel, member Olkajiado County Council, Amboseli, Olgulului Group Ranch Campground, June, 2005.

84 Ibid.

85 "Summary Report on Water Supply Investigation at Amboseli" and "Amboseli: Inspection by the chief Hydrologic Engineer, 9th–12th January, 1939" in "Amboseli investigations, including Co-ordination plan for Action," Industry of Natural Resources Department, 1958–1960, Kenya National Archive, WAT/SURV/1 Vol II and "Amboseli National Reserve," Confidential Letter from Provincial Commissioner, Southern Province, to the District Commissioner, Kajiado,

November 1, 1955, Kenya National Archive, Game Control and Preservation, 1955–57, PC/NGO/1/16/2.

86 Quote in "Amboseli National Reserve Water For Cattle," Memorandum from B.R.C. Koch, for the Chief Hydraulic Engineer, to the Permanent Secretary, Ministry of Forest Development, Game and Fisheries, January 14, 1958, in "Amboseli National Reserve," 1958–60, Kenya National Archive, PC/NGO/1/19/8.

87 The scheme would have cost 78,000 pounds, or $1.5m today. "Council of Ministers, Development Committee, Provision of 4,500 lbs for Two Exploratory Boreholes in the Amboseli National Reserve," a Memorandum by the Minister for Forest Development, Game and Fisheries, December, 1957, in "Amboseli National Reserves" 1958–1960, PV/NGO/1/16/8.

88 "Address to Governor," Statement by Chief Kisimir, Baraza Meeting at Ol Tukai, August 8, 1958, "Amboseli National Reserve 1958–60," Kenya National Archives, PC/NGO.1.16.8.

89 Ibid.

90 The crowd was reported to have been primarily from Loitokitok. "His Excellency the Governor's Speech at the Baraza held at Ol Tukai in the Loitokitok Section of Kajiado District on Friday, August 8, 1958." "Important political Events," 1958–1960, Kenya National Archive, DC/KAJ.1/3/1.

91 Interview with Daniel Laturesh, Ogulului/Olalarashi Group Ranch Chairman, and Joseph Saiyalel, member Olkajiado County Council, Amboseli, Olgulului Group Ranch Campground, June, 2005.

92 Western's involvement through the African Conservation Centre in defeating the park transfer is common knowledge, and he is also quoted here: David Western is quoted in: Constance Holden, "Kenya National Park Transfer under Fire: Conservation Groups Fear Turning the Park Over to Local Control will have Dire Consequences for Wildlife," *Science*, October 7, 2005, https://www.science.org/content/article/kenya-national-park-transfer-under-fire.

93 Mary Poole was the person who invited the community leader to the lodge and who witnessed the refusal of lodge security to allow him entry.

Chapter 5

1 This story will not be complete until the local histories of the whole of *Olosho le Maa* are given fuller attention, through the Kenya/Tanzania border, and from Samburu to all the Maa-speaking peoples.

2 Today Kerio is the name of a grassland to the west of Lake Turkana, but Maasai scholar of oral history, Naomi Kupury, wrote that Kerio may have been a second Maasai homeland of that name. Kipury says, "Although many scholars have

referred to this place as a south-eastern region of present-day Lake Turkana, some oral sources suggest that it may have been somewhere further north, probably in the northern part of Africa." Naomi Kipury, Oral Literature of the Maasai, (Portsmouth, NH: Heinemann Educational Books, 1983); Tepilit Ole Saitoti, *Maasai* (New York: Abradale Press, Harry N. Abrams Inc. Publishers) 1980.

3   The story is told in Ole Saitoti, *Maasai*, 22, and in Kipury, *Oral History of the Maasai*, 2.

4   The dates of these events would have occurred in deep history. Maasai record time by the names of age groups and periods of their initiation. Sometimes, more recent generations use the names of older generations to remember them in spite of their passage into deep history. The most recent age groups are *Irratanya*, which corresponds roughly to the years 1757–73; *Ilpetaa* (1774–89); *Isalaash* (1790–1805); *Ilmeirishari* (1806–20); *Ilkidotu* (1821–34); *Iltuati* (1835–49); *Ily'angusi* (1850–64); *Ilaimer* (1865–79); *Iltalala* (1880–95); *Iltuati* (1896–1910); *Iltareto* (1911–25); *Ilterito* (1926–40); *Ilny'angusi* (1941–54); *Ilserui* (1955–68); *Ilkitoip* (1969–81); *Ilkishuru* (1982–95); *Ilmeshuki* (1996–2014); *Ilmirisho* (2015–present).

5   During the time of the age groups Ilpetaa, Isalaash, Ilmeirishari, Ilkidotu, and Iltuati, Maasai moved north into Uasing'ishu, Entorror (Laikipia); Isampurr (Samburu); Oldoinyio Keri (Mount Kenya); and Marsabit. They moved to the west into Oldoinyio Loolkoony (Mount Elgon), Kitale, and Eldoret. They moved east into Oldama Oropil (Eldama Ravine), Nakurro (Nakuru), Kinopop (Kinangop); Enaiposha (Naivasha); Enkong'n Enchooro Emuny (Ngong); Enkare Nairobi (Nairobi); and Oldoinyio Oibor (Mount Kilimanjaro). They moved south into what is now northern Tanzania, and then into central Tanzania, to Enaiposha e yiasi, Enaiposha Emanyara, and Kiteto. A small group of Maasai established themselves at the Southern coast, continuing to maintain their Maasai identity, the Kwale.

6   Kipury says that

> Although they present a linguistic and cultural unity, there are still noticeable dialectic and cultural differences among the various Maa speakers. The Samburu or Ilooibor-Kineji, the people of the white goats, the Iltiamus who practise [sic] fishing around Lake Baringo, keep a few livestock and do subsistence farming, and the hunter-gathering group Iltorrobeo, (Dorobo), form the third group of Maa speakers, although they speak another language that sounds like a dialect of Kalenjin. But since these people speak Maa, albeit with a heavy accent, and having acquired livestock, like the pastoral Maasai, they are gradually being assimilated, as a group, into the Maasai community. The Ilkunono, who subsist on iron smithing, in addition to keeping an insignificant number of livestock, also live alongside the Maasai, and although they are said to speak a language separate from Maa, it is a

language spoken only by the senior members of the community, and risks becoming extinct. There are also other peripheral Maa groups such as the Baraguyu, Ilarusa and Ilkurman; the last two are semi-pastoral and subsist mainly on agriculture.

Kipury, Oral Literature of the Maasai, 1

7   Jim Igoe, "Clash of Two Conservation Models," in *Conservation and Globalization: A Study of National Parks and Indigenous Communities from East Africa to South Dakota* (Australia: Thomas Wadsworth) 2004, 48.

8   Archaeological evidence suggests that pastoralism has existed in what is now eastern Kenya and the Rift Valley for many thousands of years and the zebu cattle of the Maasai and "the typical Maasai economy" have been in the highlands for up to two thousand years. Archaeologists date pastoralism in East Africa to the third millennium BC and evidence of pastoralism with zebu cattle in the Rift Valley of what is now Kenya between 2000 years ago and the twelfth or thirteenth centuries. Thomas Spear, "Part One: Introduction," in Thomas Spear and Richard Waller, Eds., *Being Maasai: Ethnicity and Identity in East Africa* (Athens, OH: Ohio University Press) 1993, 9, and; J.E.G. Sutton, "Becoming Maasailand," in Spear and Waller, *Being Maasai,* 46. Linguists suggest that the Maa language could have existed separately from other Nilotic languages up to a millennium ago, though they speculate that the Maasai movement into the Rift Valley was "perhaps two to four centuries" based on assumptions of the time it would take for distinct dialects of Maa to form through migrations. Sutton, "Becoming Maasailand," in Spear and Waller, 38.

9   Gary Clayton Anderson, *The Indian Southwest, 1580–1830: Ethnogenesis and Reinvention* (Norman: University of Oklahoma Press) 1999, 106. See also James F. Brooks, *Captives and Cousins: Slavery, Kinship, & Community in the Southwest Borderlands* (Chapel Hill, NC: University of North Carolina Press) 2002.

10 See extensive examples of rituals that incorporate raiding among Comanche and Pueblo peoples in "Violence, Exchange, and the Honor of Men," in Brooks, *Captives and Cousins.*

11 She says that these include: "Cushitic-speaking pastoralists, such as the Somali, Borana, Rendille and Orwa; the Nilotic-speaking semi-pastoralists such as the Turkana, Luo, Kalenjin, Latuka, Bari, Dinka, etc., and the Bantu-speaking agriculturalists, such as the Akamba, Abaluhya, Kikuyu, Kisii, Chagga, Pare, Hehe, Swahili and others." Kipury, *Oral Literature of the Maasai,* 2.

12 British colonial records are rife with evidence of the health of Maasailand at the time of first British encounter. See especially George Ritchie Sandford, *An Administrative and Political History of the Masai Reserve* (London: Waterlow & Sons Ltd.) 1919. Scholars have described the colonial interruption of Maasai grazing systems which led to degradation of land beginning with the removal of

Maasai herding from the north. See Esther Mwangi and Elinor Ostrom, "Top-Down Solutions: Looking Up from East Africa's Rangelands," *Environment*, 51:21, January/February, 2009; Igoe, "Clash of Two Conservation Models," and for further study of the impacts on the overcrowding in the southern reserve, see Isaac Sindiga, "Land and Population Problems in Kajiado and Narok, Kenya," *African Studies Review*, 27:1, March, 1984, 23–39; Martin Rutten, *Selling Wealth to Buy Poverty: The Process of the Individualization of Landownership Among the Maasai Pastoralists of Kajiado District, Kenya* (Saarbrucken, Germany: Verlag Breitenbach Publishers, 1992).

13 Sandford, *An Administrative and Political History of the Masai Reserve,* 4.

14 *Iloikop* is not the name of a section as some historians have believed, but a word that describes the murder of one Maasai person by another, whether accidental or intentional. John Berntsen, "The Enemy Is Us: Eponymy in the Historiography of the Maasai," *History in Africa*, 7, 1980, 1–21; Richard Waller, "The Maasai and the British, 1895–1905: The Origins of an Alliance," *Journal of African History*, XVII:4, 1976, 532; Spear, *Being Maasai,* 121.

15 Mary Poole and Meitamei Olol Dapash Interview with Donkol ole Keiwa, Dopoi Center, Maasai Mara, July 15, 2018.

16 "Generally quite profitable, these expeditions constituted the economic base for a rich and complex Arab Empire" centered in Oman and Muscat, operating along the coast from Mozambique to Somalia and facilitated in East Africa by the Swahili community of the Kenyan coast. Slaves were exported to Zanzibar, the Middle East, and "European dealers." Richard D. Wolff, "British Imperialism and the East African Slave Trade," *Science and Society*, 36:4, 1972, 445–6.

17 This claim is based in Maasai oral history and is not contradicted in any known source, and supported by known published English language sources. See Wolff, "British Imperialism and the East African Slave Trade."

18 In the time of Iltuati, in the year 1848, Maasai people near Oldoinyo Oiborr, Mt. Kilimanjaro were observed and recorded by German missionaries led by Dr. Ludwig Krapf. Krapf reported that the Kamba also organized trading caravans to the Coast, and that the "most powerful merchant leader in the mid-nineteenth century, Kivoi, also exercised considerable political powers in his area." Robert Tignor, *The Colonial Transformation of Kenya: The Kamba, Kikuyu and Maasai from 1900 to 1939* (Princeton, NJ: Princeton University Press) 1976, 13.

19 A persistent question remains in the Maasai community as to whether the British deliberately introduced diseases as a tactic of war, as well as other extreme forms of violence reflected in threads of memory. This history will only be more fully known through further research that pursues these questions. The extent of British violence in North America only came to light after Indigenous historians themselves took knowledge of oral histories into a search of archival records. Roxanne Ortiz says

that the British had a reputation among Indigenous peoples in North America of killing "the unarmed and vulnerable," children, as tactics of war. An example from Pequot war in what is also now Connecticut, USA, in 1636, a "war of annihilation" where the British attacked first a fort set aside for "women, children, and old men" and slaughtered most of the people and then set the structure on fire burning the inhabitants alive. The evidence of British brutality is typically buried in stories that Indigenous peoples welcomed colonization, such as is ritualized in the Thanksgiving myth in US culture. Roxanne Dunbar Ortiz, *An Indigenous People's History of the United States* (Boston, MA: Beacon Press) 2014, 62.

20 Sandford, *An Administrative and Political History of the Masai Reserve.*

21 Ibid, 1.

22 See Dr. Lawrence Esho, "How the Maasai Labled Most of Kenya," *The Standard*, July 27, 2011.

23 On the destruction of evidence, see for example, Andrei Tapalaga, "How the Documents Proving Crimes Committed by the British Empire Were Destroyed," *History of Yesterday*, March 5, 2020, historyofyesterday.com/how-the-documents-proving-crimes-committed-by-the-british-empire-were-destroyed-262d4e589dde. Sandford's *Administrative History* makes reference to "campaigns" against most other communities in the early years of colonization. See, for example, page 3.

24 See Tignor, *Colonial Transformation,* 21. There is some evidence that the British did wage against these communities: a 1902 confrontation with the "Muraka Kikuyu" was reported to have left as many as 1,500 dead. The British are known to have waged war on the communities to the West including the "Nandi," Kalenjin in 1905–6, and others who they found difficult to defeat. G.H. Mungeam, *British Rule in Kenya, 1895–1912: The Establishment of Administration in the East Africa Protectorate* (Oxford: Oxford University Press) 1966, 84–5.

25 This quote refers to the period 1890–1902. Sandford, *Administrative and Political History of the Masai Reserve,* 1.

26 Eliot was Commissioner of the East African Protectorate, equivalent to a colonial Governor.

27 Sir Charles Eliot, "Memorandum on the subject of Native Rights in the Naivasha Province on the 7th of September, 1903," Sandford, *An Administrative and Political History of the Masai Reserve,* 21.

28 Lastly, the epidemic which lately swept over the country and destroyed the cattle was a terrible blow to them[the Maasai], and reduced them to the verge of starvation. The Wa-Kikuyu, their old enemies, have seized every opportunity of attacking their kraals, and by force or fraud have made a practice of carrying off their women and children as slaves. Some of these they have retained for themselves, some they have bartered with coast traders, and some with the neighbouring Wakamba .... It would be

impossible at present, and until the Wa-Kikuyu are more completely under
control, to prevent the raiding and kidnapping of these people in the Masai
country.

> Sandford, *Administrative and Political History of the Masai Reserve*, 14

29 Sir Arthur Hardinge, "Report on the Condition and Progress of the East Africa
Protectorate from Its Establishment to the 20th of July, 1897," quoted in Sandford,
Administrative and Political History of the Masai Reserve, 17.

30 Hardinge's report said that "The trade in Ukamba is confined to district of Kitui
… and is chiefly in Masai women and children." Sandford, *An Administrative and
Political History of the Masai Reserve*, 17.

31 Richard Wolff says that the British anti-slave-trade campaigns were in fact a
"strategy" to gain the approval of the British public for a colonial presence in East
Africa, as "means of establishing British economic and political hegemony" in
East Africa. Wolff, "British Imperialism and Slavery," 448; For a primary source, see
Sandford, *Administrative and Political History of the Masai Reserve*, 17.

32 Sandford, *Administrative and Political History of the Masai Reserve*, 13.

33 Sir Arthur Hardinge's "Report on the Condition and Progress of the East
Africa Protectorate from its Establishment to the 20th of July, 1897," Sandford,
Administrative and Political History of the Masai Reserve, 15.

34 Mary Poole and Meitamei Dapash Interview with Charles Takai, Dopoi Center, July
22, 2019.

35 Discussion with Charles Takai and other elders, Dopoi Center, Talek, July 22, 2019.

36 Sandford, *Administrative and Political History of the Masai Reserve*, 15–16. See
Lotte Hughes, *Moving the Maasai: A Colonial Misadventure* (London: Palgrave
Macmillan) 2006, 191, n. 48 for different sources on the number killed by Maasai.

37 Sandford, *Administrative and Political History of the Masai Reserve,* 15.

38 Tignor, *Colonial Transformation*, 42.

39 Ibid, 43, 53.

40 Ibid, 54.

41 Ibid, 64.

42 Ibid, 65.

43 Ibid, 65.

44 Ibid, 74.

45 Mwangi and Ostrom, "Top-Down Solutions," 42.

46 Kipury, *Oral Literature of the Maasai*, 1.

47 The British claimed that Nkapilil Ole Masikonte was a loyal "progressive," who sent
two of his sons to mission schools to demonstrate his support for education, owned
"big gardens" in Rumuruti, and also apparently supported the government's plans
to develop ghee dairies in Maasailand. Other Maasai were appointed to be chiefs by
the British, including Lengemojik ole Nakorodo, of Kekonyokie, who spoke English

and Swahili and owned a farm. The British also claimed that Karaga and Eulele in Kajiado were "progressive" chiefs. The British apparently referred to Nakorodo as a "boy" who served early colonial governor Frances Hall. This is reported in the Kenya Land Commission records, KLC, Evidence, I, 949, quoted in Tignor, *Colonial Transformation,* 64–5.

48 Tignor, *Colonial Transformation,* 64.

49 Some of the land Olonana was said to have grazed was the foothills of Ngong that became the estate of Karen Blixen, published under the name Isak Dinesen.

50 Through British eyes, Olonana was many things. Some claimed him as a loyal friend who believed in British justice, while others as corrupt and petty, a man driven by an obsession with power who would give away his community's land in hopes of gaining personal wealth and status; some described him as "noble," still others as devious, "a thoroughly mischievious and even dangerous person" (quoted in Waller, "Origins of an Alliance," 547).

51 Mary Poole and Meitamei Olol Dapash interview with Donkol ole Keiwa, Dopoi Center, Maasai Mara, June 23, 2018.

52 The British claimed that Olonana received a chief's salary, though we have not found evidence of memory in Maasai oral history about that.

53 Sandford, *Administrative and Political History of the Masai Reserve,* 15.

54 Leys was a government medical officer considered sympathetic to the Maasai. Quoted in Hughes, *Moving the Maasai,* 19.

55 Sandford, *Administrative and Political History of the Masai Reserve,* 1.

56 Sir Arthur Hardinge "Report on the Condition and Progress of the East Africa Protectorate from Its Establishment to the 20th of July, 1897," quoted in Sandford, *Administrative and Political History of the Masai Reserve,* 17.

57 Sandford, *Administrative and Political History of the Masai Reserve,* 20.

58 Waller, "Origins of an Alliance."

59 Ibid, 536.

60 C.W. Hobley, described in "no. 64, Sadler to the Colonial Office, February 6, 1906, enclosing Hobley on the Masai and their reserve," PRO CO 533/11, in Tignor, *Colonial Transformation,* 75. Also see Sandford, *Administrative and Political History of the Masai Reserve,* for the full tally of raids gathered before its publication in 1919 and presented in endnote 47.

61 The fines were significant. In 1913 four Maasai villages were fined 500 cows following a raid against the Lumbwa, Kavirondo, and certain communities in German East Africa (later Tanganyika). In 1914, a fine of 250 cows was imposed for raiding in East Africa. In 1917, three *Purko* villages were fined 60,000 rupees, an enormous sum, for sheltering warriors accused of the murder of two Kikuyu. Tignor, *Colonial Transformation,* 77.

62 The Agreements were written in the language of, and signed as, formal treaties. The second, referred to as the "1911 Agreement," was found to have treaty status

by a British colonial court in 1913, and both were deemed to be treaties by British lawyers in 1962 as the Kenyan constitution was drafted, as was described in Chapter 3.

63 The 1904 treaty needs to be investigated first through research conducted by Maasai families about the names of people listed as signers. British sources say that the treaty was signed "Lenana, Son of Mbatian, Lybon of all the Masai" and "18 representatives of eight sections" including "Legalishu, Leganan of Elburgu." Olonana, Son of Mbatian, Lybon of all the Masai. Arariu, Lybon at Naivasha. Signed at Nairobi, August 15, 1904:—Lemani, Elmura of Matapatu. Leteregi, Elmura of Matapatu. Lelmurua, Leganan of Kapte. Lakombe, Elmura of Ndogalani. Lisiari, Elmura of Ndogalani. Mepaku, Head Elmoran of Matapatu. Lambari, Leganon of Ndogalani. Naivasha, representing Elburgu, Gekunuku, Loita, Damat, and Laitutok:—Legalishu, Leganan of Elburgu. Olmugeza, Leganan of Elburgu. Olainomodo, Leganan of Elburgu Olotogia, Leganan of Elburgu. Olieti, Leganan of Elburgu. Lanairugu, Leganan of Elburgu. Lingaldu, Leganan of Elburgu. Ginomun, Leganan of Elburgu. Liwala, Leganan of Gekunuki. Lembogi, Leganan of Laitutok. Signed at Nairobi, August 15, 1904:—Sabori, Elmura of Elburgu. We, the Undersigned, were Interpreters in this Agreement:—C.W. Hobley (Swahili). Mwe s/o Lithugu (Masai). Lybich s/o Keretu (Masai).Waziri-bin-Mwynbego (Masai). Further research would involve an analysis of the specific British concessions to the Maasai and what they reveal about Maasai power to bargain, such as the road between the reservations, and the language of permanence, and whether those were typical of British treaties in other places.

64 The Agreement required all Maasai to be removed from the Rift Valley, from Nakurro (Nakuru) and Enaiposha (Naivasha), and resettled onto two reservations, one in Laikipia in the north and the other below the railroad on the border of the German East African, later Tanganyika. This would remove *Purko*, Keekonyokie, and IlDamat Maasai from their prime grazing land and the entire drought reserve of Mau Highlands, the ceremonial and medicinal core of western Maasailand. Hughes, *Moving the Maasai*, 30–3.

65 Quoted in Hughes, *Moving the Maasai*, 32.

66 The 1904 treaty does not exist in physical form but it is reproduced in colonial histories. Maasai negotiators are quoted as saying: "We, the Undersigned, being the Lybon and Chiefs (representatives) of the existing clans and sections of the Masai tribes in the East Africa Protectorate, having, this 9th day of August, 1904, met Sir Donald Stewart, His Majesty's Commissioner for the East Africa Protectorate and discussed fully the question of a land settlement scheme for the Masai, have of our own free will, decided that it is for our best interests to remove our people, flocks, and herds into definite reservations away from the railway line, and away from any land that may be thrown open to European settlement." Sandford, *Administrative and Political History of the Masai Reserve,* 181.

67 The official history of the moves, published in Sandford's account says,

> Five sections, referred to as Elburgu, Gokunuki, Loita, Damat and Laitutok
> undertook to move absolutely to Laikipia. A considerable portion, estimated
> about one quarter of the first-named section remained in the Southern
> Reserve or in the uninhabited country between the Uaso Nyiro and Mara
> Rivers. The Kakonyukye (Gekunuki) moved from the neighbourhood
> of Naivasha to Il Melili and the southern slopes of the Mau. The Loita
> continued to occupy the Loita Hills and Plains. The Damat made use of the
> country watered by the Southern Uaso Nyiro and its tributaries and the last
> named section continued to inhabit the region to the north of Kilimanjaro.
>
> Sandford, *Administrative History of the Masai Reserve*, 25

However other sources say that many Kekonyokie stayed in Naivasha or returned
to the Rift Valley after initially moving. The Loita and Damat and some *Purko* are
also reported to have retreated into Loita hills, an area at the time not included
in the Masai Reserve. The government estimated in 1911 that 2,000 *Purko* were
living there with 20,000 cattle and 500,000 sheep and goats. Apparently, only some
Purko who were led by Ole Gilisho and Ole Masikonte moved to Laikipia. Tignor,
Colonial Transformation, 34.

68 Hollis, "Memorandum on the Masai," July 5, 1910, in "Correspondence Relating to
the Masai," Sandford, *Administrative and Political History of the Masai Reserve*, 14,
25.

69 This evidence is provided in Hughes, *Moving the Maasai*, 35.

70 Hughes, *Moving the Maasai*. See also H.R. McClure, "Removal of the Northern
Masai from Laikipia to the Southern Reserve," undated, KNA DC/KAJ 1/1/1;
"Belfield to Harcourt," October 31, 1912, No. 771, PRO CO 533/107, in Tignor,
Colonial Transformation of Kenya, 35.

71 Likely a memo from Belfield to Harcourt in 1912 or 1913, quoted in Tignor,
Colonial Transformation, 36.

72 Letter from Jackson to Colonial Office, August 19, 1909, PRO CO 533/61, in
Tignor, *Colonial Transformation*, 37.

73 Sandford, *Administrative History of the Masai Reserve*, 31.

74 This important story was reconstructed through various sources by Lotte Hughes
in *Moving the Maasai*, 52. Hughes includes a quote from an interview with Thomas
Ole Mootian, who was a child at the time of the move, who said "they were pushing
us by force—it was not a joke. The askaris were holding guns. They were beating
people. When you stopped, they hit you with the butt of the gun. And if women
made a joke or became lazy, they were caned." 55

75 Hughes, *Moving the Maasai*, 65–7.

76 Litigants included "3 leading Purko *moran* and 6 *moran* from the Kakonyukie."
Tignor, *Colonial Transformation*, 37.

77 Tignor, *Colonial Transformation*, 37. The most detailed reconstruction of the suit and 1913 ruling is provided by Lotte Hughes in *Moving the Maasai*.

78 Sandford, *Administrative and Political History of the Masai Reserve*, 4.

79 Ibid.

80 Ibid, 74.

81 For a discussion of the use of such unequal education as a tactic of European colonization, see Martin Carnoy, *Education as Cultural Imperialism* (Philadelphia: David McKay Co.) 1974.

82 Tignor, *Colonial Transformation*, 79.

83 Sandford, *Administrative and Political History of the Masai Reserve*, 74.

84 Ibid, 76.

85 Tignor, *Colonial Transformation*, 76, 141; Sandford, *Administrative and Political History of the Masasi Reserve*, 76.

86 Sandford, *Administrative and Political History of the Masai Reserve*, 77–9; Tignor, *Colonial Transformation*, 78.

87 Tignor, *Colonial Transformation*, 80.

88 Ibid.

89 *Ilaitete* and *Ilkanyara*.

90 Ole Sangalle would later be made a colonial government chief.

91 The collusion of a member of the Ogiek, the same community that had likely helped to identify the clearing and with whom Maasai shared and collaborated on many fronts, is remembered as a bitter betrayal.

92 The Maasai community continues today to pay homage to those trees that protected the warriors.

93 This account is based on a tour in July 2016, in which the authors were taken to the massacre site by descendants of the Maasai communities living in 1922 on adjacent land and whose oral history contains the detailed memory.

94 "Report of the Masai Enquiry Committee," 1925, 5–6, quoted in Tignor, *Colonial Transformation*, 82.

95 Ibid.

96 Mary Poole interview with Donkol ole Keiwa, Dopoi Center, March 12, 2023.

97 Tignor, *Colonial Transformation*, 38.

98 Letter from Olgayal s/o Nanjiru, T.H. Motian, Arthur G. Tameno, and Thumb mark of Karaga Ole Saitaga A. Kaurai, to The Honorable The Officer in Charge, Masai Province Ngong, October 1, 1934, in "Officer in Charge," Kenya Land Commission-Masai District, Kenya National Archive, DC/NGO/1/7/7. Also see series of memorandums, correspondence and meeting notes, in "Officer in Charge," Kenya Land Commission-Masai District, Kenya National Archive, DC/NGO/1/7/7.

99   Petition with thirty-five signatories to the Hon. The Colonial Secretariat, Ngong
      Masai Reserve, August 28, 1934, in "officer in charge," Kenya land commission-
      Masai District, Kenya National Archive, DC/NGO/1/7/7.

100   This story is also found in Hughes' Chapter 9, "A Land No Longer Fit for Heroes,"
      PhD Dissertation, "Moving the Maasai: A Colonial Misadventure," St. Anthony's
      College, University of Oxford, 2002.

101   In his last recorded memorandum to the Independence Committee, Justice Ole
      Tipis said unless their demands were met, "the Maasai will have no alternative but
      to fend for themselves in whatever way they see fit" and that "Maasai will fight to
      protect their rights." "Memorandum to the Independence Conference Submitted
      by Justice Ole Tipis, the Member for Narok East, The Vice President of the Rift
      Valley Regional Assembly, and President of the Maasai United Front," sometime
      after September 21, 1963. David Lemomo, General Secretary of the MUF, said,
      "By their failure to implement the regional constitution KANU have forfeited all
      legal pretentions to the right of ruling the people of Kenya. What was supposed
      to be a nationalist government has in fact been turned into a Constitutional
      monster—a tribalist mouse brandishing imperialist claws, at the peace-loving,
      non-KANU African tribes of Kenya." David Lemomo, "A Open Letter" to
      Her Majesty's Secretary of State for the Colonies, Through His Excellency the
      Governor of Kenya, August 31, 1963.

102   Ole Ntimama became an outspoken advocate for Maasai land rights and identity
      toward the end of his life. At a meeting in Maji Moto in the context of government
      plans to appropriate Maasailand for the Mombasa-Kisumu railway, he was quoted
      as saying, "For over 100 years, the Maasai have been continuously and perpetually
      relegated to the dark corners of Kenyan society. For all this time, we have not had
      access to education and health facilities," he said, adding that leaders were now
      more determined than ever to have the ownership of the vast tracts of land in the
      Rift Valley from which the community was evicted by the British Government.
      "We shall enjoin every Maasai leader in the effort. We know that not all will
      come on board, but we shall approach every one of them. This is an issue that
      stems from all the ranks of the community and there is consensus on the move."
      Kipkoech Tanui, "Ntimama in new push for land rights," *Daily Nation,* Kenya
      Monday, October 2, 2000.

103   See Parselelo Kantai, "Betraying the Maasai," *The East African Standard,* Sunday
      October 5, 2008.

Bibliography

Adams, Jonathan S. and Thomas O. McShane, *The Myth of Wild Africa: Conservation without Illusion* (Oakland: University of California Press, 1997).

Adas, Michael, "Social History and the Revolution in African and Asian Historiography," *Journal of Social History*, Vol. 19, No. 2 (Winter 1985), 335–48.

Akama, John, "The Creation of the Maasai Image and Tourism Development in Kenya," in John Akama and Patricia Sterry, eds., *Cultural Tourism in Africa: Strategies for the New Millennium: The Proceedings of the ATLAS Africa International Conference, Mombasa 2000* (Arnhem: Association for Tourism and Leisure Education, 2002), 43–54.

Alvarez, Sonia E., Evelina Dagnino, and Arturo Escobar, eds., *Cultures of Politics, Politics of Cultures: Re-visioning Latin American Social Movements* (Boulder: Westview Press, 1998).

Amin, Samin, *Eurocentrism: Second Edition* (New York: Monthly Review Press, 2009).

Anderson, Benedict, *Imagined Communities: Reflections on the Origin and Spread of Nationalism*, 1983 (London: Verso, 1991).

Anderson, David, *Histories of the Hanged: The Dirty War in Kenya and the End of Empire* (New York: W.W. Norton, 2005).

Anderson, David M., "Depression, Dust Bowl, Demography, and Drought: The Colonial State and Soil Conservation in East Africa during the 1930s," *African Affairs*, Vol. 83, No. 332 (1984), 321–43.

Anderson, David M., "Cow Power: Livestock and the Pastoralist in Africa," *African Affairs*, Vol. 92, No. 366 (January, 1993), 121–33.

Anderson, David M., *Eroding the Commons: The Politics of Ecology in Baringo, Kenya 1890s–1963* (London: J. Currey, 2002).

Anderson, Gary Clayton, *The Indian Southwest, 1580–1830: Ethnogenesis and Reinvention* (Norman: University of Oklahoma Press, 1999).

Ashcroft, Bill, Gareth Griffiths, and Helen Tiffin, *The Empire Writes Back: Theory and Practice in Post-Colonial Literature* (London: Routledge, 1986).

Bender, Thomas, ed., *Rethinking American History in a Global Age* (Berkeley: University of California Press, 2002).

Benjaminsen, Tor A., Mara J. Goldman, Maya Y. Minwary, and Faustin P. Maganga, "Wildlife Management in Tanzania: State Control, Rent Seeking and Community Resistance," *Development and Change*, Vol. 44, No. 5 (2013), 1087–109.

Berman, Bruce and John Lonsdale, *Unhappy Valley: Conflict in Kenya and Africa: Book I: State and Class* (London: James Currey, 1992).

Berman, Bruce and John Lonsdale, *Unhappy Valley: Conflict in Kenya and Africa: Book II: Violence and Ethnicity* (London: James Currey, 1992).

Berman, Edward H., "American Influence on African Education: The Role of the Phelps-Stokes Fund's Education Commissions," *Comparative Education Review*, Vol. 15, No. 2 (1971), 132–45.

Berman, Edward H., *The Influence of the Carnegie, Ford, and Rockefeller Foundations on American Foreign Policy: The Ideology of Philanthropy* (Albany: State University of New York Press, 1983).

Berntsen, John L., "The Enemy Is Us: Eponymy in the Historiography of the Maasai," *History in Africa*, Vol. 7 (1980), 1–21.

Blake, Michael, "Rights for People, Not Cultures," *Civilization*, August/September, 2000.

Blaut, James Morris, *The Colonizer's Model of the World: Geographical Diffusion and Eurocentric History* (New York: Guilford Press, 1993).

Bodley, John H., *Victims of Progress* (London: Mayfield Publishing Company, 1999).

Bonner, Raymond, *At the Hand of Man: Peril and Hope for Africa's Wildlife* (New York: Knopf, 1993).

Branch, Daniel, *Kenya: Between Hope and Despair, 1963–2012* (New Haven: Yale University Press, 2011).

Brecher, Jeremy and Tim Costello, *Global Village or Global Pillage: Economic Reconstruction from the Bottom Up* (Cambridge, MA: South End Press, 1994).

Brooks, James F., *Captives and Cousins: Slavery, Kinship, & Community in the Southwest Borderlands* (Chapel Hill: University of North Carolina Press, 2002).

Bruner, Edward, "Maasai on the Lawn: Tourist Realism in East Africa," *Cultural Anthropology*, October, 2009.

Butt, Bilal, Ashton Shortridge, and Antoinette M.G.A. WinklerPrins, "Pastoral Herd Management, Drought Coping Strategies, and Cattle Mobility in Southern Kenya," *Annals of the Association of American Geographers*, Vol. 99, No. 2 (2009), 309–34.

Byrd, Jody, *Transit of Empire: Indigenous Critiques of Colonialism* (Minneapolis: University of Minnesota Press, 2011).

Cahen, Michel, "Anticolonialism and Nationalism: Deconstructing Synonymy, Investigating Historical Processes: Notes on the Heterogeneity of Former African Portuguese Colonial Areas," in Eric Morier-Genoud, ed., *Sure Road? Nations and Nationalisms in Guinea, Angola and Mozambique*, African Social Studies Series (Leiden: Brill Academic Publishers, 2012), 28.

Cashmore, Thomas H.R., "Studies in District Administration in the East Africa Protectorate (1895–1918)," Dissertation submitted for the Degree of Ph.D. in the University of Cambridge, Jesus College, November, 1965.

Cavanagh, Connor J., Teklehaymanot Weldemichel, and Tor A. Benjaminsen, "Gentrifying the African Landscape: The Performance and Powers of for-Profit Conservation on Southern Kenya's Conservancy Frontier," Department of International Environment and Development Studies (Noragric), Norwegian University of Life Sciences, Department of Geography, Norwegian University of Science and Technology (Taylor and Francis Group, 2020).

Césaire, Aimé, *Discourse on Colonialism*, 1950 (New York: Monthly Review Press, 2000).

Champagne, Duane, "In Search of Theory and Method in American Indian Studies," *American Indian Quarterly*, Vol. 31, No. 3 (Summer, 2007), 353–72.

Chua, Amy, *World on Fire: How Exporting Free Market Democracy Breeds Ethnic Hatred and Global Instability* (New York: Doubleday, 2003).

Clough, Marshall, *Fighting Two Sides: Kenyan Chiefs and Politicians, 1918–1940* (Niwot: The University Press of Colorado, 1990).

Colchester, Marcus, *Salvaging Nature: Indigenous Peoples, Protected Areas and Biodiversity Conservation* (New York: United Nations Research Institute for Social Development with the World Rainforest Movement and World Wide Fund for Nature, 2003).

Cole, Sonia, *The Prehistory of East Africa* (New York: New American Library, 1963).

Coombes, Annie E., Lotte Hughes, and Karega Munene, *Managing Heritage, Making Peace: History, Identity and Memory in Contemporary Kenya* (London: I.B. Tauris, 2014).

Cooper, Frederick, *Africa in the World: Capitalism, Empire, Nation-State* (Cambridge, MA: Harvard University Press, 2014).

Dabashi, Hamid, *The Emperor Is Naked: On the Inevitable Demise of the Nation-State* (London: Zed Books, 2020).

Davidson, Basil, *A Guide to African History: A General Survey of the African Past from Earliest Times to the Present*, Revised and Edited by Haskel Frankel (New York: Zenith Books, 1965).

Davidson, Basil, *Let Freedom Come: Africa in Modern History* (Boston: Little, Brown and Company, 1978).

Davidson, Basil, *The Black Man's Burden: Africa and the Curse of the Nation-State* (New York: Random House, 1992).

Dean, Bartholomew and Jerome Levi, eds., *At the Risk of Being Heard: Indigenous Rights, Identity, and Postcolonial States* (Ann Arbor, MI: University of Michigan Press, 2003).

Dei, George J. Sefa, *Teaching Africa: Towards a Transgressive Pedagogy* (Ontario: University of Toronto, Ontario Institute for Studies in Education, 2010).

Dowie, Mark, *Conservation Refugees: The Hundred-Year Conflict between Global Conservation and Native Peoples* (Cambridge, MA: MIT Press, 2011).

DuBois, W.E.B., *The World and Africa*, 1946 (London: Oxford University Press, 2007).

Dunbar-Ortiz, Roxanne, *An Indigenous Peoples' History of the United States* (Boston: Beacon Press, 2014).

Elkins, Caroline, *Imperial Reckoning: The Untold Story of Britain's Gulag in Kenya* (New York: Henry Holt, 2005).

Esteva, Gustavo, "Development," in Wolfgang Sachs, ed., *The Development Dictionary: A Guide to Knowledge as Power*, 1992, 2nd Ed. (London: Zed Books, 2010), 6–24.

Estes, Nick, *Our History Is Our Future: Standing Rock versus the Dakota Access Pipeline, and the Long Tradition of Indigenous Resistance* (New York: Verso, 2019).

Fabian, Johannes, *Out of Our Minds: Reason and Madness in the Exploration of Central Africa* (Berkeley: University of California Press, 2000).

Falola, Toyin, *Nationalism and African Intellectuals* (Rochester, NY: University of Rochester Press, 2001).

Falola, Toyin, *Decolonizing African Studies: Knowledge Production, Agency and Voice* (Rochester, NY: University of Rochester Press, 2022).

Falola, Toyin and Raphael Chijioke Njoku, *United States & Africa Relations: 1400s to the Present* (New Haven: Yale University Press, 2020).

Fane, Rebecca, "Nationalism in Kenya," *African Affairs*, Vol. 55, No. 221 (October, 1956), 294–6.

Fanon, Frantz, *Black Skin, White Masks*, 1952 (New York: Grove Press, 2008).

Fosbrooke, Henry A., "An Administrative Survey of the Masai Social System" (Issue 26 of Tanganyika notes and records, 1948).

Foucault, Michel, *Archeology of Knowledge* (New York: Harper & Row, 1976).

Fratkin, Elliot, "Pastoral Land Tenure in Kenya: Maasai, Samburu, Boran, and Rendille Experiences, 1950–1990," *Nomadic Peoples*, Vol. 34, No. 35 (1994), 55–68.

Fyfe, Christopher, ed., *African Studies since 1945: A Tribute to Basil Davidson: Proceedings of a Seminar in Honour of Basil Davidson's Sixtieth Birthday at the Centre of African Studies, University of Edinburgh Under the Chairmanship of George Shepperson* (London: Longman, 1976).

Galaty, John, "This Land Is Yours: Social and Economic Factors in the Privatization, Sub-division and Sale of Maasai Ranches," *Nomadic Peoples*, Vol. 30 (1992), 28.

Galaty, John, "The Collapsing Platform for Pastoralism: Land Sales and Land Loss in Kajiado County, Kenya," *Nomadic Peoples*, Vol. 17, No. 2 (2013), 20–39.

Gilroy, Paul, *"There Ain't No Black in the Union Jack": The Cultural Politics of Race and Nation* (Chicago, IL: University of Chicago Press, 1987).

Gilroy, Paul, *The Black Atlantic: Modernity and Double Consciousness* (Cambridge, MA: Harvard University Press, 1993).

Goldman, Mara, *Narrating Nature: Wildlife Conservation and Maasai Ways of Knowing* (Tucson: University of Arizona Press, 2020).

Goldstein, Aloysha, "Where the Nation Takes Place: Proprietary Regimes, Antistatism, and U.S. Settler Colonialism," *South Atlantic Quarterly*, Vol. 107, No. 4 (Fall, 2008), 833–61.

Goldsworthy, David, *Tom Mboya: The Man Kenya Wanted to Forget*, 1982 (New York: Africana Publishing Co, 2008).

Grosfoguel, Ramon, "The Epistemic Decolonial Turn: Beyond Political Economy Paradigms," *Cultural Studies*, Vol. 21, No. 2–3 (2007), 211–23.

Gruenbaum, Ellen, *The Female Circumcision Controversy: An Anthropological Perspective* (Philadelphia: University of Pennsylvania Press, 2001).

Gutkind, Peter, ed., *The Passing of Tribal Man in Africa* (Leiden: E.J. Brill, 1970).

Hall, Stuart, "The West and the Rest: Discourse and Power," in Stuart Hall and Bram Gieben, eds., *Formations of Modernity* (Cambridge, MA: Polity Press, in association with Blackwell and the Open University, 1992), 276–314 and 325–9.

Harvey, David, *The New Imperialism* (London: Oxford University Press, 2003).

Harvey, David, *A Brief History of Neoliberalism* (Oxford: Oxford University Press, 2005).

Hodgson, Dorothy, *Once Intrepid Warriors: Gender, Ethnicity, and the Cultural Politics of Maasai Development* (Bloomington: Indiana University Press, 2001).

Hodgson, Dorothy, *Being Maasai, Becoming Indigenous: Postcolonial Politics in a Neoliberal World* (Bloomington: Indiana University Press, 2011).

Hodgson, Dorothy, *Gender, Justice, and the Problem of Culture: From Customary Law to Human Rights in Tanzania* (Bloomington: Indiana University Press, 2017).

Horne, Gerald, *Mau Mau in Harlem?: The U.S. and the Liberation of Kenya* (New York: Palgrave Macmillan, 2009).

Hornsby, Charles, *Kenya: A History since Independence* (London: I.B. Tauris, 2013).

Hughes, Lotte, *Moving the Maasai: A Colonial Misadventure* (London: Palgrave, Macmillan, 2006).

Hughes, Lotte, "Rough Time in Paradise: Claims, Blames and Memory Making Around Some Protected Areas in Kenya," *Conservation and Society*, Vol. 5, No. 3 (2007), 307–30.

Hughes, Lotte, "Mining the Maasai Reserve: The Story of Magadi," *The Journal of East African Studies*, Vol. 2, No. 1 (2008), 134–64.

Hull, Richard W., *African Cities and Towns before the European Conquest* (New York: Norton, 1976).

Human Rights Watch/Africa Watch, *Divide and Rule: State-Sponsored Ethnic Violence in Kenya* (New York: Human Rights Watch, 1993).

Huntnyk, John, "African Research Futures: Post-Colonialism and Identity," *Anthropology Today*, Vol. 10, No. 4 (August, 1994), 24–5.

Igoe, Jim, "Clash of Two Conservation Models," in *Conservation and Globalization: A Study of National Parks and Indigenous Communities from East Africa to South Dakota* (Belmont, CA: Wadsworth, 2004).

International Alliance of Indigenous-Tribal Peoples of the Tropical Forests and International Work Group for Indigenous Affairs, *Indigenous Peoples, Forests, and Biodiversity: Indigenous Peoples and the Global Environmental Agenda* (London: IAITP, 1996).

James, C.L.R., *The Black Jacobins: Toussaint L'ouverture and the San Domingo Revolution* (London: Secker & Warburg Ltd., 1938).

Jewsiewicki, Bogumil and David Newbury, eds., *African Historiographies: What Histories for Which Africas?* (Beverly Hills: Sage, 1986).

Kantai, Parselelo, "In the Grip of the Vampire State: Maasai Land Struggles in Kenyan Politics," *Journal of Eastern African Studies*, Vol. 1, No. 1 (March, 2007), 107–22.

Kanyinga, Karuti, "The Legacy of the White Highlands: Land Rights, Ethnicity, and the Post-2007 Election Violence in Kenya," *Journal of Contemporary African Studies*, Vol. 27, No. 3 (2009), 325–44.

Kaplan, Jeffrey and Tore Bjorgo, *Nation and Race: The Developing Euro-American Racist Subculture* (Boston: Northwestern University, 1998).

King, Kenneth, "The Kenya Maasai and the Protest Phenomenon, 1900–1960," *The Journal of African History*, Vol. 12, No. 1 (1971), 117–37.

Kipury, Naomi, *Oral Literature of the Maasai* (Portsmouth, NH: Heinemann Educational Books, 1983).

Kitching, Gavin, *Class and Economic Change in Kenya: The Making of an African Petite Bourgeoisie, 1905–1970* (New Haven: Yale University Press, 1980).

Koshy, Susan, Lisa Marie Cacho, Jodi A. Byrd, and Brian Jordan Jefferson, eds., *Colonial Racial Capitalism* (Durham: Duke University Press, 2022).

Krishna, Sankaran, *Globalization and Post Colonialism: Hegemony and Resistance in the 21st Century* (Lanham, MD: Rowman and Littlefield, 2009).

Laher, Ridwan and Korir Sing Oei, eds., *Indigenous People in Africa: Contestations, Empowerment and Group Rights* (Pretoria: Africa Institute of South Africa, 2014).

Lekuton, Joseph Lemasolai, *Facing the Lion: Growing Up Maasai on the African Savanna* (Washington, D.C.: National Geographic, 2003).

Leonard, David K., *African Successes: Four Public Managers of Kenyan Rural Development* (Berkley, CA: University of California Press, 1991).

Leys, Norman, *Kenya* (London: Hogarth Press, 1924).

Lonsdale, John, "Agency in Tight Corners: Narrative and Initiative in African History," *Journal of African Cultural Studies,* Vol. 13, No. 1 (2000), 5–16.

Lonsdale, John, "KAU's Cultures: Imaginations of Community and Constructions of Leadership in Kenya after the Second World War," *Journal of African Cultural Studies*, Vol. 13, No. 1 (2000), 107–24.

Lonsdale, John, *Mau Mau and Nationhood: Arms, Authority, and Narration* (Columbus: Ohio State University Press, 2003).

Lonsdale, John and Bruce Berman, "Coping with the Contradictions: The Development of the Colonial State in Kenya, 1895–1914," *The Journal of African History*, Vol. 20, No. 4, White Presence and Power in Africa (1979), 487–505.

Lowe, Lisa, *Intimacies of Four Continents* (Durham: Duke University Press, 2015).

MacGaffey, Wyatt, "Concepts of Race in the Historiography of Northeast Africa," *The Journal of African History*, Vol. 7, No. 1 (1966), 1–17.

Maekawa, Ichiro, "Neo-Colonialism Reconsidered: A Case Study of East Africa in the 1960s and 1970s," *The Journal of Imperial and Commonwealth History*, Vol. 43, No. 2 (2015), 317–41.

Maloba, Wunyabari O., *Mau Mau and Kenya: An Analysis of a Peasant Revolt* (Bloomington: Indiana University Press, 1998).

Mamdani, Mahmood, *Neither Settler Nor Native: The Making and Unmaking of Permanent Minorities* (Cambridge, MA: Belknap, Harvard University Press, 2020).

Manning, Patrick, *Slavery and African Life: Occidental, Oriental, and African Slave Trades* (Cambridge: Cambridge University Press, 1990).

Matheka, Reuben M., "Decolonisation and Wildlife Conservation in Kenya, 1958–68," *Journal of Imperial and Commonwealth History*, Vol. 36, No. 4 (December, 2008), 615–39.

Maundu, Patrick, et.al, "Ethnobotony of the Loita Maasai: Towards Community Management of the Forest of the Lost Child," Loita Ethnobotony Project, People and Plants Working Paper, December, No. 8 (Paris: UNESCO, 2001).

Maxon, Robert and David Javersak, "The Kedong Massacre and the Dick Affair: A Problem in the Early Colonial Historiography of East Africa," *History in Africa*, 1981, Vol. 8 (1981), 261–9.

Michesuah, Devon A., ed., *Natives and Academics: Researching and Writing about American Indians* (Lincoln: University of Nebraska Press, 1998).

Mignolo, Walter, *The Darker Side of Renaissance: Literacy, Territoriality, and Colonization* (Ann Arbor: University of Michigan Press, 2003).

Miller, Joseph C., "History and Africa/Africa and History," *The American Historical Review*, Vol. 104, No. 1 (Feburary, 1999), 1–32.

Mohanty, Chandra, "Under Western Eyes: Feminist Scholarship and Colonial Discourses," *Feminist Review*, Vol. 30, No. 1 (1998), 61–88.

Mohanty, Chandra, *Feminism without Borders: Decolonizing Theory, Practicing Solidarity* (Durham: Duke University Press, 2003).

Momoh, Abubakar, "Does Pan-Africanism Have a Future in Africa? In Search of the Ideational Basis of Afro-Pessimism," *African Journal of Political Science*, Vol. 8, No. 1 (2003), 31–57.

Monyenye, Solomon, "Education and Development of Nationhood in Kenya," *Reinvigorating the University Mandate in a Globalizing Environment: Challenges, Obstacles, and Way Forward* (Conference Proceedings May 26–27, Kenyatta University, 2005).

Moreton-Robinson, Aileen, *The White Possessive: Property, Power & Indigenous Sovereignty* (Minneapolis: University of Minnesota Press, 2015).

Moyo, Dambisa, *Dead Aid: Why Aid Is Not Working and How There Is a Better Way for Africa* (New York: Farrar, Straus and Giroux, 2009).

Mudimbe, Valentin Y., *The Invention of Africa: Gnosis, Philosophy, and the Order of Knowledge* (London: James Currey, 1988).

Munene, Macharia, J.D. Olewe Nyunya, and Korwa Adar, eds., *The United States and Africa: From Independence to the End of the Cold War* (Nairobi: East African Educational Publishers, Ltd., 1995).

Mungai, Mbugua and George Gona, eds., *(Re)membering Kenya Vol 1: Identity, Culture and Freedom* (Nairobi: Twaweza Communications, African Books Collective, 2010).

Musembi, Celestine Nyamu and Patricia Kameri-Mbote, "Mobility, Marginality and Tenure Transformation in Kenya: Explorations of Community Property Rights in Law and Practice," *Nomadic Peoples*, Vol. 17, No. 1 (2013), 5–32.

Musila, Grace A., "Writing History's Silences: Interview with Parselelo Kantai," *Kunapipi*, Vol. 34, No. 1 (2012). Available at: http://ro.uow.edu.au/kunapipi/vol34/iss1/8.

Mwangi, Esther, "Subdividing the Commons: The Politics of Property Rights Transformation in Kenya's Maasailand" (Washington, D.C.: International Food Policy Research Institute, 2006).

Mwangi, Esther, "Bumbling Bureaucrats, Sluggish Courts and Forum-Shopping Elites: Unending Conflict and Competition in the Transition to Private Property," *European Journal of Development Research*, Vol. 22 (2010), 715–32.

Mwangi, Esther and Elinor Ostrom, "Top-Down Solutions: Looking Up from East Africa's Rangelands," *Environment*, Vol. 51, No. 21 (January/February, 2009), 34–44.

Mwesigirem Bwesigye Bwa, "Land Grabbing in Africa: The New Colonialism," *This Is Africa*, May 28, 2014. https://thisisafrica.me/land-grabbing-africa-new-colonialism/.

Naghibi, Nima, *Rethinking Global Sisterhood: Western Feminism and Iran* (Minneapolis, MN: University of Minnesota Press, 2007).

Nandy, Ashis, *The Intimate Enemy: Loss and Recovery of Self Under Colonialism*, 1983 (London: Oxford, 2009).

Ndlovu-Gatsheni, Sabelo J., *Coloniality of Power in Neocolonial Africa: Myths of Decolonization* (Dakar: Council for the Development of Social Science Research in Africa, 2013).

Neale, Caroline, *Writing "Independent" History: African Historiography, 1960–1980* (Westport: Greenwood Press, 1985).

Neckebrouck, Valeer, *Resistant Peoples: The Case of the Pastoral Maasai of East Africa* (Roma: E.P.U.G., 1993).

Newman, James L., *The Peopling of Africa: A Geographic Interpretation* (New Haven: Yale University Press, 1995).

Newman, Louise Michele, *White Women's Rights: The Racial Origins of Feminism in the United States* (London: Oxford University Press, 1999).

Nkrumah, Kwame, *Neo-Colonialism, the Last Stage of Imperialism* (London: Thomas Nelson & Sons Ltd., 1965).

Odhiambo, E.S. Atieno and John Lonsdale, eds., *Mau Mau and Nationhood: Arms, Authority, and Narration* (Columbus: Ohio University Press, 2003).

Ogot, Bethwell A., *Politics and Nationalism in Colonial Kenya* (Nairobi: East African Publishing House, 1972).

Ogot, Bethwell A., Review Article, "Britain's Gulag. Review of David Anderson, *Histories of the Hanged: Britain's Dirty War in Kenya and the End of Empire* (London: Weidenfeld & Nicolson) 2005, and Caroline Elkins, *Britain's Gulag: The Brutal End of Empire in Kenya* (London: Jonathan Cape) 2005," *Journal of American History*, Vol. 46 (2005), 493–505.

Ogot, Bethwell A., *My Footprints on the Sands of Time* (Bloomington: Trafford Pub., 2006).

Ogot, Bethwell A., "Rereading the History and Historiography of Epistemic Domination and Resistance in Africa," *African Studies Review*, Vol. 52, No. 1 (April 2009), 18.

Ogot, Bethwell A. and John A. Kieran, eds., *Zamani: A Survey of East African History* (Nairobi: East African Publishing House, 1968).

Ogot, Bethwell A. and William R. Ochieng, eds., *Decolonization and Independence in Kenya, 1940–1993* (Nairobi: East African Educational Publishers, 1995).

Okoth-Ogendo, Hastings W.O., *Tenants of the Crown: Evolution of Agrarian Law and Institutions in Kenya* (Nairobi: African Center for Technology Studies Press, 1991).

Ole Saitoti, Tepilit, *Maasai* (New York: Abradale Press, Harry N. Abrams Inc. Pub., 1980).

Osborne, Myles, "Controlling Development: 'Martial Race' and Empire in Kenya, 1945–59," *The Journal of Imperial and Commonwealth History*, Vol. 42, No. 3 (2014), 464–85.

Oyěwùmí, Oyèrónkẹ́, *The Invention of Women: Making an African Sense of Western Gender Discourse* (Minneapolis: University of Minnesota Press, 1997).

Parker, Ian and Stan Bleazard, eds., *An Impossible Dream: Some of Kenya's Last Colonial Wardens Recall the Game Department in the Closing Years of the British Empire* (Elgin, Scotland: Librario Press, 2001).

Pieterse, Jan Nederveen, *White on Black: Images of Africa and Blacks in Western Popular Culture* (New Haven: Yale University Press, 1992).

Quijano, Anibal, "Coloniality of Power, Eurocentrism, and Latin America," *Nepantla*, Vol. 1, No. 3 (Durham: Duke University Press, 2000), 533–80.

Rigby, Peter, "Time and Historical Consciousness: The Case of the Ilparakuyo Maasai," *Comparative Studies in Society and History*, Vol. 25, No. 3 (1983), 428–56.

Riley, Charlotte Lydia, "The Winds of Change Are Blowing Economically: The Labour Party and British Overseas Development, 1940s–1960s," in Andrew W.M. Smith and Chris Jeppesen, eds., *Britain, France and the Decolonization of Africa: Future Imperfect?* (London: UCL Press, 2017), 43–61.

Rodney, Walter, *How Europe Underdeveloped Africa*, 1972 (African Tree Press, 2014).

Rutten, Marcel, *Selling Wealth to Buy Poverty: The Process of the Individualization of Land Ownership among the Maasai Pastoralists of Kajiado District, Kenya* (Saarbrucken: Verlag Breitenbach Publishers, 1992).

Ryser, Rudolph, *Indigenous Nations and Modern States: The Political Emergence of Nations Challenging State Power* (New York: Routledge, 2012).

Said, Edward W., *Covering Islam: How the Media and the Experts Determine How We See the Rest of the World* (New York: Pantheon, 1981).

Said, Edward W., *Orientalism* (London: Penguin Modern Classics, 2003).

Sambu, Daniel, "Wildlife Conservation in Kenya and Tanzania and Effects on Maasai Communities," *Focus on Geography*, New York, Vol. 60 (2017).

Samson, Colin and Carlos Gigoux, *Indigenous Peoples and Colonialism: Global Perspectives* (Cambridge: Polity Press, 2017).

Sandford, George Ritchie, *An Administrative and Political History of the Masai Reserve* (London: Waterlow & Sons Ltd., 1919).

Scott, James C., *Seeing Like a State: How Certain Schemes to Improve the Human Condition Have Failed* (New Haven: Yale University Press, 1998).

Shah, Esha, "Manifesting Utopia: History and Philosophy of UN Debates on Science and Technology for Sustainable Development," STEPS Working Paper 25 (Brighton: STEPS Centre, 2009).

Shahjahan, Riyad Ahmed, "Mapping the Field of Anti-Colonial Discourse to Understand Issues of Indigenous Knowledges: Decolonizing Praxis," *McGill Journal of Education*, Vol. 40, No. 2 (Spring, 2005), 213–40. https://mje.mcgill.ca/article/view/566.

Shiva, Issa G., *Maasai Rights in Ngorongoro, Tanzania* (UK: IIED/hAKIARDHI, 1998).

Smith, Andrew W.M. and Chris Jeppesen, eds., *Britain, France, and the Decolonization of Africa: Future Imperfect?* (London: UCL Press, 2017).

Smith, David Lovatt, *Amboseli: A Miracle Too Far?* (East Sussex: Mawenzi Books, 2008).

Smith, Linda Tuhiwai, *Decolonizing Methodologies: Research and Indigenous Peoples* (London: Zed Books, 2006).

Soske, Jon, "The Dissimulation of Race: 'Afro-Pessimism' and the Problem of Development," *Qui Pane*, Vol. 14, No. 2 (Spring/Summer, 2004), 15–56.

de Sousa Santos, Boaventura, *Rise of the Global Left: The World Social Forum and Beyond* (London: Zed Books, 2006).

Spear, Thomas and Richard Waller, ed., *Being Maasai: Ethnicity and Identity in East Africa* (Columbus: Ohio University Press, 1993).

Spivak, Gayatri Chakravorty, *A Critique of Postcolonial Reason: Toward a History of the Vanishing Present* (Cambridge, MA: Harvard University Press, 1999).

Spivak, Gayatri Chakravorty, "Can the Subaltern Speak?," in Rosalind Morris, ed., *Can the Subaltern Speak? Reflections on the History of an Idea* (New York: Columbia University Press, 2010), 21–80.

Temu, Arnold and Bonaventure Swai, *Historians and Africanist History: A Critique: Post-Colonial Historiography Examined* (London: Zed Books, 1981).

wa Thiong'o, Ngũgĩ, *Decolonising the Mind: The Politics of Language in African Literature* (London: James Currey Ltd / Heinemann, 1986).

Thomas, Lynn M., *Politics of the Womb: Women, Reproduction, and the State and Kenya* (Berkeley: University of California Press, 2003).

Thompson, Michael and Katherine Homewood, "Entrepreneurs, Elites, and Exclusion in Maasailand: Trends in Wildlife Conservation and Pastoralist Development," *Human Ecology*, Vol. 30, No. 1 (March, 2002), 107–38.

Thornton, John, *Africa and Africans: In the Making of the Atlantic World, 1400–1680* (Cambridge: Cambridge University Press, 1992).

Thurston, Anne, *Smallholder Agriculture in Colonial Kenya: The Official Mind and the Swynnerton Plan* (Cambridge: African Monographs 8. African Studies Centre, 1987).

Tignor, Robert, *The Colonial Transformation of Kenya: The Kamba, Kikuyu, and Maasai from 1900–1939* (Princeton, NJ: Princeton University Press, 1976).

Torgovnick, Marianna, *Gone Primitive: Savage Intellects, Modern Lives* (Chicago, IL: University of Chicago Press, 1990).

Trask, Haunani-Kay, "Coalition-Building between Natives and Non-Natives," *Stanford Law Review*, Vol. 43, No. 6 (July, 1991), 1197–213.

Trask, Huanani-Kay, *From a Native Daughter: Colonialism and Sovereignty in Hawai'i* (O'ahu, HI: University of Hawaii Press, 1999).

Trevor-Roper, Hugh, "The Rise of Christian Europe," *The Listener*, November, 1963.

Trouillot, Michel-Rolph, *Silencing the Past: Power and the Production of History*, 1995 (Boston: Beacon Press, 2015).

Trzebinski, Errol, *The Kenya Pioneers* (London: Norton, 1986).

Tuck, Eve and K. Wayne Yang, "Decolonization Is Not a Metaphor," *Decolonization: Indigeneity, Education & Society*, Vol. 1, No. 1 (2012), 1–40.

Tyrrell, Ian, *Transnational Nation: United States History in Global Perspective since 1789* (New York: Palgrave Macmillan, 2007).

Valle, Elisabeth and Mark Nelson Yobesia, "Economic Contribution of Tourism in Kenya," *Tourism Analysis*, Vol. 14 (2009), 401–14.

Vansina, Jan, "Once Upon a Time: Oral Traditions as History in Africa," *Daedalus*, Vol. 100, No. 2 (Spring, 1971), 442–68.

Wachira, George Mukundi, "Vindicating Indigenous Peoples' Land Rights in Kenya," Submitted in fulfilment of the requirements of the degree, "Doctor of Law, LLD," Faculty of Law, University of Pretoria, 2008.

Wai, Zubairu, *Epistemologies of African Conflicts: Violence, Evolutionism, and the War in Sierra Leone* (New York: Palgrave Macmillan, 2012).

Walljasper, Jay and Nikil Aziz, "The Neo-Colonial Land Grab in Africa: Outside Nations Are Once Again Dividing Up Africa—this Time for Biofuel and Mineral Rights," *On the Commons*, April 15, 2011. http://www.onthecommons.org/neo-colonial-land-grab-africa.

Wamwere, Koigi wa, *I Refuse to Die: My Journey for Freedom* (London: Seven Stories Press, 2002).

Wamwere, Koigi wa, *Negative Ethnicity: From Bias to Genocide* (London: Seven Stories Press, 2003).

Western, David, *In the Dust of Kilimanjaro* (Washington, D.C.: Island Press, 1997).

Western, David and R. Michael Wright, eds., *Natural Connections: Perspectives in Community-Based Conservation* (Washington, D.C.: Island Press, 1994).

Wolfe, Patrick, "Settler Colonialism and the Elimination of the Native," *Journal of Genocide Research*, Vol. 8, No. 4 (December, 2006), 387–409.

Wolff, Richard D., "British Imperialism and the East African Slave Trade," *Science and Society*, Vol. 36, No. 4 (1972), 443–62.

Wood, Ellen Meiksins, *Empire of Capital* (London: Verso, 2005).

Wrena, Susie and Chinwe Ifejika Speranza, "The Struggle to Diversify Rural Livelihoods: Bio-Enterprise Initiatives and Their Impacts on Agro-Pastoralists and Pastoralists Communities in the Drylands of Kenya," *European Journal of Development Research*, Vol. 22, No. 5 (2010), 751–69.

Wrong, Michela, *It's Our Turn to Eat: The Story of a Kenyan Whistle-Blower* (New York: Harper Perennial, 2010).

Young, Robert, *White Mythologies: Writing History and the West* (London: Psychology Press, 2004).

Zeleza, Paul Tiyambe, "African Studies and Universities since Independence," *Transition*, Vol. 101, No. 101, Looking Ahead (2009), 110–35.

Zimmerman, Andrew, "Africa in Imperial and Transnational History: Multi-sited Historiography and the Necessity of Theory," *The Journal of African History*, Vol. 54, No. 3 (2013), 331–40.

Index

triple disasters (*See Emutai*)
Trouillot, Michel-Rolph 11, 14

Uganda 91, 140, 175 (En69)
Ugandan railroad 59, 60, 79, 133, 135
Ujamaa policy, Tanzania 151
Ukarih, Maasailand 87
United Nations Declaration on the Rights
    of Indigenous Peoples (UNDRIP) 6,
    38, 173–4 (En60)
United Nations Development Programme
    30, 176 (En77)
United Nations on Indigenous Peoples
    7–8, 37–8
United States 28–31, 33, 36, 75, 133,
    166 (En46), 167 (En9), 172 (En47),
    176 (En73)
  as the Centre of African Studies 14, 20,
    40–1, 47, 49–50, 178 (En91)
  Indigenous peoples 8, 36, 41, 62, 74,
    84, 162 (En23), 177 (En82 & En83),
    214 (En19), 215 (En19)
  National Park model 74–5, 107, 110,
    116
United States history 40, 41–2, 49–50,
    61–2, 77 (Fn), 177 (En82 & En83),
    214 (En19)
University of Dar es Salaam 48–50
University of Edinburgh 44, 46
University of Nairobi (Nairobi College)
    42, 44, 119

Vansina, Jan 51, 179 (En94), 186 (En147)
violence (*See also* evictions from
    Maasailand)
  in Maasai culture 20, 55–6, 127–30
  post-election in Kenya 12–13,
    160 (En8), 163 (En25), 162–3
    (En24), 172–3 (En52)
  structural violence of colonization 2,
    11, 60, 66, 69–70, 79, 83, 130–6,
    138, 139, 140–2, 147, 149–51,

    168–9 (En18), 198 (En30),
    214–15 (En19), 215 (En23)
  under nation-states 4, 6, 13, 21, 32–3,
    35–7, 74, 134–5, 152, 155–7

Wa Wamwere, Koigi 67
Waller, Richard 52–3, 185–6 (En150)
West Africa 30, 39, 169 (En18),
    173 (En55)
Western, David 16, 105, 119–20,
    123, 163 (En34), 204 (En2),
    211 (En92)
Western epistemology in African history
    17, 32, 35, 50, 186 (En147)
Western history
  role in coloniality & silencing of
    Indigenous histories 1, 11–18, 21,
    25–6, 29–30, 37–9, 50–6, 70–1,
    177 (En83 & En84)
  as a tool of resistance to coloniality
    21–2, 39–40, 48–50, 177–8 (En86),
    185 (En142)
White Highlands 57–8, 60–1, 63, 68–71,
    73, 84–5, 92, 193 (En54)
Wolfe, Patrick 36, 177 (En82)
Wood, Ellen Meiksins 29
World Bank 30, 33, 71–2, 75, 84–5,
    176 (En77), 182–3 (En116)
  Amboseli National Park Plan 119–20,
    123
  Maasai Agricultural Development
    Organization (MADO) 92–5
World Conference on Racism, Durbin
    South Africa 2001 32
World War I (*See* First World War)
World War II (*See* Second World War)
World Wildlife Fund (WWF) 116
Wrong, Michela 73

Zaphiro, Game Ranger Amboseli 114
Zebu cattle 75, 127, 213 (En8)
Ki-Zerbo, Joseph 42

www.ingramcontent.com/pod-product-compliance
Lightning Source LLC
Chambersburg PA
CBHW061723270326
41928CB00011B/2096